Counselling Children

A Practical Introduction

Kathryn Geldard and David Geldard

SAGE Publications
London • Thousand Oaks • New Delhi

First published 1997. Reprinted 1998, 1999

SAGE Publications Ltd
6 Bonhill Street
London EC2A 4PU

SAGE Publications Inc.
2455 Teller Road
Thousand Oaks, California 91320

SAGE Publications India Pvt Ltd
32, M-Block Market
Greater Kailash – I
New Delhi 110 048

British Library Cataloguing in Publication data

A catalogue record for this book is available from the British Library

ISBN 0 7619 5551 8
ISBN 0 7619 5552 6 (pbk)

Library of Congress catalog card number 97–065726

Typeset by Mayhew Typesetting, Rhayader, Powys
Printed in Great Britain by
The Cromwell Press, Trowbridge, Wiltshire

This book is dedicated to
Lavinia Leslie
and
our children
Matthew and Tomos
Edward and Alison

Contents

Note on terminology

In this book we will be writing about children and counsellors of both sexes. We could use combined personal pronouns such as 'she/he', 'his/her', and 'her/him'. However, we do not like using these combined personal pronouns because they are not consistent with our spoken language and spoil the flow of the written word. We will therefore sometimes use personal pronouns of the female gender and sometimes use personal pronouns of the male gender. Our hope is that this will be comfortable for readers.

PART 1
COUNSELLING CHILDREN

1 Introductory comments

This book is written in an interactive writing style. We have chosen this style because as counsellors we are used to interactive communication. Also, by being interactive we hope to invite readers to join with us in thinking about ideas for counselling children. This is important for us, because there are many different ways of counselling children and we each have our own theoretical bias and practical preferences. We believe that counselling children is a very personal activity in which the personality, personal qualities and professional training of the counsellor have a significant influence on the counselling relationship and consequently on counselling outcomes.

This book is intended to be useful in the training of new counsellors and as a source of ideas for experienced counsellors. In our experience, people from a variety of professions are inevitably involved in counselling children and we believe that this is appropriate and sensible. However, we do think that anyone who counsels children needs to have a sound theoretical knowledge base, together with appropriate training and ongoing professional supervision. We are both practising and experienced child psychotherapists who train others, but continue to seek regular professional supervision for ourselves.

We believe that differing professions bring different and useful perspectives to the work of counselling children. We ourselves have different professional backgrounds, with one of us being an occupational therapist and the other a psychologist. We both believe that we have gained in our understanding and competence as therapists by sharing the philosophies and ideas for practice which underpin these two professions. Similarly, we have expanded our thinking about counselling children through working closely with social workers, psychiatrists, teachers and welfare workers.

We hope that the ideas expressed in this book will be both useful and interesting. However, we expect that at times readers will disagree with us, because we are all individually different. In reading this book you may find that you have different ideas about what is important theoretically and may have a different counselling style. In this case, you might wish to use those ideas which fit for you and to reject those ideas that do not fit, and in the process generate new and useful ideas of your own.

We are aware that counsellors work in many different settings. Although we are fortunate in having well equipped counselling rooms ourselves, we know that successful counselling can be carried out with little equipment in a wide variety of environments including schools and homes. We have therefore suggested methods in this book which we believe are suitable for use in a wide variety of situations.

This is not intended to be a text on the psychological theory of counselling children. It is primarily a practical text with practical ideas about counselling methods. However, in Parts 1 and 2 we have included an overview of important aspects of theory related to counselling children so that the later practical chapters of the book can be viewed in a theoretical context.

In Chapters 2, 3 and 4, we will discuss the goals of counselling children, then the type of relationship which is required between a child and counsellor, and finally the attributes which we believe a counsellor needs in order to be effective.

◆   ◆   ◆   ◆   ◆   ◆   ◆

2   Goals for counselling children

It is probably obvious, even to people who have never been involved in counselling children, that we cannot counsel children in the same way that we counsel adults. We counsel adults by sitting down with them, and inviting them to talk with us. If we were to use the same strategy with children, it is unlikely that they would tell us anything of importance. They would probably become bored with the conversation after a short while, or would withdraw into silence. However, even if they did talk to us, they would probably deflect away from important issues.

If, as counsellors, we are to engage children so that they will talk freely about painful issues, then we need to use verbal counselling skills in conjunction with other strategies. For example, we might involve the child in play, or in the use of media such as miniature animals, clay or various forms of art. Alternatively, we might involve the child in storytelling, or take her on an imaginary journey. As a consequence of combining the use of verbal counselling skills with the use of media or some other strategy, we are able to create an opportunity for the child to join with us in a therapeutically useful counselling process. We, as counsellors, provide the child with the environment in which to undergo therapeutic change.

Because we cannot use verbal counselling skills alone, and because we are promoting the possibility of a therapeutic outcome, we will in this book, frequently refer to child-*therapy*. Clearly, therapeutic change is the outcome we hope to achieve by using counselling in conjunction with media.

Before becoming a counsellor for children it is important to have an understanding of the nature and purpose of counselling children. We need to be clear about our goals and to have clear ideas about how these goals can be achieved. As we will discover, the achievement of goals is not only dependent on the media used and on the style of working, but is critically dependent on the child–counsellor relationship. We will therefore consider goals for counselling children in this section and then move on to considering the child–counsellor relationship in Chapter 3.

Before you read further, we would like to invite you to stop, if you would like to, and to do some thinking of your own. What do you think the most important goals should be, when counselling children?

We would like to ask you another question which has some ethical implications. Should the specific goals for an individual session or a series of sessions be set by the counsellor, or by the child's parents or guardians, or by the child? What do you think?

We think that the answers to the above questions are quite complex, and we have identified four different levels at which goals can be set:

- Level 1 goals – fundamental goals
- Level 2 goals – the parents' goals
- Level 3 goals – goals formulated by the counsellor
- Level 4 goals – the child's goals

All of these goals are important and have to be kept in focus during the therapeutic process. However, at various times during the process some goals need to have preference over others. How this is achieved is the responsibility of the counsellor. We will now discuss our ideas with regard to each of the four levels of goals.

Level 1 goals – fundamental goals

These goals are globally applicable to all children in therapy. They include the following:

- to enable the child to deal with painful emotional issues;
- to enable the child to achieve some level of congruence with regard to thoughts, emotions and behaviours;
- to enable the child to feel good about herself;
- to enable the child to accept her limitations and strengths and to feel OK about them;
- to enable the child to change behaviours that have negative consequences;
- to enable the child to function comfortably and adaptively within the external environment (for example at home and at school);
- to maximize the opportunity for the child to pursue developmental milestones.

Level 2 goals – the parents' goals

These are set by the parents when they bring their child for therapy. They are related to the parents' own agenda and are usually based on the child's current behaviours. For example, if a child is smearing faeces on walls the parents' goal is likely to be to extinguish this behaviour.

Level 3 goals – goals formulated by the counsellor

These goals are formulated by the counsellor as a consequence of hypotheses which the counsellor may have about why the child is behaving in a particular way. Take the example of the child who is smearing faeces. The counsellor may have a hypothesis that the smearing is a consequence of the child's emotional issues. Hence the counsellor may have the goal of addressing and resolving the child's emotional issues.

Clearly, when formulating hypotheses about the possible causation of child behaviour, counsellors need to draw on information from their own casework experience, from their theoretical understanding of child psychology and behaviour, and from their knowledge of current research and the relevant literature.

Level 4 goals – the child's goals

These goals emerge during the therapy session and are effectively the child's own goals, although the child will usually be unable to verbalize them as such. They are based on material which the child brings to the session. Sometimes these goals will match the counsellor's goals and sometimes they will not. For example a counsellor may enter a session having a *level 3* goal that the child needs to be empowered. It may emerge during the session that the child wants to talk about a painful loss and is not ready to be empowered. In this situation the counsellor will need to attend to the *level 4* goal and allow the grieving process to occur.

If a counsellor goes into a particular session with a specific agenda, there may be times when sticking to this agenda will be effective and appropriate. However, generally, there is danger in holding rigidly to a pre-determined agenda because the child's own needs might then be overlooked rather than addressed. For the child's real needs to emerge and to be adequately dealt with therapeutically, the counsellor must stay with the child's own process. The alternative would be for us as counsellors to structure sessions which would meet our own needs rather than those of the children who come to us for help. This is clearly unacceptable, and it follows that generally *level 4* goals must take precedence.

Here is another illustration of what we mean when we talk about a child's goals or agenda being the most important. If we are working with a child who has come from a violent family, we may very strongly believe that an important goal for therapy (a *level 3* goal) is to explore strategies to help the child discover ways of staying safe. This would certainly be important, and in the long term, would be a useful and essential goal. However, the child may be more interested in exploring the fears she has with regard to her mother's safety (her *level 4* goal). Our belief is that unless the issues which are uppermost for the child are addressed first, then the likelihood of counselling having a successful outcome will be diminished.

It is important to view each child's experience as unique, so we need to be careful in setting *level 3* goals. Our assumptions about what a child needs in therapy might be wrong. We need to continually review our goals during the course of counselling, and to be open to amending them wherever necessary. Developing the skills required to discover the child's real needs takes practice and experience.

If therapy sessions are properly conducted, the child's goals will naturally emerge. If these goals are recognized by the counsellor, rather than submerged below other goals set by the counsellor or parents, then they can be formally incorporated into the process through consultation with the parents. In our view, wherever possible these *level 4* goals, involving the child's own agenda, should take precedence.

Thus we strongly suggest that, in general, the specific goals for a counselling session, or series of sessions, need to be determined by giving precedence to the child's level 4 goals while attending to the parents' level 2 goals and the counsellor's level 3 goals. Our experience is that when we follow this process the fundamental level 1 goals will automatically be achieved. Whenever possible, the goal-setting process needs to be interactive and consultative, with the full participatory involvement of the child, the parents or family, and the counsellor.

In setting goals we are implying that the child is our primary client, yet it is the parents who pay our bill! Although this may seem to raise an ethical dilemma, we find that by using the process we have proposed, the parents' goals are also achieved.

In considering what counselling children involves, we have looked first at goals. As stated before, another important aspect of counselling children is the child–counsellor relationship, which we will discuss in the next chapter.

◆　◆　◆　◆　◆　◆　◆

3　The child–counsellor relationship

It has long been recognized, going right back to the 1950s, that the relationship between an adult client and a counsellor is a critical factor with regard to therapeutic outcomes. Original research on the adult client–counsellor relationship was done by Carl Rogers many years ago. He believed that the important ingredients in such a relationship were congruence, empathy and unconditional positive regard. Since then other workers have described what they have believed to be desirable attributes of the counselling relationship, and have generally agreed that the relationship is of major importance in influencing positive outcomes from therapy.

In the same way that in adult therapy the relationship with the counsellor is of major influence, it is generally agreed that in child therapy the child–counsellor relationship is significantly important in influencing the effectiveness of therapy. There have been a number of attempts to define the important attributes of this relationship (see Virginia Axline (1947), Melanie Klein (1932) and Anna Freud (1928)). Unfortunately, there are major differences of opinion about what type of relationship is desirable for therapy to be maximally effective. We don't intend to discuss the differing schools of thought in depth because this is a *practical* guide to counselling children rather than a book about the theory of child therapy. However, we have included a brief overview of the historical background and contemporary ideas about counselling children in Chapter 5.

In this section we would like to share with you our own ideas about what we believe is important in the child–counsellor relationship. We suggest that you might like to compare our ideas with other schools of thought, and then decide for yourself what you consider to be appropriate.

We agree with other workers in child therapy that the child–counsellor relationship is crucial to the process of therapeutic change. Further, we claim that this relationship is the single most important factor in achieving successful therapeutic outcomes.

We need to acknowledge that the child–counsellor relationship is dependent on personal attributes which the counsellor brings into the relationship. These will be discussed in Chapter 4. Here we will consider what we believe to be appropriate and necessary attributes of the child–counsellor relationship. These attributes inevitably impact on the parent–counsellor relationship, so we will also comment on the parent–counsellor relationship. Additionally, we will consider the effect of *transference* on the child–counsellor relationship.

Attributes of the child–counsellor relationship (and the influence of these attributes on the parent–counsellor relationship)

To be optimally effective, we believe that the child–counsellor relationship must be all of the following:

1   a connecting link between the child's world and the counsellor
2   exclusive
3   safe
4   authentic
5   confidential (subject to limits)
6   non-intrusive
7   purposeful

We will now discuss the attributes listed above in more detail.

1 The child–counsellor relationship should be a connecting link between the child's world and the counsellor

The relationship is primarily about connecting with the child and staying with the child's perceptions. The child may see the environment in which he lives quite differently from the way in which his parents see this environment. The counsellor's job is to join with the child and to work from within the child's framework. This needs to be done without judgement, affirmation or condemnation, because to do otherwise would invite the child to move away from his perceptions, and towards those of the counsellor. It is important for the child to stay with his own values, beliefs and attitudes rather than to be influenced by the counsellor's values, beliefs and attitudes.

The child–counsellor relationship provides a link between the child's world and the counsellor enabling the counsellor to observe with clarity the experience of the child. This observation will inevitably be partially distorted by the counsellor's own experiences, and some projection of these on to the child is unavoidable. However, the counsellor must aim to minimize the influence of his own experience, so that his connection with the child's experience of the world is as complete as is possible.

We need to qualify what we have said above. Certainly, we should always join with the child's world, and try to understand that world. However, we will sometimes realize that a child is out of touch with reality. When this situation arises, it is our responsibility as counsellors to provide an opportunity, during the counselling process, for the child to test his reality so that appropriate changes can occur.

2 The child–counsellor relationship should be exclusive

The counsellor needs to establish and maintain good rapport with the child so that trust is developed. For the child the relationship should have a strong flavour of exclusivity, so that the child experiences a unique relationship with the counsellor which is not compromised by the unwanted intrusion of others, such as parents or siblings.

The child will have a personal perception of herself which will not be the same as the parents' perception. For the therapeutic relationship to be effective the child needs to feel accepted by the counsellor for the way in which she perceives herself. It won't be helpful if the child thinks that the counsellor's views of her have been influenced by the parents or by significant others. The relationship therefore needs to be exclusive.

Keeping the relationship exclusive means not allowing others to intrude or be included without the child's permission. Consequently, preparation of the child and parents for therapy requires specific attention, because there is clearly an ethical issue involved. The parents have care and control of the child, yet in therapy we are proposing that the counsellor needs to build an exclusive relationship with the child. How do you think the parents will feel about that?

The situation may be aggravated in cases where parents are using public health services or the services of large non-government agencies. Some parents may feel disempowered and overwhelmed by the system even though individual workers may try to create a personal consumer-oriented service. Such parents may be worried by the suggestion that they will not be fully included in the counselling process.

The ethical issue can only be addressed satisfactorily if the counsellor is clear with parents about the nature of the therapeutic relationship, and gains their acceptance of what is required. Therapy is generally a new experience for the child and the parents. We find that parents are likely to have a satisfactory level of comfort and to have confidence in the process, if they are fully informed about the need for the counsellor to maintain an exclusive relationship with the child.

It is helpful to warn parents that at times their child may not wish to disclose information arising from a therapy session. It is reasonable to expect that parents may feel anxious and believe that they might be left without information which they should rightfully know. Parents need to have reassurance that in time they will be given all the information that is important for them. They need to understand that children often have great difficulty sharing important and private information and that such sharing needs to be done when the child is ready and feels safe about sharing.

Sometimes, particularly at important points in the therapeutic process, a child may develop behaviours which are worse than the presenting behaviours apparent at the commencement of therapy. It is helpful to warn parents that there may be a period of improvement soon after treatment begins which is often followed by a setback or deterioration in behaviour. Passing general information to the parents, such as that mentioned in this and the previous paragraph, does not compromise the exclusivity of the relationship. However, to pass on specific details of a therapy session, without the child's agreement, would certainly compromise exclusivity.

As the child's confidence in the counsellor increases and the counsellor's understanding of the child's issues becomes broader, the trust that the child experiences becomes stronger. This trust is reinforced by the knowledge that fears, anxieties and negative thoughts towards parents, events and situations will not be disclosed to the child's parents or family members without the child's agreement. We believe that a child has a right to privacy, but do understand that it is sometimes difficult for parents to accept this.

Clearly, it's highly desirable to enlist the support and encouragement of parents, so that the child feels free to talk openly with the counsellor. We have found that if we are open with parents about the nature of the child–counsellor relationship parents will most often be very supportive of our work with their children.

We try to build a trusting relationship with the parents in the child's presence. Thus the exclusivity of the child–counsellor relationship is maintained, the child is fully aware of the parents' acceptance of that relationship, and is given permission and encouraged by the parents to join with us.

3 The child–counsellor relationship should be safe

The counsellor must create a permissive environment in which the child feels free to act out and to gain mastery over her feelings in safety. The child should feel safe to make disclosures with the confidence that doing so will not have repercussions or consequences which may be emotionally harmful or damaging. The issue of confidentiality is involved here and this will be addressed later in this section.

For the child to feel safe, structure is required. Structure gives the child a sense of security and predictability during therapy sessions. It also allows the counsellor to remind the child that indulging in repetitive non-purposeful activity will reduce the amount of time for constructive work. Structure includes the setting of behavioural limits and the giving of information about the expected length of each session. Additionally the child needs to be prepared for the termination of each session.

With regard to limit setting, we believe that limits should be imposed to protect the child, the counsellor, and property, from damage. Early in the joining process we make it clear to the child that there are three basic rules:

1 The child is not permitted to injure herself.
2 The child is not permitted to hurt the counsellor.
3 The child is not permitted to damage property.

We then make it clear that there are consequences for breaking the rules. If the rules are not complied with then the therapy session ends. However, the child is welcome to come back another time, and a new appointment will be made.

By using the three rules only, we avoid having to control and parent a child during a session. Also a uniquely therapeutic relationship is created where the child has permission to be herself with little restraint.

Although some external controls are set, this does not mean that the counsellor should anticipate a session free of acting out behaviour. Intermittent periods of testing behaviour are a normal part of the child therapy process.

Safety needs must also be considered when choosing materials for play therapy sessions. Equipment or toys which can be easily broken may be a source of anxiety for many children. Most children don't want to be held responsible for damaging property.

4 The child–counsellor relationship should be authentic

For the relationship to be authentic, it must be a genuine, and honest relationship where the interaction is one between two real people. The whole relationship must at all times be consistent with the real person who is the counsellor, and the child as the child genuinely is. It cannot be superficial, or a relationship where the counsellor pretends to be someone she is not. The authentic relationship allows the child an opportunity to give up the pretence of being someone she is not, and to allow the raw inner self to be exposed. This leads to a deep level of trust and understanding.

Authenticity in the relationship means allowing natural, spontaneous interplay between the counsellor and the child to occur, without inhibition or censorship, and without unnecessary anxiety. By being authentic, the relationship between the child and the counsellor will at times be serious, because of the gravity of the issues being discussed and the intensity of the emotions involved. However, the authentic relationship will not always be serious, it will also allow the child and counsellor to spontaneously engage in playful and enjoyable interaction. Most importantly, in the authentic relationship, the emerging issues of the child are not suppressed, avoided or violated.

5 The child–counsellor relationship should be confidential

When working with children the counsellor tries to create an environment where the child feels safe enough to share very private thoughts and emotional feelings. In order for the child to feel safe, a level of confidentiality is required. This confidentiality, and its limits, need to be discussed with the child early in the relationship building process.

Firstly, we need to consider problems which might arise from confidentiality, so that we can recognize appropriate limits.

Inevitably, there will be times when the child will share information with the counsellor which the counsellor believes needs to be shared with others: for example if a child discloses sexual or physical abuse. However, to disclose this information inconsiderately, or without giving consideration to the impact of disclosure on the child might lead the child into believing that he has been betrayed. Clearly, there is a dilemma for the counsellor here.

Take a few moments, if you will, to think about how you could satisfy the child's need for confidentiality and at the same time prepare the child for the possibility that important information might be shared with others.

Here is our approach to the confidentiality problem. Right at the start of the therapeutic process, we tell the child that what he says to us will be private, and that information will generally only be disclosed to parents or others with the child's permission. However, we warn the child that there may be times when it is important for information to be passed on. We explain that in such instances, we will discuss with the child, how and when the information is to be shared with others. We do this so that the child does not become disempowered but has control over the way in which disclosures are made to others.

When we need to pass information on to parents or others, we remind the child that we had previously said that there might be information which needed to be passed on. We tell the child that this is the case, and then ask the child what it will be like for her when the information is told to others. We then explore both positive and negative consequences of the proposed disclosure so that the child is fully aware of what outcomes there might be. We deal with the child's anxieties about sharing the information. We also give the child control of the timing and conditions surrounding the disclosure. We will ask the child questions such as the following:

Would you like to tell your parents yourself?
Would you like me to be present while you tell your parents?
Would you prefer me to tell your parents with you present?
Would you prefer me to tell your parents without you being present?
Would you like this to happen today, or at another time?

It is usually best if the child will tell the parents or others himself, but the child needs to have control over how and when this information is shared.

When working with children from families who have ongoing contact with statutory or government service agencies it is sensible to ascertain from those agencies, what they expect from the child and the family. Finding out what these expectations are can sometimes avert a child's removal from the family, or in other cases may facilitate the child's reintegration into the family. With such knowledge the counsellor may be able to tell the child about other agency expectations, and thus be in a position to warn the child that at times information may need to be passed on to the relevant agency.

We believe that counsellors should take steps to minimize the impact of a child's disclosures, particularly about abuse or mistreatment. Children often regret having made such disclosures, because the outcomes may be painful for them. Certainly, the counsellor needs to be sensitive to the child's predicament with regard to the disclosure of sensitive information.

Although we have been discussing confidentiality issues related to the disclosure of abuse of a child, confidentiality also relates to the disclosure of a child's intrapersonal issues to the family, particularly to parents. However, we have found that children will usually agree to the sharing of such information with others if they think that positive changes may occur as a consequence. We are, of course, careful to explore with children the possibility of negative aspects of disclosures.

In all cases, unless we consider that it is essential to make a disclosure to others, we will, after full discussion with the child, accept the child's decision to share or not to share information.

6 The child–counsellor relationship should be non-intrusive

When working with children the counsellor needs to join with the child in a way which is comfortable for the child. Some counsellors believe that questioning the child and inquiring about the child's family and background, during the joining process, is a useful way of getting to know the child and the child's world. Although we agree that this approach can be valuable, it needs to be used with care or it will be intrusive.

There is a danger in asking too many questions, because the child may fear being asked to disclose information which is private and/or too scary to share. If this happens the child will feel intruded upon and will withdraw into silence or will engage in distracting behaviour. Similarly it can be risky to use information about the child which the counsellor may already have obtained from parents, care-givers or other agencies. When the child discovers that important information has been given to the counsellor without his own consent or knowledge, he may feel threatened, exposed, vulnerable and uncertain about how much more information the counsellor may have. There is effectively an erosion of the child's ego boundaries, and the child is likely to feel disempowered. To intrude on the child's world in this way is likely to contribute to his anxieties about coming for counselling, and about being in the child–counsellor relationship.

7 The child–counsellor relationship should be purposeful

Children enter into the therapeutic process more willingly and confidently if they know exactly why they are coming to see the counsellor. They need time to prepare themselves for counselling, and will usually do so if given suitable notice and if told of the reasons why they are being brought to see a counsellor. Because of anxiety, parents sometimes wait until the last moment before letting their children know that they are going to see a counsellor and before telling them what to expect. Unfortunately some parents give their children no information whatsoever, but just arrive at the counsellor's door with their children feeling puzzled, uncertain, and anxious about what might happen!

It can be risky to assume that parents have given their child a truthful and clear explanation about their concerns and reasons for coming to see a counsellor. Some parents are very careful to explain to their children, in ways that are helpful and positive, that they are going to see a counsellor. However, other parents are not so skilled and say to their children things like, 'You will be seeing a doctor who will help you solve your problems,' or, 'I am taking you to see a woman who will make you behave.' Both of these approaches will certainly raise barriers for the counsellor to over-come. It is important for the counsellor to know precisely what information the child has received about coming to counselling and to clarify, affirm, or correct perceptions about what will happen. This needs to be done in the presence of both the parent and child so that there are no misunderstand-ings, or avoidable differences between expectations.

If the child clearly understands the reasons for coming to see a counsellor then the child–counsellor relationship has the potential to be purposeful. Most counselling sessions generally involve play because play is one of the most effective ways of producing change in children. It will be the counsellor's task to ensure that play or any other activity used is facilitated in a purposeful way, rather than being aimless. However, this does not mean that the play will necessarily be directed: it may well be free play, completely devised and controlled by the child. What is important is that the counsellor seeks to facilitate or engage the child in a process which will be therapeutically useful.

We recognize that undirected play can be therapeutic for some children. However, we believe that in most cases allowing a child to play endlessly over time, without appropriate counsellor interventions to promote some purposeful expression, is not useful. The skilled counsellor is one who takes advantage of opportunities which occur through play to intervene in a purposeful way.

We have discussed seven attributes which we believe are necessary in the child–counsellor relationship. You may have some additional or different ideas. Even so, we hope that our suggestions will be a starting point for your own exploration of the qualities which are required in the therapeutic relationship.

At this point we also need to consider the effect of *transference*, which is inevitable in the child–counsellor relationship. It is important for the counsellor to understand the nature of transference, to recognize it when it occurs, and to know how to respond to it.

Transference

'Transference' is a term which comes from psychoanalytic theory. In child therapy, transference occurs when the child behaves toward the counsellor as though the counsellor were the child's mother, the child's father, or another significant adult in the child's life. The behaviour occurs because the child projects her beliefs about a significant person on to the counsellor, believing that the counsellor is like that person. Transference can result in the child perceiving the counsellor either positively (positive transference) or negatively (negative transference).

Naturally, it is quite possible for the counsellor to inadvertently fall into playing the role in which the child sees her, and to respond as if she were a parent. If this happens we say that counter-transference is occurring. Counter-transference is likely to occur when the child triggers off the counsellor's own unresolved issues or fantasies from her past.

It is inevitable that transference and counter-transference will occur at times in the child–counsellor relationship, but provided this is recognized and dealt with appropriately, then it is not a problem. It certainly would be a problem if transference or counter-transference was not dealt with. Therapy would be compromised if the child continued to treat the counsellor as a parent and the counsellor continued to behave as a parent. For a fuller understanding of the nature of transference and counter-transference see Bauer and Kobos (1995).

Children will often transfer feelings or fantasies which they would like to direct at a parent, on to a counsellor. The counsellor may then inadvertently and unconsciously respond with counter-transference. For example, if a child has been rejected by a parent, that child may not feel able to face the painful truth and may instead project on to the counsellor the negative characteristics which belong to the parent, and may believe that it is the counsellor who is rejecting him (transference occurs). Consequently, the child's attitude to the counsellor may be negative, and the counsellor may unthinkingly respond as a rejecting parent (counter-transference occurs).

When we, as counsellors, suspect that transference is happening, we need to try to be as objective as possible. To achieve this objectivity we may need to discuss the case in question with our supervisor, so that we can deal with our own issues, projections and unconscious desires in connection with the child–counsellor relationship. Once we have owned our counter-transference we can then deal with it, and with the transference problem by bringing this into the child's awareness, as described in Chapter 11.

For an appropriate child–counsellor relationship to be created and maintained, the counsellor needs to bring certain personal qualities or attributes into the relationship and to engage in some specific behaviours. We will now consider these attributes and behaviours.

◆　◆　◆　◆　◆　◆　◆

4　Attributes of a counsellor for children

We know that each counsellor will bring into the therapeutic relationship her own unique personality. No two counsellors are going to be alike. Your individual personality will influence what you bring to the therapeutic relationship and you can use your own strengths and personal attributes to enhance your work. Having said this, we need to recognize that there are some basic attributes and behaviours which are desirable in the counsellor if an appropriate child–counsellor relationship is to be achieved. There are also some roles which the counsellor must play.

We invite you to think about the child–counsellor relationship, and to consider the question: 'In what ways would it be useful for a counsellor to relate to a child in a similar way to one of the following?'

- a parent
- a teacher
- an aunt or uncle
- a peer
- a blank sheet

What do you think?

None of the above would fit for us. In fact when we find ourselves behaving in any of the roles listed above, we know that it is time for us to visit our supervisor. Our belief is that there are a number of important attributes which are desirable for a counsellor.

Desirable attributes for a child-counsellor

The counsellor must be:

1　Congruent
2　In touch with her own inner child
3　Accepting
4　Emotionally detached

1 Being congruent

The child needs to perceive his relationship with the counsellor as trust-worthy and the counselling environment as safe. For this to happen the counsellor must be personally integrated, grounded, genuine, consistent and stable, so that trust can be developed and maintained. Children are very good at recognizing people who are not congruent and who are trying to play a role which is not consistent with the rest of their personalities.

2 Being in touch with our own inner child

The adult world is very different from a child's world. However, as adults we have not lost our child: it is still a part of our personality. This inner child is available to us if we learn how to access it. Accessing our inner child doesn't mean being childish, or regressing to childhood. It means getting in touch with that part of ourselves which fits comfortably with a child's world.

Both of us can remember when we ran a group for children from violent families, and an adult observer remarked that it was difficult to tell who the kids were – us, or the children in the group! We weren't offended by this remark, because we believed that a considerable amount of meaningful therapeutic work was accomplished with the children in that group. We both enjoy getting in touch with our inner child. Sometimes when we have done this in adult company we have been seen as 'like a couple of kids'. This ability to get in touch with our own inner child is important if we are to join effectively with our child clients. Otherwise we might well be perceived as like a parent, aunt, uncle or teacher, who experiences a very different world from the child.

If we are able to get in touch with our own inner child and to enter the child's world, then we are more likely to be able to join with the child successfully, to understand the child's feelings and perceptions, and to provide opportunities for the child to experience them fully. By helping the child to experience current feelings, we minimize the possibility of these feelings being stored and repressed to become the foundation of some future emotional disturbance and neurosis.

Children usually want to avoid strong unpleasant emotions. For them, as for ourselves as adults, getting in touch with feelings which haven't been accessed before may be very frightening. Consequently there will be a natural tendency for our child clients to push such feelings down, to repress them, and unfortunately to lock them in. It can be a huge leap for some children to learn that negative feelings can lessen and change when they are verbalized and shared. Similarly, as counsellors if we can get in touch with our own inner child and the pain of unresolved issues from our own childhood, then we will be better able to understand the difficulties and the release that comes from confronting those issues. If we are more open and more in touch with our own feelings, then the children we work with will come into a different relationship with us. They will be freer to be more open with us.

As counsellors we become models for the children we work with, so it is essential that we change those things in ourselves which we might want to change in our child clients. To do this we need to regularly work through our own personal issues in supervision with a competent therapist. We believe that it would be irresponsible for us to engage in counselling children without regular supervision where we can discuss case issues and personal issues of our own. It is inevitable that our own issues will be triggered off by the counselling work we do with children. If we fail to deal with these issues, they will interfere with our ability to help our clients.

3 Accepting

Right from childhood, all of us learn to respond to the verbal and non-verbal behaviour of others. When we are in the company of others we modify our behaviour to suit other people. We control our behaviours, we censor what we say, and we generally only reveal the more socially acceptable parts of ourselves. If we fail to comply with expected norms we are punished by the disapproval, criticism or withdrawal of others.

If we want to encourage children to explore the private, and maybe the darker or shadow side of themselves, then as counsellors we need to behave in the most accepting way we can so that our child clients have permission to be who they are, without restraint. In being accepting, we do not show approval, or disapproval. To do either of these things would have an effect on the child's behaviour. What we do is to accept, in the most non-judgemental way possible, whatever it is the child is saying or doing. We even avoid, as far as possible, making statements such as 'That's OK', because by doing so we give the child information about what we like and what we don't like. If we do that, the child's behaviour will change, and we will never see and be able to understand the whole child. In being accepting, we don't put our expectations on to the child, we do not withdraw or come closer in response to changes in behaviour, and we are not overwhelmed by the child's behaviour.

Naturally, it will take a child a while to trust that we will continue to be accepting. We will admit to you that being accepting, particularly with a child who is acting out, is not easy. Remember, though, the three rules mentioned earlier (see Chapter 3). When the rules are invoked, and as a consequence a therapy session ends, there still needs to be an uncritical acceptance of the child's decision to behave in the way that she did. It is essential to be non-judgemental at such a time, because the child is testing the limits which provide security in the therapeutic situation, and needs to know that it is expected that she will come back another time.

As a counsellor for children, can you put aside your parent role to accept a child in the way which we have described? We believe that such acceptance is one of the most important attributes of a counsellor.

4 Emotionally detached

In order to be accepting in the way just described, a counsellor also needs to be emotionally detached. This is often difficult for the new counsellor who might believe that being close, warm and friendly is more appropriate.

Unfortunately, there are problems for children who are clients of counsellors who are too close, warm and friendly. The child may be controlled by the relationship, because the child will not want to risk losing such a relationship by behaving in ways which might attract disapproval. Further, transference issues will be hard, if not impossible, for the counsellor to manage appropriately.

Most often, children who are being counselled deal with extraordinarily painful issues. If a counsellor becomes emotionally involved, then the counsellor is likely to become distressed by those issues in a way which is apparent to the child. The child will then experience additional pain at seeing the counsellor in pain, may believe that the counsellor is being overwhelmed by what is being shared, and will be likely to withdraw from discussing further painful material. Children find it hard to cope with a crying counsellor! They have enough trouble coping with their own pain.

The counsellor not only needs to avoid displaying emotional distress, but must also try to avoid showing other strong emotional responses in connection with the child's issues. For example, it is generally not useful for a counsellor to verbally or non-verbally give a child affirmation in connection with the child's issues or desires. To do so sets the child up to say and do things which will please the counsellor rather than encouraging the child to be authentic. Instead of giving either sympathy or affirmation, the counsellor should validate the child's experience. Nevertheless, it is both appropriate and necessary for a counsellor to affirm any sensible decisions a child may make. As counsellors, we need to discriminate between those things which need to be affirmed, and those things which should be accepted without affirmation, as belonging to the child.

Although a counsellor needs to be emotionally detached, this does not mean that the counsellor need be limp, lifeless and remote. On the contrary, the child does need to feel comfortable with the counsellor, so it is a question of balance. The counsellor needs to be present for the child as a calm and stable facilitator, who is able to participate when necessary, and always to listen, accept and understand the child.

We have considered four major attributes which we believe are important for a child counsellor. You may have others which you can add to our list. Clearly, the therapeutic relationship is multi-faceted. Counsellors need to be adaptable and to bring into play the various qualities which are needed at differing stages in the therapeutic process and at different points within a counselling session.

PART 2

THEORETICAL PERSPECTIVES

5 Historical background and contemporary ideas about counselling children

This chapter gives only an overview of the background and recent ideas about counselling children. Counsellors who wish to work with children do need to have a good understanding of the psychological theories which underpin their counselling work. We believe that it is important for counsellors to be familiar with all of the major theories and select ways of working developed from those theories which appeal to them personally and which they believe will be helpful for particular clients. We have fully referenced this section to enable you, the reader, to do further reading if you wish. Publications by the referenced authors are listed in the bibliography.

In moving from early history to the current time we will consider four overlapping periods during which significant ideas were developed relevant to counselling children:

1880 to 1940: The early pioneers developed underlying concepts.
1920 to 1975: Various theories of child development were proposed.
1940 to 1980: A number of humanistic/existentialist therapeutic
approaches were developed.
1980 onwards: Recent ideas for counselling children.

We will consider each of these periods in turn. In this discussion we will sometimes be referring to theoretical concepts and approaches which were initially developed for adults. Although there are major differences between the practical ways in which we counsel children and ways in which we counsel adults, many therapists of different orientations agree that the same underlying principles of psychotherapy apply to children and adults (Reisman and Ribordy, 1993).

1880 to 1940 – the work of the early pioneers

Sigmund Freud

The first of the early pioneers was clearly Sigmund Freud, who developed his psychoanalytic model over a period from 1880 to the 1930s (see Thompson and Rudolph, 1983). Much of psychoanalytic psychotherapy with children derives from Freud's discovery of unconscious processes and also of defence mechanisms which are employed by emotionally disturbed adults in order to protect themselves from distressing and/or unbearable experiences with which they cannot cope (Dale, 1990). Additionally, Freud introduced conceptual ideas about the formation of personality. These included the concepts of the id, the ego, and the superego. He also placed great emphasis on psychosexual development.

Some of Freud's ideas are directly useful when counselling children today. Additionally, it is important to understand them because some later theorists drew on his ideas but modified them. We consider the following aspects of Freud's theories to be the most relevant for counsellors who work with children today:

- id, ego and superego
- unconscious processes
- defence mechanisms
- resistance and free association
- transference

Id, ego and superego   Expressed simply, the id is the energizing part of us which strives to get our basic needs and drives met. The id is innate, uncontrolled and unconscious. The superego contains the qualities of conscience: it is a mixture of ideas which have been imposed by significant others, and ideas which are based on ideals. The ego is the part of the personality which seeks to strike a balance between the needs of the id and the conscience of the superego.

It is important for the contemporary counsellor who is working with children to recognize that when any stress occurs which causes anxiety or inner conflict, the child's id and superego are put into opposition. The id will strive to get instinctive and primary needs met, which may lead to unacceptable behaviours. By contrast the superego, which is said to be totally learned, imposes moral restrictions on these behaviours (Ivey et al., 1993). It is the ego's job to balance this struggle so that the id, ego and superego work together cooperatively. The counsellor's job is to help the child to gain in ego-strength so that this balance can be achieved.

Unconscious processes   According to Freud, anxiety occurs as a result of unconscious processes. These may arise as a result of the fear of memories, which may be conscious or unconscious. Other unconscious processes occur as a consequence of conflict between the id and superego. For example, the id may drive the child to satisfy sexual impulses which the superego views as taboo. If this is happening at an unconscious level then the child may become distressed because the ego is unable to resolve the situation.

Defence mechanisms   Defence mechanisms are unconscious. They protect the child from anxiety by helping him to avoid facing the consequences of unresolved differences between the id and superego. Defence mechanisms identified by Freud and described by Thompson and Rudolph (1983) include:

- repression
- projection
- reaction formation
- rationalization
- denial
- intellectualization
- withdrawal
- regression
- acting out
- compensation
- undoing
- fantasy

It is useful and necessary for counsellors who work with children to become familiar with the definitions of all of the defence mechanisms, because they are used by children as a way of dealing with their pain and anxiety (Thompson and Rudolph, 1983). Although defence mechanisms occur in normal human behaviour, Freud saw them as obstructing the ability of people to deal with the resolution of unconscious issues. Similarly, we need to recognize the ways in which these mechanisms block children from dealing directly with their issues.

Resistance and free association   Free association occurs normally in the progression of our thoughts from one topic or idea to another. However, this natural flow of thoughts and ideas becomes blocked as a consequence of the interference of defence mechanisms or resistance. Psychoanalysts see resistance as preventing the client from remembering painful experiences and preventing the client from talking about subjects which provoke anxiety. The psychoanalyst encourages the client to talk freely, looks for continuity of thoughts and feelings, identifies themes, and then interprets the client's statements. This enables the client's free association to continue so that he can continue to talk about important material. It is the analyst's job to notice when blocks to free association occur as a consequence of resistance or defence mechanisms, and to interpret these for the client. Through this process the client is enabled to discover and understand why he thinks and feels the way he does, and to make sense of his current behaviours.

Psychoanalysts place considerable emphasis on encouraging the client to talk freely by listening, and then interpreting for the client. You, the reader, may wish to train and work psychoanalytically, and if you do, we believe that you will be able to make use of many of the ideas in Part 4 for helping children to talk freely. Although we find Freud's basic theories very useful we do not generally use a psychoanalytic approach but instead invite the child to gain insight by self-discovery rather than through our interpretation. However, we do not always work in this way and are sometimes interpretive. It is probably useful for us to say at this point that we find that an eclectic approach is the most useful, in which we select our method of working to suit the child. Consequently, we think that it is important for us to include discussion of the major theoretical contributions to counselling children so that you may choose those ideas which appeal to you and are most appropriate for the child.

Psychodynamic ideas are certainly relevant today for work with children. However, an important difference between working with adults and working with children is that free association in children may be observed not only through verbal behaviour but also through non-directive free play, particularly imaginative pretend play (see Chapter 24). Just as an analyst working with an adult will interpret themes and recurring concepts for the adult, the counsellor working with a child can interpret recurring themes and concepts observed during the child's play, storytelling, or work with art.

Transference Transference and counter-transference were important concepts of Freud's. These were described in Chapter 3.

Other early pioneers of importance are:

- Anna Freud
- Melanie Klein
- Donald Winnicott
- Carl Jung
- Margaret Lowenfeld
- Alfred Adler

We will now briefly examine the contribution made by each of these.

Anna Freud

Whereas Sigmund Freud generally worked with adults, his daughter, Anna Freud, developed a method of working psychoanalytically with children by observing their play. She looked for the unconscious motivation behind imaginative play, and drawings and paintings, and interpreted the content of the child's play to the child when the relationship with the child was established (Cattanach, 1992). Waiting until the relationship with the child was established was essential in Anna Freud's view. She took great pains to establish in the child a strong attachment to herself and to bring the child into a relationship of real dependence on herself. She believed that the child would only believe the 'loved person' and would only accomplish something to please that person. She believed that this affectionate attachment or positive transference with the therapist was a prerequisite to all work which was to be done with the child (Yorke, 1982).

Anna Freud also placed importance on what she called negative transference. In children negative transference occurs when the child sees the therapist as a competitor to the mother. For more information on Anna Freud's theoretical perspectives and practical methods see Yorke (1982).

Melanie Klein

Melanie Klein worked with children in a totally non-directive way using play as a substitute for the verbal free association methods used by Sigmund Freud. She developed Freud's object relations theory (Klein, 1932). Freud believed that as children we attach to 'objects', such as our mother, and that growth and development involves separating from these objects. During the process of separation we attach to other objects, which are known as transitional objects. For example, when a child plays with a toy or a person, that toy or person becomes a transitional object because the child displaces her feelings from the mother on to the object.

Whereas Anna Freud believed that it was essential for a relationship to develop between the child and herself before using interpretations, Klein emphasized the immediate use of interpretation without waiting for the development of this rapport (Cattanach, 1992). She emphasized the object relations theory and the significance of transitional objects. Toys and other objects in the therapy room, and the therapist herself, were seen as transitional objects. Additionally, Klein sometimes recognized harmless explanations for a child's behaviour rather than always attributing symbolic meaning to that behaviour.

Contemporary counsellors of children need to understand both Anna Freud's and Klein's perspectives, particularly with regard to the nature of the counselling relationship, and the theoretical concepts of positive and negative transference. Clearly, your personal view of Freud's and Klein's differing theoretical perspectives will influence the way in which you use the counselling relationship in your work. Anna Freud's ideas can be useful in child psychotherapy which is open ended and not time limited. However, her perspective is not relevant to short-term or time-limited psychotherapy in which a long-term dependent relationship with the child is impossible. In such a situation Klein's ideas might be more suitable.

Donald Winnicott

Another important pioneer was Winnicott. His account of the treatment of a young child in *The Piggle* (Ramzy, 1978) gives a description of the treatment as it develops and a theoretical understanding of what is happening. *The Piggle* illustrates Winnicott's contribution to psychoanalytic theory. Winnicott believed that a child grows and develops through the use of transitional objects and also through the experience of the transitional space between the mother and child (Cattanach, 1992). Transitional space is the space in which the mother plays with the child in the process of helping the child to separate from her to establish a separate identity. According to Winnicott, therapy with the child parallels the transitional space. This is consistent with our view that with some children the counselling session and the relationship with the therapist is sufficient in itself to enable the child to work through unconscious issues.

Carl Jung

Carl Jung's work was not specifically targeted at children, although he did recognize the importance of childhood experiences in the process of children establishing their sense of identity. We believe that the most important contribution of Jung's work is his development of Freud's idea of the unconscious. Jung (1933) suggested that there existed a collective unconscious which came from the primal motivations of human beings. In this collective unconscious Jung believed that there were symbols which were common for all human beings. In his work he used symbolic representation, which is particularly relevant in counselling children when using the sand tray, clay, and art (see Part 4).

Margaret Lowenfeld

Although Jung placed great emphasis on symbolic representation, he worked psychotherapeutically through the use of verbal communication with the client. In 1925, Margaret Lowenfeld, who had been influenced by Jung's thinking, began working with children by using symbols in a sand tray to encourage non-verbal expression which was less influenced by rational thinking. She collected small objects, coloured sticks and shapes of paper, metal and clay, and kept them in what her young patients called her 'wonder box' (Ryce-Menuhin, 1992). Lowenfeld writes that this approach grew out of her attempts to find a way of helping children to talk without the use of language (Schaefer and O'Connor, 1983). Sand tray work is a way of helping the child to tell her story with or without the use of words (see Chapter 18).

Alfred Adler

In the early 1900s Adler was a member of a discussion group led by Sigmund Freud. This group later became the first psychoanalytic society. However, Adler broke away from that group in 1911 because he did not agree with Freud's psychosexual theories.

Adler believed that while people develop as individuals they also develop within a social structure: every individual is dependent upon other people. Adler focused on the interdependence of the person with the wider society. As a child develops, she is influenced by other people, and behaviours develop in response to the way in which other people view the child. Adler's work has an important influence on counselling children since clearly we need to take account of a child's wider environment. If we view the child in a wider context then the notion of consequences of behaviours arises. Reward and punishment are concepts rejected by Adler; instead he focused on natural and logical consequences. We ourselves favour this approach. In particular we make use of it when using worksheets and when working on social skills training (see Chapter 27).

Table 5.1 summarizes the work of the early pioneers.

Table 5.1   *The work of the early pioneers (1880–1940)*

Sigmund Freud	Developed psychoanalytic psychotherapy including the following concepts: unconcious processes, defence mechanisms, id, ego, superego, resistance, free association, transference, psychosexual development.
Anna Freud	Sought an affectionate attachment with the child (positive transference). Interpreted child's non-directed free play after an affectionate attachment with the child had been established.
Melanie Klein	Started to interpret the child's behaviour early in the therapeutic relationship. Interpreted child's non-directed free play.
Donald Winnicott	Saw the therapeutic relationship with the child as a parallel to the transitional space in which the child is separating from the mother. Thought that the relationship with the therapist was sufficient in itself to produce therapeutic change.
Carl Jung	Introduced ideas about the symbolic representation of a collective unconscious.
Margaret Lowenfeld	Used symbols in a sand tray as a substitute for verbal communication.
Alfred Adler	Introduced the need to take account of the person's social context.

1920 to 1975 – various theories of child development were proposed

In order to understand the development of therapeutic work with children we need to consider contributions to developmental psychology made by the following:

- Abraham Maslow
- Erik Erikson
- Jean Piaget
- Lawrence Kohlberg
- John Bowlby

Abraham Maslow

Abraham Maslow (1954) aided our understanding of the needs of human beings by identifying a hierarchy of needs. This hierarchy was not specifically developed for children but is very relevant to them, and includes the following levels:

1 Physiological needs – as the lowest level (the need for food, water, rest, air and warmth)
2 Need for safety
3 Need for love and belonging
4 Need for achievement of self-esteem
5 Need for self-actualization – as the highest level (achievement of personal goals)

Maslow suggested that if lower-level needs aren't met then the individual cannot direct his energies towards fulfilling higher-level needs. This has clear implications for counselling children, because, if we accept Maslow's hierarchy, it is pointless trying to achieve higher-level needs without first addressing lower-level needs.

The hierarchy does not need to be viewed or used rigidly. It may be possible to work on some higher-level needs before lower-level needs have been *fully* met. Additionally, particular levels in the hierarchy may assume greater importance at different developmental stages for the child. Understanding the hierarchy does help a counsellor to recognize when specific needs of a child have not been met and should be addressed. For example, a child who has been physically abused will have a need to work on issues of safety before being able to address issues of self-esteem, or self-actualization.

Erik Erikson

Erik Erikson believed that the individual has the potential to solve his own conflicts, and that competent functioning is achieved through the resolution of crises occurring throughout the individual's life at particular developmental stages. He emphasized the importance of the formation of an individual's personal identity; the personal identity being the way in which an individual sees himself.

Specifically, Erikson divided an individual's life-span into eight stages, each of which is represented by a personal social crisis. He believed that dealing with each crisis gives the individual an opportunity to strengthen his ego and to become more adaptive so that life can be lived more successfully.

Erikson's work is relevant to issues relating to self-concept and to the counsellor's work in helping the child to gain ego-strength through the successful resolution of developmental crises. Counsellors working with children need to be familiar with, and understand, Erikson's eight stages (see Erikson, 1967), because these stages illustrate the inevitable crises which children will meet. Each stage contributes to the ongoing process of mastery and achievement and needs to be recognized in the counselling situation.

Jean Piaget and Lawrence Kohlberg

Jean Piaget and Lawrence Kohlberg both contributed to the concept of children acquiring particular behaviours and skills at various stages in their development. Piaget (1962, 1971) noticed that a child interacts with both human and non-human objects, and the relationships which the child has with these objects allow him to become progressively more adaptive in his behaviour. As the child becomes more adaptive, he develops higher levels of cognition and starts to understand his environment in an increasingly complex way. Recognition of the child's development of cognition and acquisition of moral values is important for the counsellor when selecting activities such as games with rules (see Chapter 25).

Table 5.2   *Theories of child development (1920–75)*

Abraham Maslow	Introduced the idea of a hierarchy of needs.
Erik Erikson	Believed that the individual has the potential to solve her/his own problems. Postulated eight stages of development. Believed that ego-strength was gained through successful resolution of developmental crises.
Jean Piaget	Had a concept of children obtaining particular skills and behaviours at particular developmental stages and recognized stages of cognitive development.
Lawrence Kohlberg	Looked at the relationship between Piaget's concepts of cognitive development and the acquisition of moral concepts.
John Bowlby	Introduced theory of attachment whereby a child's emotional and behavioural development was seen to be related to the way in which a child was able to attach to its mother.

Lawrence Kohlberg (1969) was interested in the relationship between Piaget's concepts of cognitive development and the acquisition of moral values. A counsellor needs to have an understanding of the normal developmental sequence in which children come to understand moral concepts, because a child's decision-making processes will be based on his moral understanding and expectations of particular outcomes.

John Bowlby

Bowlby (1969, 1988) placed great emphasis on a child's attachment to her mother. He believed that the child's behaviours later in life would depend on the way in which she attached to the mother. He believed that children who securely attached to their mother were happy and well adjusted; where the attachment was less secure the child would be likely to become socially and emotionally maladjusted. He also believed that children who were securely attached to their mother would find it easier to separate and develop as individuals. Clearly, Bowlby's theories were culture specific and relate only to those cultures where primary attachment to the mother is socially promoted.

Ideas about attachment are relevant when counselling children who have poor attachment histories with their mothers and consequently are unable to form healthy relationships.

Table 5.2 provides a summary of the theories of child development.

1940 to 1980 – a number of humanistic/existentialist therapeutic approaches were developed

A number of humanistic/existentialist approaches for counselling adults were developed from 1940 onwards (see Corsini and Wedding, 1989). As we saw before, styles of therapy used for adults can be adapted for use with children. Important contributors to humanistic/existentialist therapies include Carl

Rogers, Frederick (Fritz) Perls, Albert Ellis, Richard Bandler, John Grinder and William Glasser. Additionally Virginia Axline and Violet Oaklander have made important contributions to ways of working specifically with children.

We ourselves, have an eclectic approach to our work, making use of those ideas which fit for us from all of the pioneers previously mentioned, and from the developmental theorists. We make considerable use of the humanistic therapies, together with some contemporary practices.

We will now consider the individual contributions of

- Carl Rogers
- Virginia Axline
- Frederick (Fritz) Perls
- Violet Oaklander
- Albert Ellis
- Richard Bandler
- John Grinder
- William Glasser

Carl Rogers

In 1942 Carl Rogers published *Counseling and Psychotherapy*, which at the time was controversial. Whereas in psychoanalysis the emphasis had been on the therapist's analysis and interpretation of the client's behaviour, Rogers (1955, 1965) believed that the client had the ability to find his own solutions in an environment where there was a warm and responsive counselling relationship. Thus he saw the counselling relationship itself as a catalyst for therapeutic change and believed that it was inappropriate for the counsellor to try to make interpretations on the client's behalf.

Rogers described desirable characteristics of the counselling relationship as congruence, empathy and unconditional positive regard, with the counsellor having a non-judgemental attitude to the client and the client's behaviour. Because Rogers believed that the client had the ability to find his own solutions he was totally non-directive, and used the technique of actively listening and reflecting back to the client what the client had said. Although Rogers's work was mainly with adults, we believe that his ideas are particularly useful when helping a child to tell her story, especially in the initial stages of therapy (see Chapters 9 and 10).

Virginia Axline

Virginia Axline's work with children in some ways paralleled Rogers's work with adults. She believed in the child's ability to solve her own problems in an environment where the relationship with the therapist was secure, and safe. She used Rogers's techniques of reflective listening based on the counselling principles of empathy, warmth, acceptance and genuineness (McMahon, 1992).

In *Play Therapy* (1947) Axline outlined eight principles for non-directive play therapy:

1 The therapist must develop a warm friendly relationship with the child.
2 The therapist accepts the child exactly as he is.
3 The therapist establishes a feeling of permissiveness in the relationship.
4 The therapist is alert to recognizing the feelings the child is expressing and reflects those back to him so that he gains insight.
5 The therapist maintains a deep respect for the child's ability to solve his own problems.
6 The therapist does not attempt to direct the child's conversation or actions in any manner.
7 The therapist does not attempt to hurry the therapy along.
8 The therapist establishes only those limitations that are necessary to anchor the therapy to the world of reality.

We find Axline's approach very useful in the early contact with the child and in the initial stages of therapy. However, later in the therapeutic process we usually become more directive.

Frederick (Fritz) Perls

Fritz Perls was the originator of Gestalt Therapy. Although he worked with adults, Gestalt Therapy can be a very valuable tool when working with children as demonstrated by Violet Oaklander. Perls initially trained as a psychoanalyst, but then challenged many of the assumptions of psycho-analysis, particularly those which placed heavy emphasis on the client's past (Clarkson, 1989). He believed that the focus should be on the client's current experience rather than the client's past and that the client should take responsibility for that current experience rather than blaming others or his past. Perls concentrated on raising the client's awareness of current bodily sensations, emotional feelings and related thoughts. By encouraging clients to become fully in contact with their current experience in the 'here and now', he believed that he could enable clients to work through 'unfinished business', sort out their emotional confusion, achieve what he called a gestalt, or 'Ah ha' experience, and thus feel more integrated.

Perls used, but modified, some of Freud's concepts. For example he redefined Freud's defence mechanisms as 'neuroses'.

Whereas the psychoanalysts dealt with resistance by interpreting the client's behaviour, Perls directly confronted resistance by raising the client's awareness of it, by encouraging the client to explore the experience of resisting, and to explore the resistance itself.

Perls used a number of counselling or therapeutic techniques which are especially useful when working with children:

• He gave the client immediate feedback about non-verbal behaviour as it was observed during the counselling process. This draws the client's attention to feelings that are being suppressed, or to resistance.

- He invited the client to get in touch with and describe bodily sensations and relate these to emotional feelings and thoughts.
- He encouraged clients to make 'I' statements and to take responsibility for their actions.
- He challenged and confronted what he saw as neurotic behaviour, for example deflection, introjection, projection and retroflexion.
- He explored polarities of the self by bringing them into awareness so that neither polarity was excluded (for example, the love–hate polarity).
- He encouraged clients to role-play different parts of themselves and to create a dialogue between these parts.
- He encouraged clients to role-play themselves and a significant other and to create a dialogue between themselves and the significant other.
- He introduced the concept of 'topdog underdog' and encouraged clients to role-play dialogue between these parts of self.
- He helped clients to explore dreams.

Parts 3 and 4 of this book illustrate ways in which we have integrated many of Perls's ideas into our work with children.

Violet Oaklander

Violet Oaklander (1988) has demonstrated a particular way to combine the use of Gestalt Therapy principles and practice with the use of media when working with children. She works therapeutically with children by encouraging them to use fantasy, and believes that usually the fantasy process will be the same as the life process in the child. She therefore works indirectly in bringing out what is hidden or avoided and relies on what is essentially a projective process.

Oaklander's book *Windows to our Children* consists of a number of excerpts from case studies, and will be of interest to those readers who would like to use Gestalt Therapy and fantasy. Her working model specifies techniques such as:

- encouraging the child to dialogue between two parts of the child's picture;
- helping the child to take responsibility or own what he has said about the picture;
- watching for cues in the child's body posture, facial expressions, tone of voice, breathing and silences;
- moving away from the child's activity with the media to work directly on the child's life situations and unfinished business as these arise from use of the media. Oaklander does this by directly asking the question, 'Does this fit with your life?'

We use Oaklander's approach sometimes when we use clay, the imaginary journey, storytelling and puppets (see Chapters 19, 21, 22 and 23). However, when we use Gestalt techniques, we usually work directly rather than through the use of fantasy.

Albert Ellis

Albert Ellis was the originator of Rational Emotive Therapy (RET), and published his first book on Rational Emotive Therapy in 1957. Originally developed for use with adults, RET is equally useful with older children from the age of about eight years. RET is now generally referred to as Rational Emotive Behaviour Therapy and is a Cognitive Behavioural Therapy. Readers interested in this style of therapy should consult Dryden (1990).

Ellis believed in giving direct advice and in direct interpretation of a client's behaviour. His method involved confronting and challenging what he called, *Irrational beliefs*, and persuading the client to replace these by what he believed were, *Rational beliefs*. The irrational beliefs were beliefs which tended to make the client feel bad about himself or left him with negative or uncomfortable feelings. Additionally they resulted in behaviours which would have negative consequences. Ellis believed that irrational beliefs had been learnt from significant others.

Ellis's ideas can be useful when counselling children, although we prefer to refer to *self-destructive beliefs* rather than irrational beliefs (see Chapter 12). Challenging self-destructive beliefs can be valuable when enhancing self-esteem, when engaged in social skills training, and when educating children in protective behaviours (see Part 5). When working in these areas, previously held beliefs may need to be challenged so that appropriate problem solving and decision making can occur.

Richard Bandler and John Grinder

Bandler (1985) and Grinder were the originators of Neuro-linguistic Programming (NLP). Although NLP was not specifically developed for children, there are some important elements of NLP which are useful when counselling children. These include:

- recognition of the different ways in which children primarily experience the world;
- the concept of reframing.

Human beings can experience the world by using one or more of three modes:

- seeing
- hearing
- feeling (kinaesthetically)

As counsellors, it is useful for us to match the mode which the child is currently using, or uses predominantly.

By using the NLP technique of reframing (Bandler and Grinder, 1982) we can help a child to see things differently. Examples of the use of reframing are given in Chapter 12.

Table 5.3 *A range of therapeutic approaches (1940–80)*

Carl Rogers	Introduced non-directive counselling and believed that the client could find his own solutions in an environment where there was a warm and responsive counselling relationship.
Virginia Axline	Believed in the child's ability to solve her own problems in an environment where the relationship with the therapist was safe and secure. Used non-directive play therapy.
Fritz Perls	Originator of Gestalt Therapy. Emphasized the current experience of bodily sensations, emotional feelings and thoughts. Gave the client feedback, challenged, confronted, used role plays and dialoguing.
Violet Oaklander	Combined Gestalt Therapy with the use of media and fantasy.
Albert Ellis	Originator of Rational Emotive Therapy. Challenged irrational beliefs and encouraged the client to replace them with rational beliefs.
Richard Bandler and John Grinder	Originators of Neuro-linguistic Programming (NLP). Recognized different modes in which people (and children) experience the world. Introduced the idea of reframing.
William Glasser	Originator of Reality Therapy. Encouraged the client to take responsibility for finding ways of getting his/her own needs met without infringing on the rights of others, and to accept the reality of the logical and natural consequences of behaviour.

William Glasser

William Glasser (1965) was the originator of Reality Therapy (later known as Control Therapy and now known as Choice Therapy) which has been used widely in school settings (as well as in detention centres and penal institutions for adults). Reality Therapy involves helping the client to willingly accept the reality of the logical and natural consequences of behaviour. In Reality Therapy the client is encouraged to take responsibility for finding ways of getting his own needs met without infringing on the rights of others.

Reality therapy is clearly useful at the point in the counselling process where children have gained insight into their own and others' behaviours, and are looking for more adaptive ways of meeting their needs by behaving differently. Reality Therapy is also useful in social skills training.

Table 5.3 summarizes the range of therapeutic approaches just discussed.

In our discussion of the historical background to counselling children we have only included reference to the work of those people whose work, in our opinion, has significantly influenced the practice of counselling children. Many other people have extended either the ideas or the working

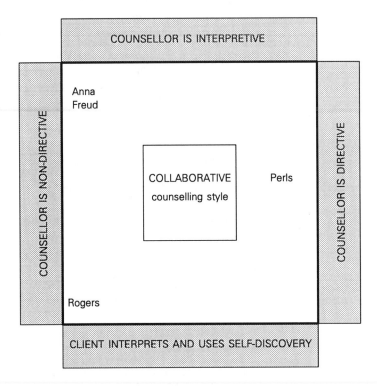

Figure 5.1 *Map of different counselling approaches*

methods of the people we have mentioned, or have introduced specific ideas related to the use of one particular medium. We have not mentioned these people because this is primarily a practical text and we want to provide only an overview of the theoretical background to counselling children.

The historical background, which we have discussed, provides the context into which recent ideas fit. Consequently, in considering recent ideas, we will summarize the historical background in two ways. Readers may wish to review Tables 5.1–5.3 to gain an overview of the historical background, before considering Figure 5.1.

Figure 5.1 provides a map which defines parameters within which counsellors work with regard to being either directive or non-directive, and interpretive or non-interpretive. The central part of the map relates to counsellors who do not take a strongly polarized position in relation to these variables, but have a collaborative counselling style. Issues about being directive or non-directive, and interpretive or non-interpretive, have been, and are, contentious among counsellors who work with children. Some counsellors, in both the past and present, have taken very polarized positions with regard to these parameters. Counsellors who take a polarized position use the approach of their choice within all of their counselling sessions.

In Figure 5.1, we wonder whether you will agree with the positions which we have allocated to the three counsellors we have shown on the map. We have placed Anna Freud in the top left hand corner, because she was non-directive and interpretive. We have placed Rogers in the bottom left hand corner because he was non-directive and left the interpretation to the client. However, we found it difficult to place Perls. We placed him towards the right hand side of the map because when he was working with clients he was very much in control of the process of the therapy, was directly confronting, and deliberately tried to frustrate the client. However, some Gestalt therapists would argue that it was the client's emerging experiences which controlled the direction of the process and would claim that Perls should therefore be further to the left. Similarly there could be argument about where to place Perls on the vertical *interpretive* versus *self-discovery* continuum. It can be difficult to place some individuals in precise positions, but we think that the map is useful for bringing into focus differences in the theoretical positions and practical approaches of the therapists we have mentioned. Readers may wish to see whether they can position the other counsellors, described in this section, on the map.

We believe that valuable work can be done in many different ways and that your individual working style needs to be one which appeals to you personally. Additionally, it is useful for us as counsellors to vary the ways in which we work to suit the individual child and the child's presenting problems. Consequently, sometimes we are directive and sometimes non-directive, and although generally we prefer the child to use self-discovery, sometimes we are interpretive. In general, with regard to methods of working, we use an eclectic approach, making use of what we consider to be the most suitable method for the child at the time. We should point out that we believe that many contemporary counsellors take a similar approach, as we will discuss later.

1980 onwards – recent ideas for counselling children

When considering recent ideas for counselling children we recognize that today there is a wide variety of viewpoints about which approach to use. We personally know a child psychotherapist who works only in a psycho-analytic way similar to that of Anna Freud, another who uses cognitive behavioural methods almost exclusively, such as those proposed by Ellis and others, and yet another who works predominantly in a Gestalt Therapy way, but without Oaklander's emphasis on fantasy. Moreover, it seems to us that all of the methods discussed in our review of the historical back-ground are still in use. Most contemporary ideas about counselling children involve the use of, or adaptation of, methods of working which were in use prior to 1980.

Perhaps the most significant new approach has been that of Richard Sloves and Karen Belinger-Peterlin, who introduced and developed time limited play therapy (1986).

Time limited play therapy

One of the most significant developments in the last few years has been the introduction of ideas about brief therapy. In contemporary society there is pressure on counsellors to be accountable by using cost effective methods (Cade, 1993). De Shazer (1985) contributed to brief therapy by placing the emphasis on the process of finding solutions rather than focusing on the origins of the problem (see Zeig and Gilligan, 1990; Walter and Peller, 1992). At the same time there were other workers such as Davanloo, Malan, Mann, Goldmann, Sifneos, Strupp and Binder, with a psychodynamic background, who embraced the idea of brief therapy without relinquishing their psychodynamic orientation (Lazarus and Fay, 1990).

Time limited play therapy (Sloves and Belinger-Peterlin, 1994) was developed as an approach for working with children using ideas from brief therapy with a psychodynamic orientation.

The approach is to make a brief assessment of the child's issues. The therapist then selects a central theme and the therapeutic work is limited to this theme. The work with the child focuses on empowerment, adaptation, and strengthening the ego. It focuses on the future rather than the past. However, the central theme will have been influenced by the child's past. Generally individual work with the child is limited to 12 sessions. This form of therapy is both directive and interpretive.

Sloves and Belinger-Peterlin (in Schaefer and O'Connor, 1994) made it clear that time limited play therapy is effective for some children and not useful for others. It is most effective for children with recent post-traumatic stress disorder, adjustment disorders, and for children who have lost a parent due to a chronic medical condition (Christ et al., 1991).

In a similar way, Millman and Schaefer (1977) pointed out that traditional psychodynamic therapy has proved most effective for intelligent moderately disturbed children, whereas more structured techniques have proven more cost effective with children who have situation-specific difficulties or traumatic reactions.

The literature demonstrates that there is no one preferred way of working which is appropriate for all children. As we have stated before, in our own work we have noticed that effective work with children depends on selecting a method of working which is specifically suitable for a particular child and relevant for that child's issues. This approach was originally proposed by Millman and Schaefer (1977) and called a 'prescriptive approach'.

In their 1983 book, Schaefer and O'Connor describe this approach. It emphasizes the therapist's responsibility for determining the most appropriate therapeutic technique for each particular child. The therapist is therefore expected to prescribe an approach which suits the child and is most relevant for the treatment of the presenting problem.

In conclusion

In writing this book we have placed a strong emphasis on helping the child to tell her story, as described in Chapter 10, and have included discussion of ways in which to use a variety of media to achieve this. However, we hope that the reader will find that the methods we have described can be adapted to the way in which you wish to work with an individual child. We adapt our way of working so that when appropriate we will sometimes be directive and sometimes non-directive. Similarly we will sometimes be interpretive and will sometimes will rely on the child's interpretations.

We believe that the most important contemporary idea is to be able to select from a range of practice methods in order to achieve the best possible outcome for the child in the most cost effective way.

We have not included methods of working with children in a group or family setting because this book is specifically concerned with counselling children individually. However, we recognize that sometimes it may be appropriate to work with a child in the context of the family, or with the parents, or by using a combination of individual and group therapy.

◆ ◆ ◆ ◆ ◆ ◆ ◆

6   The process of child therapy

Our intention is that we, as counsellors, will engage our child clients in a therapeutic process by using counselling skills in conjunction with media and other strategies. When we talk about this therapeutic process we are really referring to a number of differing processes which need to be brought into play if therapeutic change is to occur.

The flow chart in Figure 6.1 gives a simplified overview of the total process of child therapy. Each frame on the chart involves a specific process; for example *contracting with parents* is a process in itself.

Under the facilitation of a skilled counsellor, the processes described in each frame of Figure 6.1 will interact to form an integrated therapeutic process. Because each case is different, not all of the processes shown will be used for every child. Some may happen concurrently with others, and some may be repeated during the course of therapy. In this section we will describe the processes listed in Figure 6.1 in the sequence shown.

The initial assessment phase

The initial assessment phase is a time of preparation for therapy. During this phase, information is gathered about the child and the child's problems. This information enables the counsellor to hypothesize about what might be happening for the child. With a hypothesis in mind, suitable media can be selected to enable the counsellor to engage with the child and to commence working therapeutically. The initial assessment phase also includes meeting with and contracting with the parents.

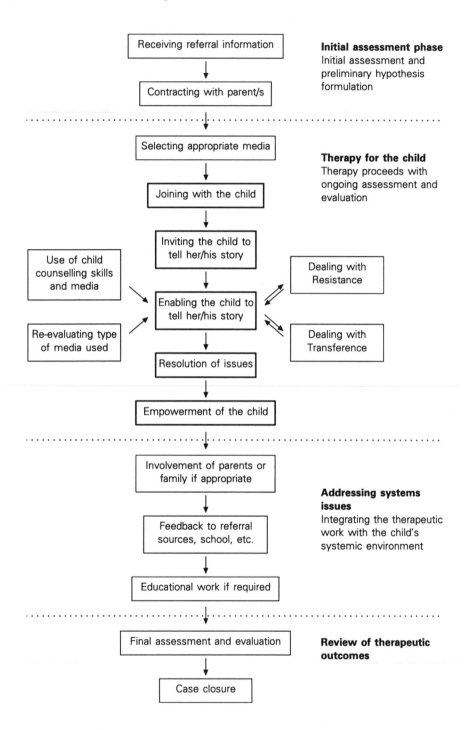

Figure 6.1 *The process of child therapy*

Receiving referral information

In order for therapeutic work to be maximally useful and effective, the counsellor needs to have as much information as possible about the child including the child's behaviour, emotional state, personality, the child's history, cultural background, and the environment within which the child lives.

Initial information comes at the time of referral, from the referral source. Sometimes the person making the referral will be a parent, but at other times referrals may come from medical practitioners, schools, other professionals, statutory bodies, and other sources. Such information can be invaluable in helping the counsellor to understand the child.

It must be remembered that the information given by a referral source may be inaccurate and distorted because of the referrer's own agenda. However, such information is still useful because it is someone else's perception of what is happening. For example, I may have been told that a child was deliberately disobedient. Later, I may discover that the child has a high-order language problem and consequently has difficulty understanding instructions, but is not generally being deliberately disobedient. Although the first piece of information was factually incorrect, it would have helped me to understand what was happening in the child's life. It can therefore be valuable to collect several different opinions with regard to the child's behaviour and problems, but to remember that these are opinions which may not be factually correct.

Part of the initial assessment phase involves meeting with the parent/s (or other care-givers) to get their picture of the situation, and to contract with them with regard to therapy.

Contracting with parents (or care-givers)

We find that it is generally useful to have a full consultation with the parents initially without the child being present. This enables the parents to talk freely and openly without being inhibited by the child. During this interview we record a detailed history, the parents' understanding of the problem, and responses to the problem. We also contract with the parents with regard to the therapeutic process.

Parents of emotionally disturbed children are likely to be anxious and concerned about their children. They may also be worried about what may happen if their child is to enter into a counselling relationship with someone who is not personally known to them. It can be quite threatening for parents to know that their child will be talking to a stranger about personal and possibly family matters. Additionally, some parents feel inadequate in their parental role and may be worried about the possibility that the counsellor will blame them for their child's problems.

Because of the likelihood of parental anxiety, it is essential that parents be given the opportunity to talk to the counsellor, not only about the child, but also about the counselling process, and at some level about their own anxieties. During interviews with parents, the counsellor needs to be an empathic listener who is seen to value both the parents and the information they provide. Although we believe it is appropriate for a counsellor to provide the opportunity for parents to talk about their anxieties in general terms, we do not believe that the child's counsellor should become counsellor for the parents also. This would compromise the child–counsellor relationship, and would make it difficult for the child to join with, and to trust, the counsellor.

It is important for parents to understand the exclusivity of the child–counsellor relationship. Therefore, we tell parents that for counselling to be effective their child will need to feel free to talk openly and confidentially with us. We also say that we realize that it may be uncomfortable for them not to be kept fully informed of what their child is telling us. However, we assure them that we will keep them informed with regard to the overall process. Further, we tell them that if information emerges which they, as parents, have a right to know, we will talk to the child about the necessity of sharing this with them.

When all of the available information has been gathered in the initial assessment phase, the counsellor is in a position to formulate a preliminary hypothesis with regard to the child's presenting issues. This hypothesis will be based not only on the information which has been received about the child from the referral sources and parents, but also on the counsellor's own understanding of child psychology and behaviour in the context of the relevant environmental climate. Thus, the hypothesis must clearly take account of racial, ethnic, cultural and religious differences in beliefs, attitudes, expectations and behaviours. Readers may wish to refer to *Counselling and Psychotherapy – a Multi-cultural Perspective* by Ivey et al. (1993) if they wish to explore the impact of cultural issues when counselling.

With a hypothesis in mind, therapy for the child can commence.

Therapy for the child

Selecting the appropriate media

Before meeting with the child, the counsellor needs to make a decision on the most appropriate media to be used. This selection will be based on age, gender, personal characteristics, and type of emotional problem. For details of the selection process see Chapter 16.

Joining with the child

Our preference is to have an initial interview with the parents, without the child being present. Subsequent sessions are generally for the child only, with the parents being included only at times when feedback is being given. However, most children are brought to therapy sessions by their parents, and it is important to make the parents feel welcome and valued when they arrive. We believe that providing a friendly and hospitable environment is important, not only for joining with the child, but also as part of the therapeutic process.

We usually offer parents a cup of tea or coffee, and the children a cold drink, when they arrive for an appointment. This is particularly appreciated by those children who come to consult with us after a busy day at school.

Children have their own unique and special personalties and needs. Some may be difficult to engage for a variety of reasons. They may have had their trust in adults betrayed, they may be hostile, they may have been frightened into silence, or they may act up and behave inappropriately. Very young children may lack the language to communicate effectively. The process of joining must be tailored to meet the individual requirements of each child. There are however some basic methods of joining which can be useful generally.

When the child arrives for the first time we start to join with the child in the waiting room. However, we start this process by joining with the parents first. By doing this we allow the child to feel safe and comfortable and in the care and control of the parents. The child observes the way that we relate to the parents, and is thus enabled to gain a level of trust and confidence in us. Additionally, the child will be encouraged by the parents and thus given permission to engage in a relationship with us. This process also allows the parents to experience the importance of their own role in the counselling process.

Asking the parents to clarify the reasons for coming for counselling, in the child's presence, is an important part of the joining process. By doing this the child and the counsellor have the same information about the reason for the child coming to counselling, and both know that the other knows what the reason is. This minimizes the possibility of misunderstandings or misconceptions.

In the process of joining the child must be provided with choices and options about how the first therapy session should begin and proceed. Initially it might be useful to allow the child to explore the building, and to let him know where his mother or father will be waiting. This approach is particularly useful if the child's anxiety levels are high.

Some children have difficulty in separating from their parents and engaging with a counsellor. When we encounter such a child, we invite the child and parents into the play therapy room. We then invite him to explore this room while we talk with his parents or care-givers in his presence. During this process we intermittently engage the child in some of the conversation, or invite the child to tell us about things of interest in the room. Occasionally we may invite the child to play with his parent in the play room until he feels safe there.

With some children, joining is easy. This is particularly so with children who do not have appropriate boundaries or are very needy. Such children may join without caution and may be inappropriately compliant. Taking note of the child's joining behaviour is useful for assessment purposes.

It is essential during the joining process to help the child to understand the nature of the child–counsellor relationship. Without this understanding, the child would not know what to expect of the counsellor and would not know what the counsellor's expectations of the relationship were, and joining would be limited.

As children grow and develop they come into contact with, and are influenced by, many adults. Each of these adults has individual characteristics or attributes. Children notice these and learn from them. For example, schoolteachers may be perceived by children as having authority: they direct children in carrying out tasks, and those tasks generally involve learning. Shopkeepers have a different type of authority, which is confined to behaviour in their shops. Aunts and uncles have authority which may not have clear boundaries, because while they don't have full responsibility for the management of the behaviours of their nieces and nephews, they may have some level of responsibility. Parents have overall authority across all areas of children's lives. Each child comes from a unique environment, and it is from their environment that the child learns the social rules for interacting with differing categories of people, such as the teacher, the shopkeeper, the aunt and uncle, and most importantly, the parent. The social rules which a child uses with any particular person will depend on the child's expectations of the relationship with that person. Hence it is essential for a child who is being counselled to have an understanding of the nature of the child–counsellor relationship, so that she knows what the expectations are; otherwise she will not feel secure and comfortable in the relationship. Counsellors need to lay down guidelines or ground-rules at the beginning of the therapeutic relationship so that the child is clear about what is permissible and what is not. The rules we use were described in Chapter 3.

Explanation of the ground-rules lets the child know what is not permissible during therapy. The child also needs to know that it *is* permissible for him to express himself in whatever way feels comfortable within the constraints of the rules, and that it is permissible to disclose and to talk about issues which are private and confidential.

The child's understanding of the relationship will develop further as the relationship is experienced. The child will learn by testing the relationship and accepting the consequences of his behaviour within the context of the relationship.

In summary, joining is primarily about creating a relationship which meets the child's needs in the therapeutic environment, so that the child will feel comfortable enough to engage usefully in the therapeutic process. Once the child is observed to be feeling comfortable in the relationship, then she can be invited to tell her story.

Inviting the child to tell her story

Counselling skills using verbal communication alone will usually be quite useless with children, especially when children have poor communication skills, high levels of emotional distress, and acute psychological disturbance. Often, it will not even be possible for the counsellor to join with the child just by talking. However, effective joining followed by effective therapy is usually possible if the child is invited to tell her story through the use of play or suitable media.

Care needs to be taken in deciding what materials to make available for play, and in selecting media. Both the play environment and the media must be appropriate for the developmental age of the child and useful in enabling the child to tell her story. These must be selected so that they provide the child with an opportunity to explore relevant emotional and psychological issues. For details about deciding what materials to make available for play, see Chapter 15, and for information about the selection of suitable media, see Chapter 16. After selection of media and play, the child can be invited to tell her story.

Inviting the child to tell her story, and enabling the child to tell her story, are the most central and effective components of any child psychotherapy process.

Through telling her story, the child has the opportunity to clarify and gain a cognitive understanding of events and issues. Additionally, she can ventilate painful feelings and gain mastery over anxieties and other emotional disturbances by active rather than passive means. The child becomes personally engaged and involved in the therapeutic experience with the consequence that intrapersonal psychological change is almost certain to occur.

It sounds very straightforward, doesn't it? We just invite the child to tell her story and therapy has begun. Unfortunately, in reality, it is not always so simple and straightforward. Problems due to factors directly related to the nature of the child's problems can arise. If these are not carefully considered and confronted, then they may undermine the therapeutic process.

Disturbed children will often behave inconsistently and have difficulty in recognizing and/or communicating their feelings. Some have poor impulse control and a decreased attention span. Others exhibit pathological defence mechanisms. The therapeutic process may be blocked by one or more of these problems, and it will be difficult to engage the child in therapy. However, with appropriate use of child counselling skills, as described in Part 3, these blocks can usually be overcome.

When inviting the child to tell her story, the issue of trust is central. Without an adequate level of trust the growth of the therapeutic relationship will be inhibited. Sometimes, because of the importance of this issue, we need to go very slowly at first. In initial sessions we might allow time for a young child to play freely, or we might engage an older child in a game to help the child to feel comfortable and safe in the environment. In other cases specific media may be used for this purpose.

Once a trusting relationship has been established in an environment which includes appropriate media, then the child can be invited to tell her story. In inviting the child, the counsellor doesn't attempt to hurry the therapeutic process, but allows the child opportunities to express herself and to explore feelings and issues which may be troubling for her. The counsellor doesn't interrogate, but instead invites the child to disclose what she wishes.

There are some counsellor behaviours which are likely to inhibit the child. These include being restricted by time, or space, or by the media that have been selected. The novice counsellor may be impatient and may want to move too quickly for the child. Sometimes inexperienced counsellors who are starting to feel frustrated by initially slow progress fall into the trap of using questioning as a way of trying to move the process along. Unfortunately, unless questioning is used sparingly, the child may shut down communication for fear of intrusion by the counsellor, into private and sensitive material.

Enabling the child to tell her story

We have already talked about the importance of trust, of creating a suitable environment, of the use of play and/or of media, in inviting the child to tell her story. However, in order to *enable* the child to tell her story we must additionally make use of appropriate child counselling skills. For the therapeutic process to be effective, the counsellor must create and/or provide the following:

- a trusting relationship;
- appropriate media;
- facilities and opportunities for free and/or meaningful play;
- the use of appropriate child counselling skills.

By using appropriate child counselling skills the counsellor enables the child to tell her story and accompanies the child as she goes on a journey of exploration, revealing her story, and in the process resolving issues. During this journey of exploration the counsellor will need to regularly re-evaluate the type of media used, and make changes if appropriate. The counsellor may also need to deal with both *resistance* and *transference* (see Figure 6.1, p. 36).

The issue of transference was discussed in Chapter 3. Discussion of approaches to use in dealing with transference and resistance are included in Chapter 11.

Resolution of issues

Sometimes a child will find that the telling of her story is in itself effective in reducing emotional pain, and in leading to the spontaneous resolution of issues. Often though, the counsellor will need to help the child to work through particular issues so that they are no longer troublesome. This may be done through play and/or through the use of counselling skills, and sometimes through educational input. When the issues are properly resolved the child will be enabled to relate to others more comfortably, to be freer of anxiety, and to live more adaptively in her social and emotional environment.

Empowerment of the child

Although in Figure 6.1 empowerment follows resolution of issues, it may have occurred spontaneously while the child told his story. Enabling the child to tell his story, in an environment where the child is accepted and believed, with understanding and without judgement, is an important part of the empowerment process.

Empowerment involves gaining mastery over issues, so that the child will no longer be excessively troubled by thoughts and memories which create anxiety and interfere with normal adaptive relationships. Empowerment adds to self-esteem and enhances social relationships. This helps the child to integrate with more comfort into his social and emotional world. Examples of ways to promote empowerment are given in Part 3.

Addressing systems issues

Involvement of parents, or family if appropriate

When we work therapeutically with a child it is essential to take account of the environment in which the child lives. The most important part of that environment is usually the family. If we work with the child alone, then the therapeutic gains we achieve may be limited by what we call *circular processes* which inevitably occur within the family.

Consider the circular process shown in Figure 6.2. In this example, the child initially feels rejected and misbehaves in order to get attention. Because of the misbehaviour the parent becomes angry and withholds affection. This increases the child's feelings of rejection. Consequently, there is an escalation of both the child's acting out behaviour and the parent's withdrawal behaviour. The process is circular, with each behaviour being a response to the previous behaviour. Because of the inevitability of circular processes occurring, it is often advantageous for siblings as well as parents to understand the changes and issues that have confronted the child during individual therapy.

Often when change occurs there is resistance to this change and it is helpful for families to understand this. The child may experience periods of setback and regression, and the family need to be prepared for these. Other family members may either intentionally or unintentionally try to sabotage newly acquired behaviours. Involvement of the family in the therapeutic process gives the opportunity for individual family members to express their feelings and emotions regarding the process of change.

Feedback to referral sources

Following a period of therapy, after a child has resolved issues and become empowered in some ways, it may be desirable for a counsellor to integrate

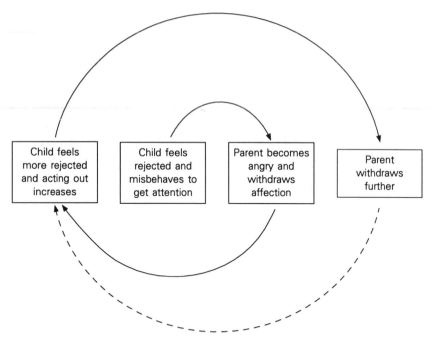

Figure 6.2   *A circular process*

the therapeutic work with the child's wider environment, with the parents' permission. Referral sources (schools and other agencies) may benefit from feedback about the child's movement through therapy. This needs to be general feedback which does not break confidentiality by divulging specific information of a private nature. A child can benefit if significant others understand past behaviours and are able to cooperate constructively with regard to changes in behaviour. Such cooperation can enable the child to continue experimenting with new behaviours and to practise newly discovered adaptive skills.

Educational work if required

Following the resolution of complex unconscious issues it may be desirable to address specific generic issues such as safety, and relationships. This requires educational work which is often best done in groups. Group work allows the child to feel less stigmatized and makes it easier for the child to integrate new ideas into her wider environment.

Review of therapeutic outcomes

Final assessment and evaluation

Final assessment and evaluation is best done in collaboration with the child and family. The assessment is to confirm that further work is not required or appropriate at the time. Evaluation is required to evaluate the effectiveness of the work which has been done and to make recommendations.

Case closure

After the final assessment and evaluation, the counselling process can be terminated and the case can be closed. Counselling skills for termination are discussed in Chapter 14.

In describing the process of child therapy our greatest emphasis has been on inviting and enabling the child to tell her story. If this becomes central to the process, then we believe that the possibility of therapeutic change occurring is maximized. In order to engage the child in the telling of her story, we need to use not only child counselling skills but also play and/or media.

In the next section we will look at other processes which also occur. These are the internal processes of therapeutic change which occur within the child.

◆ ◆ ◆ ◆ ◆ ◆ ◆

7 The child's internal processes of therapeutic change

In the previous chapter we dealt with processes which the counsellor must set in motion and facilitate in order to bring about therapeutic change in a child. In a sense these are external to the child, because they involve action by the counsellor, and not by the child. As those processes occur, there will simultaneously be processes occurring within the child. These directly result in the child experiencing therapeutic change. These internal processes either occur spontaneously in the counselling environment, or occur in direct response to the counsellor's interventions.

We will describe the child's internal processes by using a model which we have developed. We call this model the Spiral of Therapeutic Change. It is shown in Figure 7.1.

Because each child is different, and because human behaviour is complex, the Spiral of Therapeutic Change needs to be seen as offering only a general understanding of the types of processes which are likely to occur within the child; it is not an exact model of how therapeutic change occurs.

We will now discuss each frame on the Spiral of Therapeutic Change, starting with 'Child is emotionally disturbed'. To illustrate our discussion we will use a fictional but typical case study. To protect the confidentiality of our clients we have combined information from several cases and have changed all identifying information.

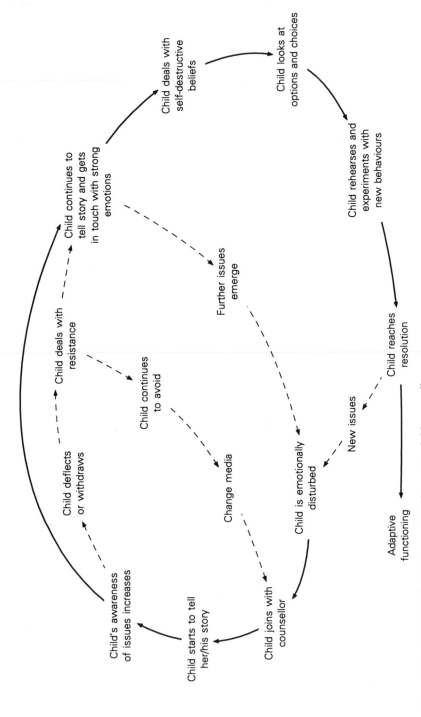

Figure 7.1 *The Spiral of Therapeutic Change in child counselling*

A case study – background information

Amy is 11 years old, but immature for her age, and lives alone with her mother. She was brought by her mother for counselling help because she was depressed, anxious, over-sensitive, and was getting into conflict at school. She cried easily, wasn't concentrating and was disobedient.

During an initial interview with the mother it emerged that Amy was the result of an unplanned and unwanted pregnancy and at first Amy was rejected by her mother. However, for the last few years Amy had been treated like an adult companion to, and confidante for, her mother. When 18 months old Amy was sexually interfered with by her maternal grandfather. It also became clear that Amy's mother had unrealistically high expectations with regard to Amy's behaviour and emotional maturity.

In the initial interview, it also emerged that Amy's mother had been neglected and physically abused by her own mother, sexually abused by her father, and subjected to rigid and strict rules in her family. Although Amy's mother was abused by her parents, her brothers and sister were not subjected to the same level of abuse. Amy's mother had decided that she did not want to parent Amy in the same way that her mother had parented her, and was making a determined effort to provide Amy with a better quality of life.

Child is emotionally disturbed

Children are unlikely to be brought for counselling unless they have emotional problems. However, sometimes referral sources may not recognize that the child is emotionally disturbed, but may instead see the child as having behavioural problems.

In our case study, the mother recognized the behavioural problems, that is the child's lack of concentration and disobedience, and also recognized the presence of emotional problems, including anxiety and depression.

Child joins with counsellor

The relationship between a child and counsellor is in some ways reciprocal although in other ways it is unequal. It is reciprocal with regard to joining. If a child is to join with a counsellor, then the counsellor must join with the child. If joining is successful, then the child will experience a level of comfort with the counsellor, and this will enable the therapeutic process to proceed.

Initially Amy was encouraged in free play. The counsellor joined with her as the child played with the dolls' house and the puppets. Through observation of Amy's free play and through interaction with Amy, the counsellor was able to discover Amy's strengths. She had a rich imagination, was good at abstract thinking, was friendly, but at times was over-compliant and eager to please. Initially, Amy expected to be reprimanded by the counsellor for the misbehaviour which her mother had described, and she agreed with her mother's negative descriptions of her behaviour.

However, when the counsellor explained the nature and purpose of the counselling relationship Amy was able to feel more comfortable, and to allow the counsellor to join with her.

Child starts to tell her story

Given an appropriate environment, with suitable media available, and with the counsellor using the required counselling skills, the child will become spontaneously involved in telling her story. This may be done in a direct way with the child openly recounting her story, or it may be done indirectly through play.

In Amy's case, the counsellor chose to use the miniature animals (see Chapter 17). The counsellor's choice was based on the assumption that the child's emotional problems might be related to her relationship with her mother. This assumption arose from the counsellor noting that the child had at first been unwanted and rejected by the mother, that the mother had experienced an unsatisfactory relationship with her own mother, and that Amy's impression was that she was being brought by her mother to counselling to be reprimanded for her misbehaviour.

By using the miniature animals Amy was able to projectively demonstrate her relationship with her mother, her grandmother and her grandfather. She then moved on to discuss these relationships more directly. During this discussion her story started to unfold and it emerged that:

1 Amy believed that her mother continually pushed her away.
2 Amy was worried by her grandfather but was also curious about him.
3 Amy believed that she could only get near to her grandmother when she was good.

Child's awareness of issues increases

As a child recounts her story, her awareness of strong emotions and/or painful issues will be intensified. As a consequence the child may either continue to tell her story, thus enabling the therapeutic process to move forward, or may deflect or withdraw.

Work with Amy continued, using the puppets to role-play a fantasy story about a princess and fairies (see Chapter 23). As Amy developed the story, the princess took a mothering role. From this story, it emerged that Amy wanted a closer relationship with her mother based on positive warm interactions, with a lot of physical touching and cuddling. However, she realized that her mother did not respond to her attempts to achieve such a relationship. She also became aware that the times when her mother did respond to her was when she was naughty, or when she was being victimized by other children. This is understandable because Amy's mother was responding to her own needs to parent in a particular way.

Amy also became aware of the fact that she couldn't satisfy her curiosity about her grandfather because her mother wouldn't let her get near to him.

The mother wanted to protect her child from the threat of sexual abuse. She started to recognize that her grandmother and mother would fight whenever she got close to her grandmother, and that she felt to blame for their fighting. She also realized that she sometimes deliberately disobeyed her grandmother to distance herself from her grandmother and get closer to her mother.

Child deflects or withdraws

When children are dealing with strong emotions or difficult issues they may naturally deflect away from dealing with their pain or withdraw into silence. In their daily lives this behaviour may, at times, be adaptive because it helps the child to cope. However, such avoidance interrupts the therapeutic process and is referred to as the child's resistance. When resistance occurs the counsellor needs to be careful not to pressure the child to continue with the story, but instead needs to help the child to deal with the resistance in a way which is acceptable to the child.

As Amy's awareness of the importance of her relationship with her mother started to increase, she began to avoid talking about that relationship. If the relationship was mentioned she would move away and engage in some unrelated activity such as drawing on the whiteboard in order to avoid facing her pain.

Child deals with resistance

The problem for a child in dealing with resistance is the choice about whether to continue to tell her story or whether to avoid telling that story. Questions in the child's thoughts might include, 'Is it safe for me to talk about these issues?' and, 'What might happen if I do?' Alternatively the child might be thinking, 'This is too scary' or, 'This is too painful for me to talk about.' If appropriate counselling skills are used the child may feel OK about continuing. However, it is equally possible that the child will avoid continuing. If this happens, then the counsellor needs to change strategies and probably to change the media being used, in order to create a new opportunity for the child to tell her story (see the dotted arrows on the Spiral of Therapeutic Change, Figure 7.1, p. 46).

When Amy started to deflect and avoid painful issues the counsellor made a decision to work differently in order to allow the child to continue telling her story. The counsellor invited the child to use clay (see Chapter 19). Once the child was familiar with using the clay, the counsellor invited the child to make a clay baby. Amy was then encouraged to experience nurturing and separating from her creation (the baby). She was invited to put the baby in a part of the room remote from herself and encouraged to explore what that felt like. This activity moved her spontaneously into the next stage of the Spiral of Therapeutic Change.

Child continues to tell story and gets in touch with strong emotions

If the outcome of dealing with resistance is positive, then the child will continue to tell her story and is likely to get in touch with strong emotions. Having done this, the child might continue around the spiral or might return to the beginning in order to address new issues.

When Amy had moved the baby away from herself, she had started to experience what it was like to be close and to be separate from her baby. The counsellor then encouraged Amy to dialogue with the baby, and during this dialogue to reverse roles, so that, as the baby she could say things to 'the mother figure' (Amy). While role-playing the baby she was able to express her fear to the 'mother' that the 'mother' did not love her and might never love her. She expressed her fear that her mother might abandon her, and her concern about who would look after her then. While participating in the dialogue between the baby and mother, Amy started to talk about her own personal experiences with her own mother, to cry, and to get in touch with her own sadness. She continued by talking about her experience of being rejected by her mother and her fear of being abandoned.

Amy explored possible reasons why her mother might not like her. She believed that her mother did not love her because she wasn't a good child and wasn't lovable.

Child deals with self-destructive beliefs

Once the child has experienced the strong emotions associated with her story, questions will arise with regard to beliefs which are troubling the child. If appropriate counselling skills are used, then the child will be able to discard self-destructive beliefs and to replace them with more adaptive beliefs.

Amy's belief that she was not good, and that this could be why her mother rejected her, was clearly self-destructive. Unfortunately this belief was reinforced by Amy's recognition that she didn't have friends at school and that her relationship with her grandmother was dependent on her being good. The counsellor encouraged Amy to look at other children's behaviours and to recognize that all children are sometimes good and sometimes not. Work on replacing Amy's self-destructive beliefs by more positive beliefs included work on Amy's self-esteem. This was done by providing evidence of Amy's strengths discovered during the counselling process, by using worksheets (see Chapter 26), and by inviting Amy's mother into a counselling session so that Amy could discuss important issues with her with the help of the counsellor.

It was clear to the counsellor that Amy's mother's issues were creating problems for Amy, so that her mother was invited to enter into a counselling relationship with another counsellor.

Child looks at options and choices

The child is now in a situation where options and choices for the future can be considered.

As a result of the work which had occurred up to now, Amy started to look at her options and choices and to explore different ways of relating to her mother and to the children at school. She realized that her mother was either not able, or not willing, to provide her with physical closeness or a great deal of time. Amy saw that one option was for her to continue to struggle to gain the closeness which she would have liked, in the way that she would have liked, with her mother. An alternative option was for her to negotiate with her mother to achieve a different sort of relationship where she joined with her mother in different ways. She decided to do the latter.

Amy also looked at her choices with regard to her relationships with peers at school. She decided that she did want to improve her relationships but didn't know how to do this (because she lacked the basic social skills).

Child rehearses and experiments with new behaviours

During this phase, the child is able to act on selected options by rehearsing chosen behaviours or by putting these behaviours into practice.

Amy found that she could take action by engaging with her mother in some common interests. This turned out to be satisfying for both Amy and her mother, with the consequence that their relationship changed and Amy felt more secure.

The counsellor also helped Amy to develop social skills through the use of work-sheets and role plays where direct verbal communication was rehearsed and practised (see Chapter 23). These role plays were based on unsatisfactory incidents which had occurred at school with other children and which had been recorded in Amy's diary. Amy was later involved in a social skills group to enable her to develop her skills further.

Child reaches resolution and moves towards adaptive functioning

Having completed the journey around the Spiral of Therapeutic Change a child reaches resolution. She can now either move into normal adaptive functioning, or return to the beginning of the spiral in order to deal with new issues.

Amy had now resolved her issues relating to her fear of rejection and abandonment by her mother. Her relationship and ability to communicate with her mother improved because she was no longer afraid to express her feelings openly. Consequently, Amy was also able to resolve issues relating to her grandparents by talking these through with her mother. She was now functioning adaptively, having discovered that she could talk directly to her mother instead of having to deal with issues in counselling sessions.

Using the Spiral of Therapeutic Change

We have illustrated the use of the Spiral of Therapeutic Change by using an example where all of the stages were involved and required. We would caution readers that the treatment described might suggest that counselling is an easy process without the complication of related issues. In practice this is rarely the case. Counselling is often complicated, with new issues being raised during the process. Sometimes only parts of the spiral will be needed to achieve desired goals, and sometimes the child will travel around the spiral more than once. However, we find that it can be useful for us to refer to the spiral when we are evaluating the progress of our work with a child. By doing this we make decisions regarding changes which might be needed during the therapeutic process in order for the child to reach the point of resolution of issues.

PART 3
CHILD COUNSELLING SKILLS

Children come to therapy with different personalities and different problems, and at different ages, so we need to decide what is the best way of working with each individual child. With some children we may choose to be active and direct in our approach, whereas with others a gentle self-discovery style may be more useful. However, regardless of the differences between children and any differences in working style, there are a number of basic child counselling skills which are generally useful.

Counselling skills need to be relevant for the various stages of the therapeutic process. Generally this therapeutic process will span a series of sessions during which the counsellor will need to perform a number of different counselling functions:

- joining with the child;
- observation of the child;
- active listening;
- awareness raising and the resolution of issues to facilitate change;
- dealing with the child's beliefs;
- actively facilitating change;
- termination of counselling.

Each of the above functions involves one or more counselling skills. In this chapter we will deal with each function and related skills, starting with *Observation*. (The function of joining was dealt with during our discussion of the child–counsellor relationship.)

◆ ◆ ◆ ◆ ◆ ◆ ◆

8   Observation

Observation begins early in the joining phase when the counsellor observes the child's relationship with his parents, the ease with which the child separates from his parents and the child's general behaviour. The observed information is valuable in helping the counsellor to make a decision as to how to proceed.

One way to carry out effective observation is to refrain from interacting actively with the child, and instead to stand back and observe unobtrusively.

When observing in this way we usually invite the child to play with the toys, games and materials set out in the play therapy room, and tell the child that we will sit quietly while he plays. While observing the child, we monitor our own behaviour to ensure that we are refraining from making judgements and interpretations about the child's presentation.

Other ways of making valuable observations are to watch what happens when you, as the counsellor, intrude on the child's space, or insist on interacting with the child, or act in a directive way.

If you, the reader, were asked to observe a child, what sort of things would you observe? We suggest that before reading the following pages, that you might like to try to draw up a list of useful things to observe.

Some of the most important things to observe when counselling children are as follows:

- General appearance
- Behaviour
- Mood or affect
- Intellectual functioning and thinking processes
- Speech and language
- Motor skills
- Play
- Relationship with counsellor

Observing general appearance

Observation of general appearance includes observation of the way the child is dressed, the child's level of alertness, and any obvious discrepancies from normal: for example physical differences. The degree of attractiveness of the child may be relevant, as well as information relating to physical development and level of nutrition. Peculiar mannerisms of the child may also be noted (for example facial tics).

Observing behaviour

When observing the kinds of behaviour the child exhibits, a counsellor might ask any of the following questions:

- Is the behaviour quiet and careful, or noisy, boisterous, aggressive and destructive?
- Is the child distractable, or does the child have a good attention span?
- Does the child try to engage in behaviour which is dangerous?
- Is the child willing to take risks?
- Is the child affectionate and dependent on the interaction of the counsellor?
- What is the child's response to physical contact?
- Is the child defensive, responsive or searching for contact?
- Does the child have appropriate boundaries?
- Does the child show approach-avoidance tendencies; for instance by showing initiative and then waiting for cues?

During observations of behaviour the counsellor may note the presence of defence mechanisms such as suppression, avoidance, denial, and indications of dissociation.

Observing the child's mood or affect

Observing the child's mood or affect during the session gives clues to the child's underlying emotional state. Generally children can be observed to be happy, sad, angry, depressed, excited, etc. Some children will be observed to show little or no emotion, being flat in affect. Others will be self-absorbed. Sometimes behaviours already observed will also give information about the child's internal mood or emotional state. (For example, aggressive play might indicate that the child is angry.)

It is also useful to observe any changes in mood during the counselling session and to observe the child's awareness of his own moods, and his level of emotional reactivity during the session.

Observing intellectual functioning and thinking processes

For a young child between the ages of four and eight, an initial indication of intellectual functioning can be obtained by inviting the child to engage in specific tasks such as doing puzzles, naming body parts, and identifying colours. With an older child, general conversation will give an indication of the ability of the child to solve problems and to conceptualize, and will give an indication of her level of insight. Whether or not a child is oriented with respect to time, place or person can be determined by asking about recent events. By checking a child's sense of reality, and organization of thoughts, the counsellor may become aware of any abnormal thought patterns including the presence of delusions and hallucinations.

Observing speech and language

Engaging in conversation with a child enables the counsellor to make an initial assessment of speech and language skills. For example, a counsellor might notice that a child experiences frustration at not being able to communicate adequately, or that the child tends to rely on non-verbal methods of communication. Additionally it may be observed that a child's speech is not clear or that the child lisps, stammers or stutters.

Observing motor skills

Gross and fine motor coordination should be observed during the child's involvement with activities in the play therapy room. Observe whether the child sits most of the time, or walks, jumps, runs or squats, and observe how the child moves in and out of positions; with ease, or with difficulty. Observe whether the child appears constricted in his physical expression or free. Anxious children sometimes show differences in their breath control, so take note of breath holding, sighing or gasping.

Observing play

Children's play differs according to age and development, so an understanding of the play of normal children is essential when making comparisons through observation. Generally speaking, it is helpful to observe whether or not a child's play is age appropriately creative or is stereotypic, repetitive and limited. An example of the latter would be if a child were to repeatedly pour sand in and out of a container in the sand tray, and do little else.

If a child can initiate play, then the counsellor does not need to be involved in the play except when wanting to influence it. The counsellor is then free to withdraw and observe the development of themes that arise in the content of the play. Additionally the counsellor can observe the quality of the play, and can notice whether the play is goal directed and following an understandable sequence and whether play materials are being used appropriately.

Whether play is creative or stereotypic will give an indication of the child's level of developmental maturity. For example, the counsellor might notice that a child can use object substitution in play, by using a box as a shopping trolley. The counsellor should notice whether the child's play is regressed, infantile, or maybe pseudo-mature.

The normal play of three- to five-year-olds is highly imaginative and creative. When observing the play of children of this age the counsellor should recognize that the expression of fantasies and themes may well be a developmentally appropriate behaviour.

The child's mode and intensity of affect in play is also an important observation.

Observing the child's relationship with the counsellor

An important aspect of observing the child's relationship with the counsellor is related to the issue of transference (see Chapter 11).

The child's warmth and friendliness, eye contact, social skills level and predominant interactional style all contribute information which the counsellor may require during the therapeutic process. The counsellor should notice whether a child is mainly withdrawn, isolated, friendly, trusting, mistrustful, competitive, negativistic, cooperative, etc. Much of this information can be obtained by observing the child's relationship with the counsellor.

While the counsellor is observing the child, the child may be starting to tell his story. If so, the child must be made fully aware of the counsellor's interest in that story. In order for this to happen the counsellor needs to make use of active listening skills.

◆　◆　◆　◆　◆　◆　◆

9 Active listening

As counsellors, we gain information about the child by observation and by listening. By performing these counsellor functions we are able to help the child to tell her story and to identify troubling issues. In doing this the child must know that we are paying attention and valuing the information which we are receiving.

How will the child know that we are paying attention? How will the child know that we are taking in, and valuing, the information which he is giving us?

Unfortunately, some children are used to spending time alone, and to being treated without respect, or ignored, by adults. How can we let these children know that we are willing to enter into their world, and to respect their view of that world? We can do this by active listening.

There are four major components to active listening.

1 Matching body language
2 The use of minimal responses
3 The use of reflection
4 The use of summarizing

Matching body language

An effective way to enhance the child–counsellor relationship is for the counsellor to match the child's non-verbal behaviour. This matching helps to give the child a message that the counsellor is listening attentively. For example, if a child is sitting on the floor beside the sand tray, then it may be helpful for the counsellor to sit on the floor with the child and to mirror the child's posture. This needs to be done in a way which is natural and comfortable for the counsellor, or it will look contrived and the child may well be disconcerted by incongruent behaviour on the part of the counsellor.

Matching the speed of talking and tone of voice of the child is also useful in enhancing the child–counsellor relationship. When the child talks rapidly, the counsellor needs to respond similarly. When the child slows up, the counsellor can be more leisurely.

There is an additional advantage to be gained if a counsellor is able to match a child's non-verbal behaviour and posture. Not only will the child feel that the counsellor is joining with him and attentively listening, but also after a while the situation can be reversed: after the counsellor has been matching the child for a while, the child is likely to follow the counsellor in any significant change. Imagine that a counsellor has been matching the speed of speaking, tone of voice and rate of breathing of an agitated child. When the counsellor wants to do so, she can slow down her breathing and speaking speed, and sit more comfortably. It is quite likely that the child will follow the counsellor's behaviour and start to relax.

Matching behaviour includes matching levels of eye contact. Eye contact is important in establishing rapport with children, but each child will be different with regard to the amount of eye contact which they find comfortable. The counsellor needs to observe the child's behaviour in this regard and to respond appropriately. Some children feel more comfortable, and are able to talk more freely, if they avoid making eye contact and instead engage in an activity while talking.

The use of minimal responses

The use of minimal responses is something that happens automatically in our conversation when we are predominantly listening rather than talking. Minimal responses indicate to the talker that the listener is attending. These responses are sometimes non-verbal and include just a nod of the head. Verbal minimal responses include expressions such as 'Ah-ha', 'Uh-hm', 'Yes', 'OK' and 'Right'.

Some longer responses serve a similar function. For example the counsellor might say 'I hear what you say', or 'I understand'.

Both minimal responses and this type of longer response are very useful in encouraging the child to continue to tell his story. It is important when making both verbal and non-verbal minimal responses that they are not likely to be interpreted as judgemental in either a positive or negative way. If the child is to tell her story accurately, then the story must not be significantly influenced by the child's perception of the counsellor's approval or disapproval. For example, powerful exclamations like 'Wow' may lead the child to draw conclusions about the counsellor's beliefs and attitudes. These conclusions may inhibit the child, or may influence the child into distorting her story in order to gain the counsellor's approval, or to avoid the counsellor's disapproval. In a similar way some non-verbal minimal responses may be perceived as expressions of judgement about the content of what the child is saying.

As a counsellor, space your minimal responses appropriately. If you give them too frequently, they will become intrusive and distracting. Remember that the minimal responses are not just an acknowledgement that the child is being heard. They can also be a subtle way of passing on other messages. Minimal responses must be used with care, or messages which are not useful therapeutically may be communicated inadvertently.

The use of reflection

Matching and minimal responses set a climate in which the child gains a sense that the counsellor has joined with and is attending to him. The child also needs assurance that the counsellor is attending to the content and detail of the story which is unfolding. Generally, the most effective way of giving the child this assurance is by using the skill called reflection.

There are two types of reflection – *reflection of content* (sometimes called *paraphrasing*), and *reflection of feelings*. We can combine these two types of reflection and *reflect both content and feelings*.

Reflection of content (paraphrasing)

Using this skill the counsellor literally reflects back to the child what the child has said to the counsellor. The counsellor does not just parrot or repeat word for word what the child has said but instead paraphrases it. This means that the counsellor picks out the most important content details of what the child has said and re-expresses them in a clearer way, and in her own words rather than in the child's.

It should be noted that reflection does not necessarily occur during conversation with children, but can happen during the therapist's observation of the child in play.

The following are some examples of paraphrasing.

Example one

Child statement: My mum and dad are always working. My dad leaves home a lot to go to work, he goes to Cairns and all over the place. Mum is the boss where she works and has to stay back sometimes and tell other people what to do.

Counsellor response: *Sounds like your mum and dad aren't around very much for you.*

Example two (child playing with miniature animals in the sand tray)

Child statement: Come on dinosaur, jump over the fence; it's nice over here. Come on, watch me, look, come on Spiky, come over here, I'll help you, I'll come back and get you, look.

Counsellor response: *Looks like your animal wants Spiky to come and join him.*

Example three (while child is playing in the dolls' house, with the dolls' house family)

Child statement: I told you not to make that mess on that floor. You'd better clean it up. You've put stuff all over the floor, you naughty boy.

Counsellor response: *That mother wants the little boy to clean up the mess.*

Example four

Child statement: I got all my spelling words right in my test but Tiffany didn't. She got into trouble for talking too. When you get naughty you have to go to the time-out room. I never go to the time-out room.

Counsellor response: *Somehow you don't seem to get into trouble but Tiffany does.*

What the counsellor does, when reflecting content, is literally to tell the child clearly and briefly the most important things that the child has just told the counsellor. By doing this the child feels as though the counsellor has heard her. By using reflection of content the counsellor also makes the child more fully aware of what he has just said, thereby intensifying the child's awareness of this. The child is then able to more fully savour the importance of what she is talking about and to sort out any confusion. Thus, reflection of content is useful in helping the child to move forward in her exploration.

The use of reflection of feelings

As well as reflection of content, the counsellor may also reflect feelings. This involves reflecting back to the child information about emotional feelings which the child is experiencing. When a child is involved in play, reflection of feelings can also be used in relation to emotional feelings which the child attributes to imaginary people, symbols, or toy animals involved in the play.

Reflection of feelings is one of the key counselling skills because it raises the child's awareness of feelings. It encourages the child to deal with significant emotional feelings rather than to avoid them.

A counsellor must be clear about the difference between thoughts and feelings and must not confuse the two. If we were to ask you, the reader, to tell us the difference between thoughts and feelings, what would you say? If we said, 'We feel that caring people make better counsellors', we would be expressing a thought; it would have been better if we had said, 'We *think* that caring people make better counsellors.'

Thoughts generally require a sentence to describe them, whereas feelings usually only need one word. Feeling words such as the following describe an emotional state:

happy	despairing	rejected
sad	overwhelmed	betrayed
angry	frightened	helpless
confused	worried	responsible
disappointed	contented	powerful
surprised	insecure	

When you look at this list you might notice that most of these feelings have opposites. As therapists, we should help children to deal with negative and uncomfortable feelings in ways which will be adaptive for them. We need to be realistic and to recognize that it will not be possible to 'take away' a child's negative feelings. However, we can help the child to deal with these, so that they either change or can be managed appropriately.

Reflecting feelings involves making statements which include feeling words, such as 'You're sad', 'You seem to be angry', or 'You look disappointed'. The following are some examples of statements made by children with the appropriate reflection of feelings by the counsellor.

Example one

> Child statement: Every time I ask Mum if I can go to Aunty Karen's,
> she says, 'No'. Kelly's going this weekend, and it was my turn.
> Possible counsellor responses: *You're disappointed*, or *You sound angry*.
> [The correct response would depend on the context and on non-verbal
> cues.]

Example two (child's brother was killed in car accident)

> Child statement: My brother didn't even have his favourite dog with him
> when the car was hit.
> Counsellor response: *You're very sad*, or, *You sound very sad*.

Example three (child is involved in imaginary pretend play)

> Child statement: Let's get out of here before they find out. Quick they're
> coming.
> Counsellor response: *You sound scared*.

Example four (child is playing in the dolls' house, with the dolls' house family)

> Child statement: I told you not to make a mess on that floor. You'd
> better clean it up. You've put stuff all over the floor, you naughty boy.
> Counsellor response: *That mother sounds very angry*.

Frequently children will try to avoid exploring their feelings because they
want to avoid the pain associated with strong emotions such as sadness,
despair, anger and anxiety. However getting in touch with feelings usually
means moving forward to feeling better emotionally, and then to being able
to make sensible decisions.

Sometimes children will tell us directly how they are feeling. For example,
a child might say, 'I'm very angry with my brother.' However, usually
children will not tell us directly how they are feeling emotionally, but instead
will give non-verbal cues, and will talk indirectly about their situation.

If you, as a counsellor, attend closely to a child, your own feelings will
begin to match those of the child, and it will become easier for you to
identify what the child is feeling. With practice, it is possible to notice
feelings such as distress, sadness or anger from the child's posture, facial
expression, movements and play behaviour.

Be aware that if you correctly reflect a child's feelings, then the child is
likely to get in touch with those feelings. If the feeling is a painful one the
child may start to cry. As a counsellor, how will that be for you? For us it
is sometimes difficult. Certainly, counsellors need to deal with the feelings
generated in themselves by children's tears.

Reflecting back anger to a child can sometimes have a dramatic outcome. If the counsellor reflects back the anger by saying, 'You're angry', or

perhaps, 'You sound very angry', then the child may respond by angrily snapping back, 'I'm not angry', followed by a period of acting out in the play room. If this happens the counsellor should not feel alarmed but should be satisfied in knowing that the child has been able to express anger which he did not wish to own openly. The counsellor may then encourage the child to direct his anger more appropriately through the use of media.

In summary, reflecting feelings allows the child to fully experience his emotions and to feel better as a result of releasing these feelings. Once feelings have been released, the child is then able to think more clearly and be able to consider constructive options and choices about the future. Reflection of feelings is therefore one of the most important of the counselling skills.

The use of reflection of content and feelings

With experience you will find that you can quite often combine the reflection of content with the reflection of feelings. For example you might combine, 'You feel sad', with 'You're telling me that Dad wasn't around for you at the weekend', into the response, 'You're sad because Dad wasn't around for you at the weekend.' Here are some examples of combined reflection of content and feelings.

Example one

Child statement: Steven and I used to play princes and princesses in the garden. He always wanted to be the king and sit on this rock which was the throne. He can't do that now he's in heaven.

Counsellor response: *You're sad because you can't play with Steven any more.*

Example two

Child statement: Even when you walk away the big kids just follow you. If you tell the teacher they get you after school. Nothing really works.

Counsellor response: *You feel helpless because you can't deal with these bullies.*

Example three (an older child)

Child statement: I wrote all my subjects down with my preferences next to them. I posted it off to my mother so that it would get there in time, and she still hasn't taken it up to the school.

Counsellor response: *You're angry because your mother has let you down.*

In reflecting content and feelings, it is desirable for a counsellor to keep his responses short so as not to intrude unduly on the child's inner processes. Long statements will take the child away from his current experience and will bring him out of his own world and into the counsellor's.

Counsellors need to use their judgement in deciding when it is best to reflect content, or to reflect feelings, or to reflect both. Sometimes it will be more appropriate in the interests of brevity to use either reflection of content or reflection of feelings, rather than both.

It can be useful, in helping a child to own a feeling which he is trying to suppress, if reflection of feeling alone is used. The child may then focus on that feeling, and be better able to deal with it. For example, if a counsellor says to a child, *'You are really sad'*, then that statement focuses on the child's pain, rather than encouraging the child to escape from the experience of the pain by dealing with the content of what has been said. The pain is not avoided by the child moving into a cognitive rather than a feeling mode: instead it is appropriately addressed in the therapeutic situation.

Whenever possible, help children to experience their emotional feelings, rather than to suppress them by operating at a 'head' or cognitive level. Experiencing feelings fully is often painful, but is cathartic and consequently therapeutically desirable.

The counselling skills of minimal responses, reflection and summarizing are those which are most useful for creating a good counselling relationship. Through the use of these skills the child is encouraged to open up and to share with the counsellor the issues which are causing emotional distress.

From time to time the counsellor should provide the child with a review of the ground which has already been covered. This review is carried out by using the skill of summarizing.

The use of summarizing

The counsellor summarizes by reflecting back to the child information from a number of statements which the child may have made over a period of several minutes. The summary draws together the main points in the content, and also takes into account the feelings which the child has described. The summary is not a complete re-run of the ground covered; but it picks out the most salient points, or the most important things that the child has been talking about.

Frequently children can become confused by the detail of their own stories. Summarizing clarifies what the child has been saying and puts the information into an organized format, so that the child has a clear picture and can be more focused.

Imagine that over a period of a few minutes a child gave you a lot of information. Included in this were several specific examples of times when the child would have liked one of his parents to be present, but they were absent. Further, the child gave more than one example of his father breaking promises and the child's tone of voice and facial appearance indicated to you that the child was very sad. How would you summarize what you had learnt from the child?

A possible summary would be to say: *You have told me how you are sad because your mum and dad aren't around very often when you need them, and because your dad promises things and doesn't seem to be able to keep his promises.*

This kind of summary enables the child to put a lot of confusing information together to create a clear picture. The child can be more focused, and thus has an opportunity to move towards finding some resolution of the issues.

Summarizing is also useful when a counsellor wishes to move towards terminating an individual counselling session. It allows the child to integrate what has been shared and experienced during the session, before leaving.

The active listening skills described in this section encourage and enable the child to tell his story. In the next section we will look at those skills which are required to raise the level of the child's awareness, so that the possibility of emotional and behavioural change is increased.

◆ ◆ ◆ ◆ ◆ ◆ ◆

10   Helping the child to tell her story

Much of the information which a counsellor needs to know about a child will emerge naturally and spontaneously if the counsellor uses the reflective listening skills described earlier. These skills help to create a good counselling relationship and encourage the child to share the issues which are causing emotional distress.

Unfortunately, many children who come to counselling have issues which are too painful for them to confront. Sometimes these issues are known to the child, but often they are hidden, or partially hidden, in the child's unconscious. Some children have misconceptions about past traumatic events as a result of information which has been repressed and is missing from their consciousness, because it is too painful. If a child is to become aware of issues which are partially or fully buried in the unconscious, then the counsellor will need to raise the child's awareness of these issues. This must be done with skill and care, so that the child is allowed to confront painful issues at a pace which is acceptable to her, and which does not produce further trauma.

Referring back to Figure 7.1 (p. 46), we can see where our present discussion fits on the Spiral of Therapeutic Change. In Figure 7.1, initially the child joins with the counsellor, and then moves on to tell her story. The next stage, as the child moves around the spiral, is for the child's awareness of issues to rise as she tells her story. Unfortunately, this increase in awareness will not always happen spontaneously.

Children are experts at deflecting away from emotional pain and at avoiding the issues which relate to that pain. However, for therapy to be effective, the child does need to focus on the relevant issues with raised awareness and to experience the associated pain.

Generally, a child will only stay focused on the issues and emotions relevant to his story if the counsellor uses appropriate counselling skills so that the child's awareness of the relevant issues and emotions is raised. The child may then experience strong emotions and can move forward around the Spiral of Therapeutic Change toward resolution.

Because children often find it difficult to talk freely with an adult about troubling issues, the counsellor needs not only to join with the child and to invite the child to tell her story, but also to create an environment in which the child is enabled to continue telling her story even when to do so is difficult or painful. This environment is created by the use of the following:

- observation and active listening skills
- questions
- statements
- media

Observation and active listening skills

These have already been discussed in Chapters 8 and 9. They are useful in both inviting the child to tell her story and also in enabling the child to tell her story.

Use of questions

Children generally live in a world where adults expect them to have answers to many questions. However, if you observe children at play, you will notice that they rarely ask each other questions. Instead, they make statements about what they are doing or what they observe their playmates doing.

When children are confronted by adults they are usually required to answer many questions. Inquisitive aunts and uncles, schoolteachers, mothers, and friends of the family, all with the best of intentions, ask children questions. Many children, in response to such pressure for answers, become very adept at producing what they consider to be the 'right' answers. These are answers which the child thinks will satisfy the questioner. They are not necessarily what the child believes to be true, and they may not fit with the child's experience or with what the child is thinking. Consequently, if a counsellor relies on asking questions he may never discover what the child is really thinking and/or experiencing, but instead may be given misleading answers which are useless in the therapeutic process.

A further problem with asking questions is that the direction in which the counselling session heads is likely to be influenced and controlled by the questions the counsellor asks, instead of following the direction in which the child's energy leads her. What is worse, if a counsellor asks too many questions, the child will quickly learn to expect questions and will wait for more questions to be asked instead of thinking for herself and talking about what is important for her. The counselling session will then degenerate into an interrogation session, with the child being less likely to be open and communicative, and more likely to avoid distressing issues.

If, as a new counsellor you find yourself repeatedly asking questions, then it is important for you to discover what your goal is in asking these questions. If your goal is to stimulate the child into talking, then you are almost certainly using the wrong approach. More often than not, reflective counselling skills will encourage a child to continue telling his story without the need for questioning.

Having given the above warnings, we need to say that questions are a powerful tool for raising awareness if used appropriately and sparingly. There are two major types of questions: *open questions* and *closed questions.*

Closed questions are questions which lead to a specific answer. Usually, the answer will be very short because closed questions invite answers such as 'Yes' and 'No', or answers which give a small piece of specific information such as 'Twenty-three'. Let us look at some examples of closed questions:

1   Did you come here by car today?
2   How old are you?
3   Would you like a felt pen?
4   Are you frightened of your brother?
5   Are you angry?
6   Do you like school?

The answers to the above questions might be as follows:

1   Yes.
2   Six.
3   No.
4   No.
5   Yes.
6   Yes.

Obviously, some children might choose to expand on these answers, but other children might not. The problems with asking closed questions are as follows:

● The child may give a short factual answer and may not enlarge on that answer.
● The child may feel limited and may not feel free to answer the question in a meaningful way.
● The child may wait for another question instead of feeling free to talk openly.

Sometimes it is appropriate to ask a closed question in order to obtain some factual information. However generally, our intention as counsellors is to encourage children to talk openly about important issues, without feeling restrained by our agendas. This is where the open question is useful.

The open question is very different in its effect. It gives the child lots of freedom to explore relevant issues and feelings, instead of inviting a single-word answer. Consider the following open questions:

1   How did you travel here?
2   What is it like living with your brother?
3   Can you tell me about your family?
4   How do you feel?
5   What can you tell me about your school?

Each of these open questions allows the child to think freely about the question and invites the child to give a full and expansive answer without being restrained by the counsellor's agenda. For example answers to the question, 'What can you tell me about your school?' could include:

• My school is large and crowded.
• Some of the boys at my school are wimps.
• My school is a long way from home.
• School is good fun.
• My school is very hot in summer.

Notice that with the open question, a wide range of different answers is possible. Compare these answers with the answer to the closed question, 'Do you go to a big school?' With the closed question, the answer may simply be 'Yes' or 'No', and if the child does expand on his answer, the range of answers will be limited by the question.

Not only are the answers to the open questions likely to be rich in information, but they often include information which allows the counsellor to use reflection of content and/or feelings to encourage the child to continue. Open questions allow the child to talk about those things which are of most interest or of most importance to him, rather than those things which are of most interest to the counsellor. For example, in responding to the open question, 'Tell me about your brothers and sisters' a child might focus on one particular sibling. Such a response might give rich information, which the counsellor did not directly seek, about the significance of that sibling in the child's life.

If we were to ask you the closed question, 'Are you finding this book useful?' your answer would probably be less helpful in providing us with feedback than if we asked you the open question, 'What can you tell us about this book?' However, both the open and closed questions might equally stimulate an open and informative response. But we need to remember that you are an adult, and are not being invited to discuss intimate personal details with us. Children in therapy are in quite a different situation. They are often reluctant to talk, particularly about very personal matters, so we are wise to use those counselling skills which are most likely to encourage open communication.

There are times when closed questions are *more* suitable than open questions. Closed questions lead to a specific answer, confine the child to a limited response, help the child to be more precise, and are useful in eliciting specific information.

We have found that it is generally wise to try to avoid asking questions which begin with 'Why'. The problem with asking 'why' questions is that the child is likely to respond with an intellectually contrived answer, rather than giving an answer which is centred on what is happening to her internally. 'Why' questions tend to generate answers which relate to matters or events external to the child, aren't connected to the child's inner experience, are lacking in emotional content, and are often trivial or unconvincing. The answers to 'why' questions frequently fall into the categories of excuses or rationalizations.

When working with children, we are generally most successful in enabling them to tell their stories if we stick to the following rules:

1 Ask only those questions which are needed.
2 Wherever appropriate, use open questions in preference to closed questions.
3 Avoid using 'why' questions, unless there is good reason to do so.
4 Never ask questions just to satisfy your own curiosity.

With regard to the fourth rule, as a counsellor, before you seek information, check whether you really need it. Before you ask a question, ask yourself, 'If I don't have this information, will I still be able to help the child effectively?' If the answer to that question is 'Yes', then asking the question is unnecessary. The desire to ask the question probably stems from your own needs and/or curiosity.

When questions are used sparingly and appropriately, they can be powerful in helping to raise the child's awareness of important issues so that he can move forward around the Spiral of Therapeutic Change towards resolution.

Use of statements

Statements made by the counsellor can be very valuable in helping a child to stay on track in telling her story, and in helping to raise the child's awareness of important issues and associated emotions. Statements can be used in a number of different ways:

- Statements give permission for the child to feel and express a particular emotion. For example, a counsellor might say to a child who is suppressing his anger and talking quietly, *When I am angry I talk in a loud voice.* This might give the child permission to get in touch with his anger and to express it.
- Statements help a counsellor to float ideas about what might be happening for the child at a particular moment. For example, a counsellor might suspect that a child is experiencing embarrassment and say, *If I were you, I would feel embarrassed.*

- Statements provide counsellors with a tool with which to affirm a child's strengths. For example, the counsellor might say, *You must be really brave to have done that.*
- Statements can be used to highlight significant events during an activity. For example if a child is having difficulty in choosing objects for the sand tray, the counsellor might make a statement like, *You have a hard time choosing objects,* or, *It's really hard for you to find the objects that you want.* By making this statement, the counsellor gives the child feedback about the difficulty she has in making choices, and the opportunity has been created for the child to explore this aspect of her behaviour.
- Statements can be used to give feedback, without judgement, about what the child is doing. For example, the counsellor might say, *I see that you have made a cave with the clay.* In a similar way to reflecting content, this feedback invites the child to talk about what he has done.
- Statements can be used to raise the child's awareness of an element of her activity, and/or to float an idea which the counsellor has about the child's issue. For example, if a child was working with puppets, and a mouse-puppet was hiding, and the counsellor suspected that the child was feeling vulnerable, the counsellor might say, *That mouse is hiding. I wonder if he is afraid of being caught.*

Use of media

In Part 4 we will discuss the use of media in some detail. While doing this, we will also consider the ways in which counselling skills and media are used together to help the child to tell her story, and thus to raise the child's awareness of both current and past unresolved issues.

The media provide the child with activity to hold her interest and to help her to stay focused. Through using them, the child tells her story either directly or indirectly. She may do this by talking directly about issues which are troubling her, or indirectly by projecting elements of her story on to the media. Media may also allow the child to connect with her emotions and may act as a vehicle through which she can express these emotions. This is a two-stage process: the child needs to get in touch with her emotional feelings, and then to express them.

During the therapeutic process, the counsellor may initially invite the child to talk about how it feels to use the media, and will also focus directly on what the child is doing with the media. Later in the therapeutic process, the focus will move away from discussion of the content of the activity involving media, and instead will focus directly on the child's life situation and unfinished business. Sometimes, when a child is working with media, and telling a story through the media, it is appropriate for the counsellor to ask directly: *Does this fit with your life?* or *Does this sound like something that might be happening to you?*

Sometimes though, a child will spontaneously recognize the association between the story she is telling through the media, and her own life story. At other times a child may suddenly become very silent. When this happens we might ask her: *What has just happened?* The child may then begin to talk about something she has remembered which relates in some way to her present life.

In some situations it is useful to go with the opposite of what the child is discussing, or with what may have been omitted. For example, if a child is discussing the excitement and pleasure of a situation, it might be appropriate to say: *Maybe your life doesn't have much fun in it.*

Often it is easier for children to share the happy experiences in their lives. Once they have told us about the happy ones, then they can often talk about the sad ones.

As the child continues to talk, he may find that he has expressed contradictory feelings related to his memories. He may become puzzled, troubled or confused by the variety of different feelings which he has expressed. Helping the child to recognize that it is OK to have differing, varied and apparently contradictory feelings can help the child express himself more clearly and accurately.

It can be useful to invite the child to engage in a dialogue between different parts of his story, or his drawing, or whatever other work he is involved in.

Watching for cues from the child's voice-tone, body posture, facial and body expression, breathing and silences can give the counsellor information. For example, the child may be censoring, remembering, thinking, repressing anxieties or fears, or becoming aware of something new. As a counsellor, if you observe the non-verbal behaviours mentioned, you may be able to use these as cues to promote further expression. For example if a child sighs while telling her story you might say: *I noticed that you just gave a big sigh. What's it like when you let all that air out at once?*

Many children who experience emotional difficulties seem to have some impairment in their contact functioning. The tools of contact are looking, talking, touching, listening, moving, smelling and tasting. Sometimes by focusing on a contact function we can encourage a child to put her feelings into words. Helping the child to get in touch with bodily feelings and sensations may enable her to connect with the emotional feelings she may be experiencing. For example we might say to a child: *Watching you move around quickly and being very busy makes me feel exhausted. I imagine that you must feel very tired, being so busy.*

To summarize: we can help the child to tell her story, and thus to get in touch with important issues and emotions, by using media, together with appropriate counselling skills. In this process, we might do any of the following:

- Encourage the child to talk about what she is currently doing in the therapy session.

- Help the child to relate current experiences in therapy to current and past life issues.
- Encourage the child to explore important unresolved issues.
- Encourage the child to experience fully and express her emotional feelings.
- Explore opposites and absences in the child's story.
- Give permission for contradictory feelings to exist.
- Focus on contact functions to help the child to access suppressed emotions.
- Give the child affirmation.

As a result of this process the child may get in touch with strong emotions (see Figure 7.1, p. 46). We will then help the child to move further round the Spiral of Therapeutic Change by dealing with self-destructive beliefs, options and choices, and rehearsal for subsequent action, as discussed in Chapters 12 and 13.

◆ ◆ ◆ ◆ ◆ ◆ ◆

11 Dealing with resistance and transference

Resistance and transference are phenomena which interfere with the therapeutic process, so the counsellor therefore needs to know how to respond to them appropriately.

Dealing with resistance

In Chapter 10 we discussed the way in which children tend to avoid emotional pain, and the way in which painful information is sometimes partially or completely repressed into the child's unconscious. As a child's awareness starts to rise, she may start to become aware of repressed material or of other emotionally painful material. When this happens, the child is likely to become spontaneously blocked from further exploration.

In practical terms, when a child becomes blocked, the counsellor is likely to realize that the child is deflecting away from discussing anything connected with emerging painful issues. This deflection may involve the child becoming silent and withdrawn, or may involve the child distracting away from the painful issues by becoming loud and boisterous.

When a child becomes blocked in this way, psychodynamic counsellors and Gestalt therapists refer to this as the child's *resistance* to the therapeutic process. We believe that resistance may be either conscious, or it may happen without the child realizing that it is happening and with the process occurring at a sub-conscious level.

Again refer back to the Spiral of Therapeutic Change (Figure 7.1, p. 46). Notice how some children will continue around the spiral to tell their stories, and to get in touch with strong emotions without meeting resistance, as shown by the thick dark arrow which forms the top of the spiral. Other children will deflect or withdraw, as shown by the dotted arrow. These children need to deal with their resistance if they are to gain from the therapeutic process. It is the counsellor's job to help them to do this.

Consider an example of how a child might become blocked in therapy, and consequently resist further exploration of painful issues. During therapy a child's awareness might have been raised with regard to issues of rejection by his parents who have put him into foster care. It could be too scary for this child to face these issues, and the child might demonstrate his resistance by deflecting, withdrawing or acting out. It is tempting for the counsellor to pressure the child to continue talking about the painful matters he is avoiding, but to do this will usually be therapeutically disastrous.

If, as counsellors we try to pressure a child into talking about painful issues we will raise the child's level of anxiety. The result will be that the child will almost certainly withdraw further, and will shut down meaningful communication with us. What is worse, the child may no longer feel safe in the counselling situation, so the possibility of engaging her in further useful work is minimized.

If a child meets a block we need to help the child to deal with the block, rather than to try to ignore the resistance and to push on. In order to help the child to deal with the resistance we need to raise the child's awareness of the resistance. We need to identify the resistance and to give the child feedback about it. For example, in the case mentioned previously, the counsellor might identify the resistance as being related to the child being scared to talk about issues of rejection. Having identified the nature of the resistance, the counsellor then gives the child feedback. For example, the counsellor might say to the child, *It might be a bit scary to talk about not going home to Mum and Dad*, and *When I get scared I like to run away, just like you*. The counsellor has validated the child's fear, made it clear that it is legitimate to feel that way and that it is acceptable to respond by withdrawing.

Paradoxically, once a child has permission to withdraw, he will be more likely to continue. This is because the child knows that his wish to withdraw will be respected, if it intensifies or recurs, and thus he will feel safer about continuing.

If the child is able to continue, then the counsellor might ask a question to help the child to understand and work through the resistance. Using our previous example the counsellor might ask, *When you think about Mum and Dad, what is the scariest thing that you think about?* This question is designed to help the child to fully confront the fear associated with the resistance and to deal with it.

The child might respond by saying, 'I'm scared that Mum and Dad won't love me any more.' The counsellor has now enabled the child to face the most painful issue underlying the resistance and can help him to get in touch with the sadness related to this issue. The child has moved around the spiral to the point labelled, *Child continues to tell story and gets in touch with strong emotions.*

It is possible that the process described above, in which the child moves through the resistance and continues to tell her story, may not occur. Instead, when the counsellor draws the attention of the child to the resistance by giving the child feedback, the child may continue to withdraw. This situation is shown on the Spiral of Therapeutic Change by a dotted line. The child we have described might say 'I'm not scared', and continue to avoid talking about useful material. If a child does continue to avoid in this way, the therapist needs to change the media being used, and to return to the earlier point on the spiral entitled *Child starts to tell her/his story.* The change in media gives the child time to process what has happened, and provides a new opportunity for her to tell her story and to re-confront the resistance.

The processes described above for dealing with resistance need to be used in conjunction with the reflective and summarizing skills described in the previous section. By using these combined skills to confront the resistance, the child will then be enabled to move through the resistance and to continue telling her story.

Although we have not specifically included it on the Spiral of Therapeutic Change, the process of the child telling her story can be effected not only by resistance but also by transference.

Dealing with transference

As discussed earlier, it is inevitable that transference and counter-transference will occur at times during the counselling process. Unfortunately, if transference and counter-transference are ignored when they occur, then the quality of the child–counsellor relationship will be changed. This change in the quality of the relationship will then interfere with, and undermine, the therapeutic process.

When we, as counsellors, suspect that transference and/or counter-transference is occurring we need to step back from the immediacy of the counselling relationship and to be as objective as possible. This is best done by talking to a supervisor about the transference, so that we can effectively deal with those issues of ours which predispose us to move into the counter-transference position. Within the counselling situation we then need to be vigilant, so that we can remain sufficiently detached and objective to avoid behaving like a parent. We also need to raise the child's awareness of the transference process.

We have noticed that in the transference process there are often two dimensions in which material is projected on to the counsellor. These dimensions involve the child's experiences and fantasies with regard to firstly a 'good' mother and secondly a 'bad' mother. Naturally, transference relating to a mother figure generally occurs with female counsellors; for male counsellors, transference will generally relate to the father figure.

Additionally, there are a number of different scenarios for male counsellors, some of which strictly relate to transference and some of which relate to broader issues of projection.

Consider transference related to the child's experiences and fantasies of a 'good' mother. In this case, the child may have expectations that the counsellor will meet all her needs. Clearly, the counsellor cannot do this. However, the counter-transference might involve the counsellor *wanting* to meet the child's needs by, for example, protecting, cuddling or nurturing the child. If a counsellor were to respond in this way, the child would be set up for disappointment in the long term, and diverted from facing the painful issue of not getting her needs met by her real mother.

Now consider transference related to the child's experiences and fantasies of a 'bad' mother. In this case, the child will project the negatively perceived behaviours of his mother on to the counsellor. As a consequence, the child might be aggressive, or abusive to the therapist, and counter-transference might result in the counsellor becoming angry or punitive to the child. Alternatively, as a consequence of transference, the child might be withdrawn, submissive or compliant, and counter-transference might result in the counsellor becoming impatient or exasperated.

The appropriate counsellor behaviour for dealing with either type of transference is for the counsellor to:

1 Recognize and deal with her own feelings and issues as they arise in response to the child's behaviour.
2 Resist the temptation to respond as a parent and try to remain objective (without compromising safety – see rules in Chapter 3).
3 Raise the child's awareness of his behaviour. For example the counsellor might say, *It seems as though you want me to be like a good mother to you*, or in dealing with the negative case, *I'm wondering if you are angry with me (or frightened of me) because you think that I am like your mother*.
4 Use the situation to explore the child's perceptions about mother–child relationships in general, and then to look at the mother–child relationship which the child actually experiences at home.

Steps 1 and 2 deal with the counter-transference and its associated behaviour. Step 3 raises the child's awareness of the transference behaviour, and makes it clear to the child that the child–counsellor relationship is different from the mother–child relationship. Thus the child is less likely to have unrealistic expectations of the counselling relationship. Instead of escaping into an inappropriate relationship with the counsellor, in step 4 the child is encouraged to focus on the real life issues relating to his own mother's relationship with him.

We need to point out that sometimes, at step 3 children will deny the truth of the transference projection. In this case we explore what the child's feelings are related to, and/or move on to step 4.

Transference behaviours will inevitably recur during the counselling process. Vigilance is needed to ensure that the issues are consistently being effectively addressed.

◆ ◆ ◆ ◆ ◆ ◆ ◆

12 Dealing with inappropriate and/or self-destructive beliefs

As children grow up, they naturally and adaptively absorb ideas and beliefs from the adults and children around them. This is the normal way in which children learn what is acceptable, and what is not acceptable, with regard to personal and social behaviour. Unfortunately some beliefs which children absorb may not be appropriate or useful, but instead may result in emotional problems. For example, a parent might teach a child to be polite to all strangers. That child may then find herself in a situation where, because of her belief that she should be polite, it becomes difficult or impossible for her to refuse the inappropriate advances of a stranger.

If a child holds on to inappropriate beliefs she may become disempowered, anxious, compliant and neurotic, and also have difficulty with interpersonal relationships. Inappropriate beliefs will often be recognized by the counsellor when the child has moved around the Spiral of Therapeutic Change to the point where strong emotions are experienced (see p. 46). Clearly, for useful therapeutic change to occur, the child must be able to discard those beliefs which are maladaptive. The counsellor needs to use strategies which will enable the child to replace inappropriate and/or self-destructive beliefs with more useful beliefs.

It may sometimes be necessary for the counsellor to involve parents in helping the child to discard and replace unacceptable beliefs. This is because it is usually parents who have the responsibility for helping their children to learn beliefs which will be useful and appropriate for them. Further, it would be quite destructive, and would set the child up for failure, if the counsellor challenged beliefs that were important to the parents.

Below are a list of beliefs which in all or some situations would be inappropriate or self-destructive for a child:

- I'm responsible for my father hitting my mother.
- I'm no good.
- I don't have any control because I'm too little.
- Boys are better than girls.
- It's not fair when I get treated differently from my brother.
- I'm naughty; that's why my mother doesn't love me.
- I am unlovable.
- You have to be tough to be popular.
- Parents split up when kids misbehave.
- My parents should never punish me.

- If you tell the truth you get into trouble.
- My mum and dad will always look after me.
- You should always be good mannered.
- You should always be polite to grown-ups.
- It's bad to show that you're angry.
- You should never say no to a grown-up.
- I must never make mistakes.
- I must always win.
- I must not cry.

In addition to beliefs similar to those listed above, there is a common self-destructive belief related to the effect of trauma. Following trauma, children sometimes believe that an irreversible negative change has occurred which will prevent life returning to normal. Thus the possibility of something new and different is ruled out, and the child believes that there is no way in which to start living in an adaptive and comfortable way. This is a very destructive belief, because it prevents the child from leaving the trauma behind and moving forward into a space where life can once again be enjoyed.

Challenging beliefs

Challenging inappropriate and/or self-destructive beliefs allows the child to replace them by more adaptive beliefs and to move around the Spiral of Therapeutic Change to the next stage, which is *child looks at options and choices*.

The first step in challenging an inappropriate belief is to reflect back to the child what the counsellor perceives to be the child's belief. We will use an example of a child who believes that he is to blame for his father hitting his mother. In this case the counsellor might say to the child, *You believe that you are responsible for your father hitting your mother.*

The next step is to help the child to test out the validity of the belief. To do this it is necessary to identify to what extent the belief comes from the child's own experience and to what extent it comes from what others have told him. For example, the counsellor might ask, *How do you know that it is your fault that your dad hit your mum?*

The child's reply might indicate that his belief has come from his parents, who have told him that it was his fault. In this case the child's parents will need to be involved in the therapeutic process so that this belief can change. Alternatively, the child's response may indicate that his belief relates to his own perceptions of the connection between his behaviour and his father's behaviour. The counsellor then needs to explore the logic behind the child's thinking, and to invite the child to consider alternative beliefs. This can be done by asking questions such as, *If you hit someone, would it be your fault or someone else's fault?* Thus the counsellor raises the child's awareness of other possible beliefs which in some way the child is overlooking or failing to identify for himself. The counsellor might also help the child to compare his experiences with his perceptions of other children's experiences.

Challenging self-destructive and/or inappropriate beliefs may involve bringing into the child's awareness, in an acceptable way, information which might be unpalatable to him and which is being avoided or is just not being noticed. The child may need to accept information he may not want to hear. For example, this child may not want to accept that his father is capable of behaving abusively and violently. Patiently, and with care, the counsellor needs to help the child to accept reality.

During this process a child may need to own and accept responsibility for some parts of the events which have troubled him. It is important to help the child to separate out those parts of the events for which he was responsible from those parts for which he was clearly not responsible.

To summarize: challenging inappropriate or self-destructive beliefs involves the following:

- reflecting back the child's current belief;
- helping the child to check the validity of that belief by identifying where the belief comes from;
- exploring the logic behind the child's thinking;
- helping the child to explore possible alternative beliefs;
- raising the child's awareness of unpalatable information;
- helping the child to separate out who is responsible for what behaviours – himself or others;
- enabling the child to replace maladaptive beliefs with more appropriate beliefs.

We will now consider two more examples of challenging inappropriate and/ or self-destructive beliefs.

Example one

Imagine that a child has been in a violent home, in which there have been strong messages that females are inferior and should not have the same rights as males. The counsellor might reflect back the child's belief by saying, *You believe that boys are better than girls.*

To help the child to check the validity of the belief, the counsellor might ask, *How do you know that's true?* The child might give an answer which suggests that the males in his family get preferential treatment.

The counsellor now needs to float alternative ideas. For example the counsellor might ask questions like, *What things can Mum do that Dad can't do?* or make statements such as, *Boys and girls are different.* The counsellor can then help the child to recognize that difference does not imply better or worse, but that each gender has different attributes. This information is likely to be unpalatable for the child when initially presented, but can hopefully be accepted after some exploration of the issues. Once the child has accepted the alternative belief, he can examine how his behaviour contributes to relationship problems for him.

Example two

Consider a child who believes that her parents should never punish her. In this case, the counsellor would reflect back the child's belief, then check its validity by finding out where the belief came from. The child might say, 'My mum does things that she shouldn't do, and she doesn't get into trouble.' The counsellor could then explore the child's logic, which includes an underlying assumption that children and parents are equal. To do this the counsellor might ask questions such as, *Does your best friend, Trudy, get punished by her mother?* and *Who makes the rules in families, parents or children?* Thus the child's awareness of unpalatable information is raised, and hopefully the child will realize that in reality parents control children. The counsellor can then help the child to see how her own behaviour inevitably results in punishment.

Two useful techniques which can be used in the processes described above for challenging inappropriate and/or self-destructive beliefs, are reframing and normalizing.

Reframing

The idea behind reframing is to alter the way the child perceives her situation. This is done by accepting the child's picture of her world and expanding that picture to include additional information so that the child will perceive her situation differently and more constructively. For example, a child might be complaining that her older brother is continually telling her to keep her room tidy. A reframe might be: *Is it possible that your brother cares about you so much that he wants to prevent you from getting into trouble because your room is untidy?*

Normalizing

Sometimes it is helpful for a child to know that her thoughts, feelings and/or behaviours are similar to those of other children. Giving a child this information is called normalizing the child's experience. For example, a counsellor might say: *Many children whose parents have split up believe that it is their fault that their parents have separated.*

When normalizing it is important not to invalidate the child's feelings and associated discomfort.

◆ ◆ ◆ ◆ ◆ ◆ ◆

13 Actively facilitating change

Earlier we described those skills which are required for joining, observation, active listening, and helping the child to tell her story. These skills will help the child to integrate thoughts and emotions, will provide some catharsis for the child, and will enable the child to re-enact traumas and to gain some level of mastery or control over past traumatic events. This facilitative counselling approach is likely to help the child to spontaneously experience psychological and emotional change.

To help the child to cognitively understand all the elements of her trauma, the child needs to explore and challenge inappropriate and self-destructive beliefs. She also needs to own and accept what were her contributions, and what were other people's contributions, to the events that led to her emotional disturbance. Having done this, the child can move around the Spiral of Therapeutic Change to the point of *Child looks at options and choices*, and then to the point of *Child rehearses and experiments with new behaviours* (see p. 46).

Exploring options and choices

As a result of the child's past experiences, he may have learnt behaviours which are unhelpful for him and unacceptable to others. For example, the child may have learnt to be excessively compliant, or aggressive, or deceitful, or to behave in a regressed way. Consequently, he may now need to learn how to behave differently, and will need to look at his options and choices.

We might expect that parents, family members and others would be pleased if a child learnt to behave more adaptively. However, we human beings dislike change, and if a child changes his behaviour, then those who interact with the child will also need to change their behaviours. For example, if a child has been behaving in a compliant way, parents and others may have difficulty accepting the behaviour of the child if he becomes more assertive with regard to his own needs. The other people in his life will need to learn to respond differently and initially may not like doing this. Consequently, as the child's behaviour changes he may have to deal with some unpleasant reactions by others. He may find that he is unable to cope with those reactions, and, that without help, he lacks the skills to carry out the newly discovered behaviours.

If a child does decide to behave differently, then he takes a risk, because he cannot predict what will occur. It may well be easier for him to go on behaving as he did in the past. Certainly, if he makes no changes, he will continue to experience the pain he knows, whereas if he takes a risk and behaves differently, then he will face new and unknown pain. Clearly, making a decision to change is hard: the child has to cope not only with his own feelings, but also with other people's reactions.

Another difficulty is related to the loss or cost component which may result from the decision to change. Frequently, we have found that deciding whether or not to accept the loss associated with a decision is more difficult than choosing between the positive gains associated with the decision. Consider a child who has behaved in an angry, aggressive way, and has been stubborn, and uncooperative with adults. Because of these behaviours, the child may have gained the respect of peers and have assumed a leadership role. As a result of counselling, the child may have gained insight into her behaviour and may have recognized how destructive it is for herself and for others around her. However, to give up her maladaptive behaviours would involve a loss: she might lose her leadership role, her power, and the respect and control of her peers. The child may see the decision about whether to change or not more in terms of the things she would lose than the positive things she would gain. Unless the counsellor validates the importance of the child's losses then the child may be blocked from making the desired change in behaviours.

Some children have difficulty in making decisions because they have been taught that there is always a right choice and a wrong choice. Unfortunately, in real life, decisions are often complicated, with differing options having advantages or positive qualities, and also costs or disadvantages. The counsellor needs to help the child to understand that making decisions does not generally involve deciding between right and wrong or between black and white. Most decisions involve a choice between shades of grey.

Consider again the child we have been discussing. In considering her options, she may initially decide to suppress her anger, to be more cooperative, compliant and submissive, and to become a follower instead of a leader. However, it is incumbent on the counsellor to introduce some new ideas so that the girl has more choices. As an alternative to suppressing her anger, the counsellor can raise the option of the child dealing with her anger differently and being assertive. The counsellor might introduce the concept of showing initiative, instead of submissiveness and compliance. Thus the child is offered options which will allow her to continue to gain respect from others, but in a different way, by using different behaviours. Consequently, she may be able to continue to exercise a leadership role and to have an appropriate level of control in some situations. We must remember, however, that the counsellor can only *suggest* alternative options and must never try to persuade the child. A child is only likely to carry through on choices which she has made herself and which fit for her.

In summary, exploring options and choices involves the following:

- weighing up advantages and disadvantages of options;
- looking at the risks involved in making behavioural changes;
- being realistic about possible losses or costs;
- understanding that there may be reactions from others to changed behaviour.

It is the counsellor's job to help the child to work through the issues related to the above. After the child has made decisions about future behaviours, the counsellor needs to help the child to rehearse and to practise the desired behaviours.

Rehearsing and experimenting with new behaviours

Some children find it helpful to use action plans when deciding how to experiment with, or to implement, new behaviours. By using an action plan the counsellor can help the child to identify the goals she hopes to achieve, and can look at how these goals can be achieved. In doing this the child may initially believe that she lacks the skills to carry out the desired behaviours, and may need assistance from the counsellor to acquire these skills.

Using our previous example, as a result of counselling the child may have gained insight into how destructive her aggressive behaviour has been in the past. She may then have decided that she wants to be less aggressive (goal one), but also wants to maintain some control so that her needs can continue to be met (goal two). Now that she has identified her goals, she needs to work out a plan so that these goals can be achieved. That plan might include the following steps:

1 Identifying the signals which will warn her of her rising anger.
2 Learning how to deal with that anger (by challenging self-destructive beliefs and using other anger control techniques).
3 Learning to be assertive.
4 Practising the above in role play.
5 Experimenting with the new behaviour in her family, school or social setting.
6 Adjusting her behaviour in response to other people's reactions.

Having made a plan, the counsellor can help the child to implement it. In the above plan the counsellor would deal with steps 1 to 4 in counselling sessions. The counsellor would then need to help the child to make a decision with regard to the timing of step 5.

We wonder if you, the reader, are sometimes like us? When we have to carry out a new or difficult task, we often delay doing what we have decided to do by using the excuse that the time is not right. As a result, delayed action sometimes results in no action. When working with children we need to be aware that they too may have a tendency to put off doing what is new and possibly difficult. It is useful to explore with children the desirability of choosing a suitable time and place for practising new behaviours. This exploration serves a dual purpose: it helps the child to avoid procrastinating, and it alerts the child to the risks of using the new behaviour at an inappropriate time.

For a child to use newly learnt assertive behaviour in the morning, when the family is preparing to leave for work and school, might be inappropriate. Use of the new behaviour at this time might prove unsuccessful, because parents and other family members may not be expecting it, and will probably be feeling pressured with regard to keeping to their normal routine. The counsellor should discuss with the child the need for sensible timing when trying out new behaviours.

After the child has tried out the new behaviour, the counsellor can look at the outcomes, and help the child to make necessary adjustments to the behaviour. The counsellor must help the child to feel good and to recognize his courage in trying out the new behaviour. A child who has attempted to use a new behaviour, but failed to achieve a positive outcome, is more likely to continue making further attempts to change if he receives praise for having had the courage to try out a new way of behaving. Frequent discussions with the child's parents can assist in ensuring that the child is affirmed and rewarded when using new and more appropriate behaviours.

Sometimes, as the result of counselling, children develop unexpected behaviours which were previously non-existent. These behaviours may well be adaptive, but they may not always suit the parents and family. The counsellor should remind the parents that the child is maturing and developing during the counselling process. Children are by their nature continually developing and changing, so it is almost inevitable that a child's behaviour will change significantly when participating in counselling. When unexpected behavioural change occurs it may be necessary for counselling to focus on helping the parents to manage these behaviours. Sometimes counselling strategies might need adjustment in order to address these changes.

◆　◆　◆　◆　◆　◆　◆

14　Termination of counselling

The decision about when to terminate a series of counselling sessions can sometimes be a difficult one for a counsellor. If we look at the Spiral of Therapeutic Change (see p. 46), we might assume that the time for termination would be obvious. Once the child has reached the point of *resolution* on the spiral, then counselling will no longer be required and the child will move ahead, functioning adaptively. However, in practice the decision is often not so easy. There are a few ways in which the question of termination can be made difficult for the counsellor. Any of the following may cause problems:

1　Regression, with the child relapsing into previous behaviours, is common with children who are anxious about ending the therapeutic relationship.
2　As termination approaches, the child may raise new and different issues.
3　The counsellor may have unwittingly become dependent on the counselling relationship.
4　The child may seem to have reached a plateau in the therapeutic process, with the counsellor believing that more change is required.

With regard to item 1 (the problem of the child regressing), the counsellor needs to raise the issues of separation, abandonment and rejection with the child. This will enable the child to recognize his response to the impending termination and to explore new ways of managing his response now and in the future.

With regard to item 2 the counsellor needs to make a decision about whether or not to allow the child to re-enter the Spiral of Therapeutic Change, starting at the beginning again. This decision will depend on an assessment of the importance of the new issues, and an assessment of the child's ability to deal with them independently without the assistance of counselling.

Item 3 is a matter of ongoing importance to any counsellor. When counsellors do become dependent they often have difficulty in recognizing this. The best way to identify such dependency is for counsellors to have regular supervision where their cases are discussed with an experienced counsellor.

With regard to item 4, reaching a plateau may be an indication that the child needs an opportunity to integrate and to assimilate the changes which are taking place as a result of the counselling process. This is often a good time to terminate counselling.

While a few children may require long term therapy, we believe that generally children should not be engaged in a counselling process over a long period of time. Adults are different: they may have accumulated many years of unresolved issues. These tend to compound each other, so that the counsellor needs to help the adult client work through many layers of unfinished business. Because of their more limited life experience, children generally don't seem to accumulate the same complexity of neurotic or maladaptive behaviours.

Responsible counselling requires the counsellor to continually review the progress of therapy to check whether goals have been achieved, and if so, to terminate the counselling process. Certainly, except in unusual cases, if a child continues coming to counselling over a period of several months, then the counsellor should review the case with a view to revising goals and moving towards termination. Generally we work with children, on a weekly basis, over a period of two to three months. However, some children need only two or three visits before termination.

As counsellors we do have clues which give us an indication that the time is right for termination. Here are some possible clues:

1 The child may have reached a plateau (see earlier discussion).
2 Sometimes the child will remain blocked and unable to deal adaptively with resistance. This needs to be respected, so that the child does not feel pressured but can return to counselling later knowing that he will not be forced to do work which is too painful.
3 Sometimes the child seems to have an inner sense that to continue would need more strength than he is able to provide at that time.
4 The child may have become involved and happily engaged in social activities with friends, in sport, or in a club. Further, he may be starting to see counselling as an unnecessary intrusion into his life and may not want to attend.
5 The focus of counselling may shift and the child may begin to 'play', instead of doing useful therapeutic work, with the counsellor recognizing

that the counselling sessions no longer seem to be achieving therapeutic goals.

6   The child has gone far enough in the counselling process so that he can continue making progress on his own. This is especially true when parents are involved and committed to the process of change.

7   The child's behaviour may have changed as reported by the parents or school.

With regard to the last item on the above list, we should point out that improved behaviour on its own may not be sufficient reason to terminate the counselling process. Changes of behaviour can also be due to the child opening up and expressing deeper material to the counsellor, so it is important to look at what is happening in the counselling process at the time.

Even though, as counsellors, we try to help children to gain as much independence as we can, it is inevitable that many children will form a caring attachment to their counsellor. There will therefore be a loss for a child when the counselling relationship ends, so the child must be adequately prepared for termination. In this preparation we need to talk openly with the child about the impending separation, and to explore the child's feelings with regard to this. It might be useful to engage the child in an activity that focuses on what it is like to be leaving the counselling relationship. Children might sometimes feel ambivalent about leaving and it is important to allow them to share their mixed feelings. Finally, to say 'Goodbye', we may want to have a special closing session so that the child is enabled symbolically to let go of the counselling relationship.

Sometimes a counsellor may decide to ease the situation for the child by maintaining contact for a limited period of follow up. This could be in the form of further assessments, letters or phone calls.

During the termination process the counsellor needs to be in touch with her own feelings and reactions, so that these do not interfere with appropriate termination at the right time. Where a counsellor recognizes some dependency on her own part, she needs to talk with her supervisor.

PART 4

PLAY THERAPY – USE OF MEDIA AND ACTIVITIES

15   The play therapy room

We have found that counselling children is easier and more effective when we work in a room which has been specifically set up for the use of media and for play therapy. Whenever possible, counsellors who work with children should work in a room which is specifically designed for the purpose. This is not always possible, and useful therapeutic work can take place in less suitable places and with limited equipment. For example, effective and useful counselling of children occurs in schools, hospitals and in government offices, where special facilities for counselling are usually not available. However, in this chapter we will describe what we believe to be the requirements for a well designed play therapy room.

Ideally, a play therapy room should be soundproof, so that extraneous noises do not distract the child. This also helps the child to believe that what she is saying is not being overheard by others. However, it is desirable that the room should have a window: internal rooms can be troubling for children who feel trapped and claustrophobic.

The room needs to have a warm and comfortable feel about it, as distinct from the ambience of most clinical rooms, and should have sufficient space for active, constructive and dramatic play. The sketch in Figure 15.1 shows a typical play therapy room.

Ideally the play therapy room should have a sink in a wet area for messy play. This enables children to use water and to clean up after using media such as clay and paint. The wet area needs to have vinyl floor covering, whereas the remainder of the room is preferably carpeted so that sitting on the floor is comfortable.

In Figure 15.1 you will notice that the room has a one-way mirror and a video camera. The mirror allows an observer in a viewing room to see what is happening in the play therapy room without intruding on the process of counselling or causing a distraction. When a one-way mirror is installed a sound system is also required so that the observer can hear what is being said, as well as observe what is happening. In some situations the sound system is linked in with the video system.

A one-way mirror can be used for the following purposes:

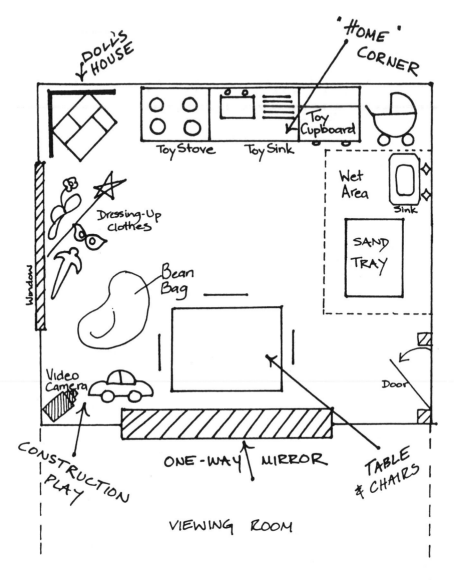

Figure 15.1   *The play therapy room*

- To enable the counsellor to observe the child's play without distracting the child. This is particularly useful when a parent or siblings are in the room with the child. The counsellor can then observe the child's play, and also observe parental and/or family interactions.
- To work with a co-therapist in the observation room. By using the mirror the co-therapist does not intrude on the counselling process and does not distract the child.
- To enable a supervisor to directly observe a counselling session.

We recommend that the one-way mirror should be curtained, so that the curtains can be drawn when the viewing room is not in use. Thus, the child can be sure that no one is watching and that his privacy is assured.

A video camera is another very useful tool to assist in the practice of counselling children. It can be used for the following purposes:

- To help a child to learn and practise new behaviours. For example, when teaching a child to be assertive the child can role-play and see for herself whether her behaviour is assertive or not.
- To help parents to discover new and more effective ways of parenting their children. By watching video-taped interactions with their children, parents are enabled to recognize both helpful and unhelpful parenting behaviours.
- To improve counselling skills through supervision. By watching video-tapes of our own counselling sessions we have often been able to recognize ways in which we could have been more effective. The process is even more helpful when peers or a supervisor are involved in the tape review.

Before a one-way mirror and video camera are used, the child and parents must be informed and their consent must be obtained. We generally find that parents realize the advantages, and are happy to give their consent. Our practice is to ask for written consent, with the parents having a choice of three levels of consent.

Level one consent: the video-tape is only to be used for the purposes of counselling, and will then be erased.

Level two consent: the video-tape is to be used for counselling purposes and for counsellor supervision purposes, and will then be erased.

Level three consent: the counsellor can use the tape for educational and training purposes, as well as for level one and two purposes. This consent may be withdrawn at any stage at the parents' request.

Furniture, equipment, toys and materials

The play therapy room should be equipped with a variety of toys, play materials and media, because different toys, materials and media tend to elicit different forms of play. Materials such as wooden blocks, Lego and cardboard boxes inspire constructional play. By comparison, dress-up clothes and housekeeping effects encourage make believe, imaginative play.

The following is a list of the furniture and other items which we have included in our own play therapy room.

Furniture and associated items

Toy stove
Toy kitchen cupboard

Toy washbasin
(The above items should be large enough for a small child to use when engaged in family role plays.)
Child's table and chairs
Bean bags

Toys

Dolls' house and dolls' house family
Doll's bed
Doll's pram
Pillow and sheets for pram, etc.
Rag doll
Baby doll
Teddy bear
Dolls' clothes
Plastic crockery and cutlery
Feeding bottle
Dolls' nappies
Telephone
Mirror
Toy vehicles
Shopping basket
Empty food packets
Play money

Equipment and materials

Sand tray
Symbols for use in the sand tray
Clay
Play-Doh
Paper
Crayons
Felt pens
Finger paints
Puppets
Cardboard boxes
Spools
Pipe cleaners
Glue
Scissors
Sticky tape
Coloured paper and cardboard
Wool
Wooden spatulas
Glitter
Wooden blocks

Miniature animals and figures

Farm animals
Zoo animals
Assorted dinosaurs of different sizes
Miniature figurines to include superheroes and other current characters

Dress-up materials

A variety of clothes and materials for dressing up, including jewellery, wigs,
  swords and handbags
Doctor's or nurse's set
Assorted masks

Books

Story books

Games

Assorted games such as Connect Four, Playing cards, and dominoes

The play therapy room should preferably be uncluttered, or children will be distracted by seeing a large number of toys and several different types of media. This is particularly important for children who are especially disturbed, or who have attention deficit problems or poor impulse control. Most of the toys and media should be stored in cupboards, with a selected number of items being available for each counselling session.

The way in which the play therapy room is set out should enable the child to move freely between activities so that she does not feel restricted. However, it is an advantage to have a space in the room where the child can retire and sit quietly. In this regard, bean bags are not only useful for sitting on generally, but may also be used by the child during relaxation, or when going on an imaginary journey, or at other times when the child needs to sit in a quiet place.

The play environment should preferably be left unaltered from session to session so that the child is immediately at ease and has a sense of belonging when coming to a new session. It is as though the child sees the room as her own. Sometimes it may not be practicable to leave the room unaltered. In this case, it can be useful to put a significant toy, materials or media from the previous session into the room, to help the child to re-join easily from where she left off in that session.

Clearly, from our discussion of the play therapy room, the appropriate selection of toys, materials and media is important in counselling children. Issues relating to selection of appropriate media or activities will be dealt with in the next section.

◆　◆　◆　◆　◆　◆　◆

16 Selecting the appropriate media or activity

We use media, or an activity, as a way of engaging the child and enabling the child to tell her story. In selecting media or activities we need to remember that each child is different, both as an individual, and with regard to the issues and behaviours which need to be addressed. Each of the media or activities available has different and particular properties. We need to match up the media or activity with the individual child and with that child's abilities and needs.

Factors which are of importance when selecting media or activities include the following:

- the child's developmental age;
- whether the child is being counselled individually or in a group;
- the current counselling goals for the child.

To assist in the selection of media and activities, we have constructed five tables (Tables 16.1 to 16.5). These tables identify the suitability of media and activities in various domains.

Table 16.1: Suitability of media or activities for various age groups
Table 16.2: Suitability of media or activities for different counselling
    situations
Table 16.3: Suitability of media or activities for achieving goals
Table 16.4: Properties of media or activities
Table 16.5: Behaviours likely to occur when using specific media or activities

In Tables 16.1 to 16.5 the media or activities which are most suitable are indicated by clear cells, those which are moderately suitable are indicated by lightly shaded cells, and the least suitable are indicated by darkly shaded cells.

Table 16.1: suitability of media or activities for various age groups

Table 16.1 can be used to assist in the selection of media or activities which are most appropriate developmentally for the child. For example, *imaginative pretend play* is an activity which is highly appropriate for pre-school children between the ages of two and five years. This activity is less likely to appeal to pre-adolescents or adolescents, because of their cognitive maturity and ability to engage in abstract thinking. They are likely to find working with miniatures and symbols more appealing.

We have found that, regardless of age, gender differences rarely influence the selection of media or activities. Both girls and boys join easily with the listed media and activities.

Some children are regressed emotionally, socially and cognitively, as a consequence of past traumas and emotional issues. Not surprisingly, these

Table 16.1　*Suitability of media and activities for various age groups*

MEDIA \ AGES	Pre-school 2 to 5 years	Primary school 6 to 10 years	Early adolescence 11 to 13 years	Late adolescence 14 to 17 years
Books/stories			Suitable	Least suitable
Clay	Suitable			
Construction			Least suitable	Least suitable
Drawing	Suitable			
Finger painting			Suitable	Suitable
Games	Suitable			Least suitable
Imaginary journey	Least suitable	Suitable		
Imaginative pretend play	Suitable			Least suitable
Miniature animals	Least suitable			
Painting/collage	Suitable	Suitable	Suitable	
Puppets/soft toys	Suitable		Suitable	Least suitable
Sand tray	Suitable			
Symbols/figurines	Least suitable			
Worksheets	Least suitable			Least suitable

Most suitable	(white)
Suitable	(light grey)
Least suitable	(dark grey)

Table 16.2　*Suitability of media and activities for various situations*

MEDIA \ SITUATION	Individual counselling	Family counselling	Group work
Books/stories		Least suitable	Least suitable
Clay		Suitable	Suitable
Construction		Least suitable	Suitable
Drawing		Suitable	Suitable
Finger painting		Suitable	
Games		Suitable	
Imaginary journey		Least suitable	Least suitable
Imaginative pretend play		Least suitable	Suitable
Miniature animals		Least suitable	Least suitable
Painting/collage		Least suitable	Suitable
Puppets/soft toys		Least suitable	Suitable
Sand tray		Least suitable	Suitable
Symbols/figurines		Least suitable	Least suitable
Worksheets		Least suitable	Suitable

Table 16.3 *Suitability of media and activities for achieving goals*

MEDIA \ GOALS	To gain mastery over issues and events	To be powerful through physical expression	To encourage expression of emotions	To develop problem-solving and decision-making skills	To develop social skills	To build self-concept and self-esteem	To improve communication skills	To develop insight
Books/stories		░	░		░	░		
Clay	░			▓		▓	▓	░
Construction	▓	▓	▓	░	▓	░	▓	▓
Drawing		░		▓	▓		░	
Finger painting	░			▓	▓		▓	
Games	▓	▓		▓	▓		░	▓
Imaginary journey		░	░			▓		
Imaginative pretend play			░					
Miniature animals	▓	▓	░			▓		
Painting/collage		░		▓	▓		░	
Puppets/soft toys			░			░		
Sand tray			░		░	▓		
Symbols/figurines								
Worksheets	▓	▓	▓				▓	▓

Most suitable	(white)
Suitable	░
Least suitable	▓

children may be more suited to activities which would normally be appropriate for younger children.

Table 16.2: suitability of media and activities for various situations

Most often counsellors work with children individually, but they sometimes work with sibling groups, or groups of children who have similar issues or have had similar experiences. At other times, counselling occurs in a family setting.

Table 16.2 describes the suitability of media for these differing settings. While all of the media and activities are suitable for use in individual counselling sessions, some are not as suitable for group or family work.

Table 16.3: suitability of media and activities for achieving goals

Table 16.3 shows some broad goals, each of which is relevant for different stages around the Spiral of Therapeutic Change (see p. 46). The table indicates which media or activities are most suitable for assisting children to achieve the goals.

To gain mastery over issues and events

To gain mastery over past events and current issues, the child needs to do one of the following:

- To re-experience past events or traumas of concern by re-enacting them, acting them out, or re-explaining them. In this process, the child may need to imagine how he could have changed his role in those events so that he would have felt more comfortable. He might also need to engage in an activity which will enable him to experience, in his imagination, the effect of his changed role. In this way he can experience a sense of mastery over the event or trauma.
- To simulate an event which will allow him to experience the feelings of power and /or control which he may not have experienced in previous instances.

It follows that in order to gain mastery over past events, the child needs to use media which allow for the creation of imaginary environments in which there can be powerful roles. These roles might sometimes be fantasy roles which give the child superhuman abilities for dealing with social and physical situations. Examples of the use of suitable media are:

- Books and stories can encourage the child to alter the story. The child can project outcomes which he would have liked for himself, on to characters within the story.
- Drawing allows the child to make pictures which depict traumatic events. In these pictures the child can depict himself as powerful or in control.
- In the imaginary journey the child is invited to revisit significant life situations. He can, in his imagination, introduce new behaviours for himself in order to achieve some sense of control or mastery in situations where he was previously powerless.
- In imaginative pretend play dramatic representation of powerful roles can be enacted.
- Painting and collage can be used in a similar way to drawing.
- Puppets and soft toys allow the child to assume powerful roles.
- Sand-tray work allows the child to create fantasy environments in which she can feel in control.
- Symbols and figurines can be used in the same way as puppets, and are suitable for older children.

To be powerful through physical expression

Children feel empowered when they witness their ability to powerfully impact on their environment. In counselling this can be achieved by providing activities and media that enable them to control the media and to alter them, or to act out powerful roles. For example:

- A child might punch a lump of clay until it becomes flat.
- When using finger painting the child can dramatically alter her drawing or destroy the images in her picture.
- In imaginative pretend play the young child can attack a bean bag with a toy sword.
- Mock battles can be acted out between 'good' and 'evil' puppets. Similar work can be done with older children using figurines.
- In sand-tray work a child can bury figures or objects in the sand to obliterate or conceal them.

Engaging in these types of activities can be cathartic for the child, as they symbolize in a concrete way her ability to impact on her environment.

To encourage expression of emotions

We have discussed the importance and benefits of encouraging and helping children to express their emotions. Some media and activities lend themselves to the expression of emotion much more effectively than others. For example:

- Clay tends to promote the expression of anger, sadness, fear and worry.
- Drawing allows the child to get in touch with not only her projected thoughts, but also her emotional feelings.
- Finger painting tends to generate the emotions of joy, celebration, and happiness.
- In painting and collage the child may connect the texture of the material with emotional feelings.

To develop problem-solving and decision-making skills

At some point around the Spiral of Therapeutic Change the child will be required to explore options, to make choices, to take risks, and to experiment with challenges and changing behaviours. Appropriate media might include:

- books and storytelling, where alternative solutions can be explored, for example, Little Red Riding Hood might trap the wolf so that she can rescue her grandmother before she gets eaten!
- puppets and soft toys: the child can make up a dialogue to solve problems between two or more characters;
- sand-tray work, where a child can rearrange a visual picture to accommodate different needs;
- symbols and figurines: these can be used similarly to puppets and soft toys and are more suitable for older children;
- worksheets: these can be used to directly address problem-solving and decision-making skills.

To develop social skills

In order to feel better in the future, many children need to develop social skills. Often this involves learning different ways of relating to others so that they can make friends, get their needs met, be appropriately assertive, identify and live within sensible boundaries, and cooperate with others.

To develop adaptive social skills a child needs to understand and experience the consequences of social behaviour. This can be achieved by the use of:

- an activity such as playing a game with the child and giving the child feedback;
- imaginative pretend play, which can help younger children to learn about and practise social skills;
- puppets and soft toys, which can help children to learn about and practise socially acceptable behaviours;
- worksheets to address specific social skills issues.

To build self-concept and self-esteem

We have found that a child's self-concept and self-esteem are almost inevitably affected adversely whenever she experiences troubling events or trauma. In order to build self-concept and self-esteem the counsellor needs to select activities and media which will promote self-fulfilment and independence in the child, and will enable the child to explore, accept and value her strengths and weaknesses. Suitable media and activities are as follows:

- Drawing, where comic strips can be created to illustrate the development of the child's own strengths. For example, a child might show her progression from infancy to the present, highlighting memorable milestones.
- Finger painting. This doesn't require skill, so anything the child produces is likely to be an acceptable product.
- Games can be selected which target the child's specific skills and give her an opportunity to perform well.
- Imaginative pretend play allows the child to experience roles such as being a leader or helper, and to discover his unique strengths.
- Painting and collage can be used similarly to finger painting.
- Specifically designed worksheets can be used to address issues related to self-esteem and self-concept.

To improve communication skills

Often when a child tells her story to friends and significant others, the story will sound confusing, incongruent, and sometimes difficult to believe. Activities which assist in highlighting the sequence of the story, important themes related to the story, the child's understanding of significant events, and how the child felt at different times, are helpful. For example:

- Storytelling helps the child to develop communication skills.
- The imaginary journey allows the child to get in touch with memories and then to relate his perception of events more easily.
- Imaginative pretend play encourages communication through dramatic role play.
- Miniature animals provide a visual picture which usually encourages the child to talk about his perceptions of relationships.
- Puppets and soft toys help the child to use words to express the feelings and perceptions of characters, and allows the child to project his perceptions on to the characters.
- Using symbols in the sand-tray can help a child to develop a visual picture of events she has experienced and to place these in chronological order. The visual picture then enables the child to tell her story, and thus to practise her communication skills.

To develop insight

If a child is to develop insight and understanding of himself and others, he may need to understand how his involvement in significant events occurred, and how his experience fits into his wider social system. For example:

- Books and storytelling can be used to develop insight by illustrating the reality of human behaviour, and the inevitability of consequences of behaviour.
- Drawing allows the child to gain insight into her own involvement in events. This can be achieved by inviting the child to draw a comic strip showing the sequence of past events.
- The imaginary journey allows the child to retrieve memories of his involvement in events and experiences, and thus to gain insight.
- Imaginative pretend play allows young children to take on the role of others in play. Consequently, they can develop insight into the motives and behaviours of themselves and others.
- The use of miniature animals enables the child to gain insight into relationships as animals are placed near to each other or are absent from each other.
- Puppets and soft toys can be used with younger children, and symbols and figurines with older children, in a similar way to imaginative pretend play.
- Use of the sand tray allows the child to develop insight into events by developing a visual picture of the way in which events may have, or could have, occurred.

Table 16.4: properties of media and activities

Each type of medium and activity has its own unique and inherent properties. We have divided these into four major categories as shown in Table 16.4.

Table 16.4   *Properties of media and activities*

MEDIA / PROPERTIES	Open ended and expansive	Functional and contained	Familiar and stable	Educational
Books/stories		▨		
Clay		█	█	▨
Construction	▨			▨
Drawing	▨			▨
Finger painting		█	█	█
Games	█			
Imaginary journey		█		▨
Imaginative pretend play		█		▨
Miniature animals	▨			
Painting/collage	▨			▨
Puppets/soft toys		▨		
Sand tray		▨		
Symbols/figurines	▨		▨	▨
Worksheets	█		█	

Most suitable	
Suitable	▨
Least suitable	█

Table 16.5   *Behaviours encouraged by media and activities*

MEDIA / BEHAVIOURS	Interactive and adventurous	Introspective and private	Simple and stereotypic	Cognitive
Books/stories	▨	█	▨	
Clay		▨		█
Construction	▨	█		▨
Drawing			█	█
Finger painting		▨		█
Games		█	█	
Imaginary journey	█		█	▨
Imaginative pretend play		▨		
Miniature animals	█		█	█
Painting/collage	▨	▨		
Puppets/soft toys		▨	█	
Sand tray	▨			█
Symbols/figurines	▨		█	
Worksheets	▨	▨	█	

Open-ended and expansive media and activities

Primarily activities and media which are open-ended and expansive allow freedom of expression with no particular boundaries or restrictions. They are activities which are flexible and moveable, and often contain a tactile or kinaesthetic element. For example, children can use their imagination to make any changes they like while on an imaginary journey. In imaginative pretend play an unstructured drama can be created, developed and changed at will. Finger painting and clay have kinaesthetic and tactile qualities. No special skill is required for any of these media and activities so there is very little experience of failure.

Media and activities which are functional and contained

These activities and media allow the child to experience a sense of containment and challenge. They demand attention to detail and often have an end product or result. For example, if we invite a child to construct a sculpture with Lego blocks, the child is focused on a specific task, needs to think and plan the construction, and we can expect a sculpture as the end product.

Media and activities which are familiar and stable

These provide an opportunity for simple, repetitive and sometimes stereotypic interaction. Using them provides a sense of stability and predictability. For example, when using imaginative pretend play, familiar and stable themes which are already well known to the child can be continually replayed. This is especially useful for children who come from chaotic and unstable backgrounds.

Media and activities which are educational

These offer an opportunity for learning, and for the acceptance and rejection of rules. They are structured, don't require lateral thinking, and are progressive in that they require work towards an objective. For example, when using worksheets the child builds on her knowledge of the content of the worksheet.

Table 16.5: behaviours encouraged by media and activities

Table 16.5 enables the counsellor to choose material which is likely to elicit particular behavioural and/or emotional responses from the child. These are responses which are required to promote a healthy resolution of issues. Table 16.5 is best used in conjunction with Table 16.4, because the behaviours generated by media and activities are clearly related to their properties.

Media and activities which encourage the child to be interactive and adventurous

These allow the child to interact with media, and encourage the child to cooperate with the counsellor or with others in a group counselling setting.

Use of the media encourages the child to experiment with new behaviours which require risk taking and provide an opportunity for adventure and challenge.

Media which allow introspective and private behaviour

These media allow the child to focus inwardly and exclusively on herself and her own issues with safety and seclusion. A good example of such media is the imaginary journey. In the imaginary journey, the child only needs to share what she chooses to share with the counsellor, and can keep to herself whatever information she wishes.

Media and activities which invite simple and stereotypic behaviour

Some activities offer the child an opportunity to experience simple predictable behaviours. Here the child's expectations are usually fulfilled and consequences are predictable. For example, in imaginative pretend play the child will role-play themes which are known to him and will use known consequences of role-played behaviours. The child can also experiment with simple changes to his or other people's behaviours.

Media and activities which encourage cognitive responses

These encourage the child to think about specific issues. They allow the child an opportunity to debate and compare ideas which are similar to, and different from her own, and to evaluate consequences of behaviour. For example, the use of books like, *It's OK to say NO* (Ayers and James, 1986) invites the child to explore the issue of saying 'No'.

In conclusion

In this section we have provided an overview of *how to select* media and activities. In the following sections we will deal with *how to use* the various media and activities.

◆ ◆ ◆ ◆ ◆ ◆ ◆

17   The use of miniature animals

We will write about the use of miniature animals under five headings as follows:

1   Materials needed
2   Goals when using miniature animals
3   How to use miniature animals
4   Counselling skills needed when using miniature animals
5   Suitability of the medium

Materials needed

A variety of small toy animals and other creatures is required, including the following:

- Domestic animals
- Farm animals
- Jungle animals
- Zoo animals
- Dinosaurs
- Reptiles (snakes, crocodiles, lizards)
- Insects (spiders, grasshoppers)
- Sea creatures (turtles, dolphins, whales)

The animals and other creatures should preferably be made of plastic and be appropriately coloured so that they look realistic. They should be of various sizes, with some having a benign appearance, some an aggressive appearance, and others being friendly. It is desirable to have both male and female animals, and baby animals in some species. The inclusion of dinosaurs is important: children like to make use of them, particularly the very large aggressive-looking ones.

All the animals must be able to stand freely without support; children become frustrated and distracted when animals fall over. We generally limit our animal collection to about 50, because some children find it over-whelming if they are asked to choose from a larger set.

A large flat work space is required when working with miniatures. This can either be a table or floor. Generally we prefer to sit and work on the carpeted floor of our play therapy room.

Goals when using miniature animals

The main goal is to enable the child to tell her story about her perceptions of her personal relationships, and her perceptions of other relationships within her family. Working with miniature animals enables the child to do the following:

- explore past, present and future relationships with others;
- gain a fuller understanding of her place in her family;
- explore fears related to her own future relationships;
- fantasize about possible future relationships;
- explore fears with regard to future relationships between others;
- explore possible solutions to relationship problems.

Miniature animals can also be used to explore the child's relationships in other systems and situations, for example in school, in foster placement, during access visits, and during visits to hospital for medical procedures.

Miniature animals can also be used in conjunction with sand-tray work (see Chapter 18).

How to use miniature animals

The counsellor's task, when using miniature animals, is to encourage the child to focus on the important relationships in her life and to tell her story with regard to these. From this storytelling the counsellor can help the child to identify important themes and issues, and can allow the child to experience any emotions which emerge.

The counsellor begins by introducing the child to the animals. The counsellor might say something like: *I thought that we might play with my toy animals today. We are going to play with them in a special way. First of all, I would like you to choose an animal which is most like you.*

In making this request, it is important for the child to understand that he is being asked to choose the animal which is most like him, as he is at the present time, rather than choosing an animal which represents how he would like to be. For example, a child might believe that he is submissive and compliant, but might have fantasies about being more powerful. If such a child chose a lamb to represent himself, that would be appropriate, but it certainly would not be appropriate if he chose a Tyrannosaurus Rex. In a similar way it would not be useful for a child to choose an animal on the grounds of physical similarity alone (for example a tall thin child might choose a giraffe). The intention is to invite the child to choose an animal which he believes is most similar to him in personality, behavioural and emotional characteristics. We find that by making the above request we generally get the required response from the child.

Once the child has chosen his animal, the counsellor should invite him to tell her what the selected animal is like, by asking: *Tell me about that lion* (or whatever animal is chosen) or, *What is that lion like?*

Some children respond by making obvious and concrete statements about the size and physical attributes of the selected animal. This is not useful, so in order to encourage the child to describe personality traits of the animal, the counsellor might say: *I wonder what this animal is like inside* or, *Tell me more.*

Notice that the counsellor refers to *'the animal'* or uses its name (for example *the lion*). The counsellor does not call the animal by the child's name, and does not imply that the animal is the child, even though the animal has been chosen as being *most like* the child, and will be used to represent the child. Referring to it 'the animal' or by its name allows the child to distance himself from the chosen animal, so that although it represents him in some ways, it is not the same as him. He can then project qualities, characteristics and behaviours on to the animal with safety. The animal – not the child – becomes the owner of negative, positive and unacceptable attributes. This enables the child to feel freer in attributing negative and undesirable behaviours which he may recognize in himself, but may not be ready to own.

Sometimes a child might choose an animal which the counsellor thinks has particular qualities. For example the child might choose a panther, which the counsellor sees as aggressive. However, the child might see the panther as powerful but friendly, and not aggressive. The counsellor therefore needs to be careful not to project his own ideas on to the child's chosen animals.

Occasionally a child will want to choose more than one animal to represent himself. This can be useful, because the two animals might represent different aspects of the same child. For example, a child with a secret might choose a hen for the part of himself which wants to keep the secret and a bull for the part of himself which wants to tell others about the secret.

Once the child has selected the animal which is most like him, the counsellor encourages the child to select other animals to represent each member of his family. Additionally, he is invited to select animals to represent absent or deceased members of his family. The same procedure is used as before, with the counsellor making requests such as: *Now choose the animal which is most like your mum.* As each animal is chosen the counsellor asks the child: *What is that animal like?*

As each animal is selected the child is encouraged to place it in front of him. Eventually the child will have a group of animals to represent his family. When the group is complete, the counsellor should note the placement of the selected animals and make a statement about how they have been arranged. For example, the counsellor might say: *Your animals are all in a straight line* or, *Your animals are all in a circle with the zebra in the centre.* Often, when a counsellor makes such an observation, the child will spontaneously talk about the meaning which is associated with the arrangement of the animals. For example, the child might say, 'All the other animals are watching the zebra because she likes to play tricks on them.'

Sometimes a child will not respond to the counsellor's feedback statement about the arrangement of the group of animals. In this case, the counsellor might say to the child: *Arrange the animals so that they make a picture.*

Perhaps, 'make a sculpture' would be more accurate, but many children don't know what the word 'sculpture' means. Once the child has arranged the animals, the counsellor can comment on the arrangement.

At this point, the counsellor can begin to explore the relationships between the animals in the group. For example the counsellor may begin to explore the relationship between the dog (representing the child) and the dinosaur (representing the child's father). The counsellor might ask questions like: *I wonder what it is like for the dog to be next to the dinosaur?*

Later the counsellor might ask: *What is it like for the dinosaur to have the dog next to him?* and *How does the horse* [representing the child's mother] *feel about the dog and dinosaur being together?* It could also be useful for the counsellor to ask the child how he thinks the other animals in the group feel about this arrangement.

The process can be extended by asking the child to move the dog (if that is the animal he chose for himself) to a new position near another animal. Similarly, the child can be asked to move other animals into different positions in the group. In this way the various relationships within the group can be explored.

Notice that the counsellor does not move the animals herself, but asks the child to move them. We believe that by doing this the child develops a greater sense of ownership about the story which she is telling, and is more likely to feel in control of the process and be more in touch with her perceptions.

Sometimes a counsellor may notice that a child is reluctant to move an animal into a particular position. The counsellor might then use reflection to feed this observation back to the child by saying: *You seem to be unhappy about moving the duck next to the snake.* By feeding back this information to the child, the counsellor is able to raise the child's awareness of important feelings. After each animal is moved, the child is again asked questions about the feelings of various other animals with regard to the altered position. Thus, the child, in an indirect way, shares his picture of his family, and of his family's relationships, with the counsellor. However, remember that the whole process of using miniature animals is primarily projective.

The projective nature of working with miniature animals

Throughout the process involved in working with miniature animals, the counsellor never refers to the group of animals selected as 'the child's family', and never uses the names of members of the child's family. This might inhibit the child in the allocation of attributes, behaviours, thoughts and feelings to the animals, and might block the child's ability to freely explore the relationships between the animals. The whole process is projective, with the child projecting ideas from his family on to the animals, but having the freedom to exaggerate or modify those projections. By using this projective technique, the child is likely to access ideas and beliefs which may have been suppressed into her unconscious because of fears about the consequences of recognizing those ideas and beliefs.

Because the process is projective, the child will make connections between relationships and behaviours in the animal group, and relationships and behaviours in his own family. In so doing, he is likely to make important discoveries about relationships within his family, and to want to talk about these. When this occurs, it is appropriate for the counsellor to use the counselling skills described in Part 3, to enable the child to continue telling his story. At this stage of the process the child may experience strong emotions (as indicated on the Spiral of Therapeutic Change, p. 46).

Further discussion on the use of the medium

As well as exploring current relationships the counsellor can explore how the child might feel about absences of family members. For example the counsellor might say to the child: *I would like you to move the dinosaur and put him behind your back.* The visual picture that appears for the child is now one where there is an absent dinosaur (Father).

The miniature animals can be used to help the child to explore her ideas about what would make relationships within the family more comfortable. This can be done by inviting the child to put her animal in a place where the animal will feel most comfortable in relation to other members of her family.

It can be useful to invite the child to place her own animal close to an animal which has already been identified as worrying for her. Thus, the child can fully experience the resulting feelings and deal with them.

When the counselling session is drawing to an end, we find that it is useful to invite the child to arrange the animals in a way that will enable all the animals to feel most comfortable. The counsellor might say: *I'd like you to rearrange your animals into a new picture so that all of the animals will feel happy and comfortable.* This enables the child to leave the session feeling comfortable about his work and with a sense of closure around the issues of relationships within his family.

Generally, when using miniature animals, the counsellor shouldn't advise, interpret, or congratulate the child while she is telling her story. Similarly, expressions of surprise, approval or disapproval would intrude on the storytelling and might influence it, so that it would cease to be authentically the child's. The counsellor needs to take the child's story seriously and to communicate respect for it. This is true even when it is clear that factual information in the child's story is completely wrong. It is only by having the opportunity to tell her story, in her own way, that the child can later move forward to test her perception of reality. It is interesting to note that when we have used miniature animals with different children in the same family, we have usually heard quite different and unique stories from each child, even though some important elements of these stories were the same.

Counselling skills required when using miniatures

All of the counselling skills dealt with in Chapter 3 are required when using miniature animals. The following skills are particularly useful:

1   Observation
2   Reflection of content and feelings
3   Use of statements (for feedback of observations)
4   Open questions

Here are some examples to demonstrate the common use of the above skills.

Use of observation and reflection of feeling: The counsellor might say, *I noticed that you looked happy when you put the monkey and the goat together.*

Use of observation and a statement: The counsellor might use a statement to feed back to the child an observation of significance by saying, *I notice that the chicken is the furthest one away from the rhinoceros.*

Use of an open question: The counsellor might ask, *What is it like for this animal when the dinosaur is standing in front of him?*

At times, while working with miniature animals the counsellor may repeat word for word, phrases used by the child, to encourage the child to tell more of his story. Consider an example where, after moving a cat next to a hen, a child says, 'The elephant doesn't like that.' If the counsellor repeats *The elephant doesn't like that*, then the child is likely to think about what he has said and to explore his ideas and feelings more thoroughly.

We need to remember that the goals of counselling do not include investigating. If a counsellor starts to ask unnecessary questions to satisfy her own agenda, then the authenticity of the child's story will almost certainly be compromised. The counsellor continually needs to remember not to intrude, but instead to gently provide opportunities for the child to continue telling her story. Any questions the counsellor asks should be to seek further information about the child's story rather than to move the story in a particular direction. Questions should be carefully phrased to encourage the child to talk about events and the meanings the child ascribes to those events.

'Why' questions aren't useful when working with miniature animals because they invite interpretative answers which tend to deflect the child away from her internal processes. 'What' and 'how' questions are useful, because they invite the child to share information which is not contaminated by contrived explanations. Explanations distract the child from the true essence of the story and allow her to deflect away from painful experiences.

Suitability of the medium

Miniature animals are most successfully used in the way which we have described, with children from about seven years of age and onwards. With younger children, their use tends to produce concrete responses and the child is not likely to project his ideas about various family members on to the animals. Instead the child is likely to talk directly about the selected animals and their characteristics. Further, children under the age of seven have limited ability to abstract and predict. They have little understanding of motive or intent, and therefore find it difficult to project other people's behaviours on to the animals.

Miniature animals are more suitable for use in individual counselling than group counselling, because use of this medium targets an individual's perceptions about others and relationships between others.

Working with miniature animals requires some direction or guidance by the counsellor. Miniature animals encourage behaviours in the child which are introspective and sometimes private because the child is required to project thoughts and feelings on to the animals. However, this medium can, in some instances, be used to expand the child's exploration of options and alternatives.

Where a child is regressed and/or emotionally blocked a warm up period may be required during which the child is encouraged to play freely with the miniature animals.

◆   ◆   ◆   ◆   ◆   ◆   ◆

18   Sand tray work

We will discuss sand tray work under the following headings:

1   Equipment and materials needed
2   Goals of sand tray work
3   How to use the sand tray
4   Counselling skills when using the sand tray
5   Suitability of sand tray work

Equipment and materials needed

The only equipment required is the sand tray itself. Materials required are symbols, figurines and miniature animals.

The sand tray

The sand tray may be made of wood or plastic. Preferably, it should be square with sides of about a metre in length, and about 150mm high. Wooden sand trays should have a waterproof lining.

The sand should be clean washed sand. We have discovered from our own practical experience that it is a mistake to use very light fine sand. It can create a miniature sandstorm in the room when used by active children. The depth of sand in the tray should be about 75mm, with a 75mm space between the surface of the sand and the top edge of the tray. This makes it easy to work in the sand without the sand spilling out of the tray.

Sometimes, access to water is useful, although this is not essential. Wet sand can be used to make caves, tunnels, hills and other shapes.

We keep our sand tray on the floor and sit, with the child, on the floor beside it.

Symbols

The symbols used in sand tray work consist of a variety of small objects which are chosen because they have properties which enable them to easily assume symbolic meaning. We have collected our symbols over a period of time, so that they include many different types of objects.

The symbols may be used to represent concrete things such as roads, houses, schools, shopping centres and individual people. Additionally, they may be used to represent less tangible concepts such as secrets, thoughts, beliefs, wishes and emotional barriers. Thus, the symbols can be used to represent anything concrete, or intangible, or abstract, which has a place in the child's story.

A useful set of symbols might include the following items:

General items

Rocks, stones and pebbles	Feathers
Shells	Wood
Small boxes with lids	Marbles
Candles	Small paper flags
Old jewellery	A key
Paper	A padlock
Ornaments	A torch battery
A tin of spaghetti	A crystal ball
A small mirror	Buttons
Beads	A horseshoe
A small pyramid	Gold stars
A notebook	A pencil
A chain	A large nail

Small toys

Plastic trees	Toy fences
Planes	Trains
Boats	Cars

Figurines and superheroes

Male and female figurines	Toy soldiers
Medieval knights	Catwoman
Batman	Power rangers

Toy animals

Dragons	Farm animals
Zoo animals	Jungle animals
Domestic animals	

Objects which have universal symbolic meaning, for example those which are funny, frightening, endearing, magical or religious make ideal symbols.

Goals of sand tray work

Sand tray work provides the child with an opportunity to use symbols, within a defined space, to tell her story. While telling her story, the child has an opportunity to re-create in the sand tray, and in her imagination, events and situations from her past and present. The child may also explore possibilities for the future or express her fantasies in the sand tray. Consequently the child is enabled to do all, or any, of the following:

- explore specific events, past, present and future;
- explore themes and issues relating to these events;
- act out those things which are not, or were not, acceptable to her;
- gain a cognitive understanding of the elements of events in her life, and thus gain insight into those events;
- integrate polarities;
- alter her story, as created in the sand tray, by projecting her fantasies on to it;
- experience a sense of power through physical expression;
- gain mastery over past and current issues and events;
- think of what might happen next;
- find resolution of issues through the development of insight.

How to use the sand tray

Because of the tactile and kinaesthetic experience of working in the sand tray most children seem to engage readily in the task. We usually start by inviting the child to use any of the symbols she wishes to make a scene or picture in the sand. In inviting the child to make her picture, we take into account goals for the counselling session. Here are several different examples of instructions which might be useful when starting sand tray work.

Example one

Sometimes we leave the child with freedom to make whatever picture she chooses without any specific direction. This non-directive approach can be useful, because it allows the counsellor to observe the way in which the child engages in the task and constructs the picture. The counsellor can then look for any themes and issues that emerge during the creation of the picture so that these can be discussed with the child. Using this approach, the counsellor might start the sand tray work by saying: *I'd like you to use these things (symbols) to make a picture in the sand.*

Example two

In some cases, the counsellor may suspect that the child's issues concern relationships with others. The counsellor can then be more specific in her direction, and might say: *Make a picture about all the people that you know.*

As the picture develops, the counsellor can notice the qualities of the various relationships, taking particular notice of strengths, weaknesses, distances, closeness and boundaries. Additionally, the counsellor should note any absences of significant others from the picture. The use of feedback statements by the counsellor will then help to raise the child's awareness of her situation so that she can deal with related issues.

Example three

Some children present with a very high level of anxiety. With these children it can be useful to give them the following instruction: *Make a picture about the things that frighten you most.*

Later, as the picture develops, the counsellor might say: *Find something that reminds you of* [ghosts, spiders, or whatever is relevant].

These instructions can be useful for the child, because by concretizing the fear itself, the child can then deal with it symbolically. For example, the child might bury it, or put it outside the sand tray.

Example four

Some children who have been emotionally deprived when younger present with issues related to rejection and abandonment. It is important for these children to explore their perceptions of the way in which they were nurtured. In such cases the counsellor might say: *Make a picture about what it was like when you were a baby.*

Through constructing the picture, the child may be enabled to recognize and experience the pain associated with not having had closeness and nurturing as a young child. By owning and experiencing this pain, the child may, with help from the counsellor, be enabled to discover ways to nurture himself. Sometimes, in cases where a mother has been absent or neglectful, the child may recognize that another person did provide some nurturing. After dealing with the pain related to his mother's behaviour, the child may be able to gain positive feelings as a consequence of recognizing the nurturing he received from the other person.

As a result of the counsellor's instructions, the child is likely to begin to create a miniature picture, in the sand tray, of her perception of part of her present, or past, or future world. While this is happening, the counsellor should stay quietly alongside the child, without interrupting the child's story unnecessarily. As a counsellor, be aware of the developing story and support its evolution. Try not to interpret, but instead try to recognize the symbolic representation, in the way that the child understands it.

Sand tray work is powerful because it provides a visual structure in the form of a sand tray picture together with feedback from an observer (the counsellor). Hence, the child is able to gain an understanding of his world by directly viewing the scene he has created in the sand tray, and also through the feedback statements made to him by the counsellor.

As the sand tray picture develops, there may be several stages of construction. For example, a child may create a picture in which she puts a fence around the house. As the child develops her story, she might put a barrier of trees around the fence. Later, as the story continues, the child may sculpt the sand beyond the trees into hills and gullies. As the child's story has developed, her picture in the sand tray has undergone three different stages, each one seeming to increase the barriers around the house. Clearly, it is likely that issues of safety are emerging. However, the counsellor should not make that interpretation because it could be wrong. Instead the counsellor should give the child accurate feedback of what has been observed by saying: *I notice that you have put a fence, and some trees, and also some hills and gullies around the house.* Through progressively constructing her picture in the sand tray, and with her awareness raised by the feedback from the counsellor, the child is now likely to recognize her issue (be it safety or something else), and may then go on to address it.

It is important for the counsellor to allow the developing process to occur without interpretation or intrusion. Equally it is important for the counsellor not to make assumptions about the meanings of symbols or objects in the sand tray story. It is better to explore the meaning which the child gives the symbol. For example the counsellor might ask: *Can you tell me about this rock?* In response, the child might say, 'That's the church, where we get lots to eat.' In this way the child's awareness of issues and developments in her story is raised.

We have already introduced some examples of counselling skills while describing how to use the media. However, we would now like to look more specifically at the types of skills which are most important when doing sand tray work.

Counselling skills when using the sand tray

When intervention is necessary while the child is telling his story, the counsellor should make use of the counselling skills described in Chapter 3. The skills detailed below are most useful and relevant to sand tray work:

1 Observation
2 Use of statements
3 Use of questions
4 Giving instructions
5 Termination skills when using the sand tray

Observation

A counsellor can learn a great deal about a child, the child's life, and the child's issues, by observing the child as she tells her story while working in the sand tray. The counsellor can use the observed information by making feedback statements to the child so that the child is able to get more fully in touch with troubling issues and developments in his life. You might find it useful to bear in mind the following while making your observations:

1 Notice which symbols the child chooses.
2 Identify the special qualities and meanings which the child attributes to the symbols.
3 Be aware of any commonly used or collective meanings of some symbols, and consider whether these are relevant.
4 Observe the placement of symbols in the sand tray: which are in the middle, and which are at the edges of the sand tray. Notice which symbols are separated from others, and which symbols are close to others. Take note of any symbols which are buried, and of any symbols which are in dominating positions.

5 Notice any vacant spaces in the sand tray, because these may be significant.
6 Observe how the child works. Does he work spontaneously, hesitantly, lethargically, aggressively or forcefully?
7 Observe the way in which the symbols are chosen. Are they chosen thoughtfully and carefully, or are they snatched and carelessly placed?
8 Identify emerging themes, for example nurturing, secrecy, disintegration, victimization, power, etc.
9 Observe inconsistencies in the child's story.

Use of statements

Sometimes, while a child is working on his picture, he will talk about it spontaneously. Generally, the counsellor observes quietly as the child creates his picture. However, if the child does not talk about what he is doing, after observing for a while, it is appropriate for the counsellor to indirectly invite the child to talk about his story by using a statement to feed back what the counsellor has observed. For example, the counsellor might say: *You've been very careful when making your picture* or, *Your picture looks very crowded* or, *Your picture is very busy.*

These statements are non-intrusive and are likely to encourage the child to talk about the picture, without directing him to one particular part of the picture. Sometimes, however, statements like the above are not sufficient, and a question will be needed.

Feedback statements not only allow the child to talk about the picture, but also raise the child's awareness of her internal processes as she constructs the picture. Her awareness of issues, thoughts and feelings, is intensified, and consequently she is able to bring these into focus so that they may be addressed.

Use of questions

Before asking questions, the counsellor should remember that it is important to sit quietly and to observe rather than to interrupt the natural flow of the child's process. However, at appropriate times, during pauses, questions can be used to help the child to explore more fully or in more depth certain parts of his picture or story.

Here are some examples of the use of questions.

When using the sand tray it can be helpful to ask a general question such as: *Can you tell me about your picture?* If there are empty spaces in the sand tray, the counsellor could draw attention to this by pointing to the empty space and making a comment such as: *I wonder what's happening over here?* If the sand tray picture contains symbols and figures which are big and strong, the counsellor might say to the child: *These things look big and strong. Do you ever feel big and strong?*

Giving instructions

Earlier in this chapter we gave examples of instructions which may be used to invite the child to start to create a picture or to tell her story by using the symbols in the sand tray. During the process, other instructions may be required. Consider the following examples.

Example one: A child might develop her story by making verbal suggestions about what might happen next. However, she may not move the symbols in the sand tray to illustrate the change. For example, the child may have set up a scene where children are playing in the park. Later, she may talk about the children going home. However, the child has left the symbols set up the way they were when the children were playing in the park. In this case the counsellor might say: *Show me what happens when they go home.* In response, the child is likely to rearrange the symbols and to continue telling her story. As a consequence, new and important issues might emerge, which otherwise could have been missed.

Example two: If a child were to show more interest in, or to concentrate on, a particular part of her picture, the counsellor might ask: *Tell me about what is happening here* or, *Tell me about this shell* [where the shell is in the relevant part of the picture].

Termination skills when using the sand tray

The counsellor needs to judge when the time is appropriate for ending a piece of work in the sand tray. Good indications of this are if:

1   The child stops work spontaneously.
2   The child is unable to develop the story any further.
3   The time allocated for the counselling session is drawing to an end.

At the appropriate time, the counsellor should summarize what has emerged from the work, and check what the child needs to do to finish working. The counsellor then needs to affirm the child for completing the current piece of work, and to give the child an opportunity to dismantle the picture himself or to leave the picture for the counsellor to dismantle after he has left. It would be inappropriate for the counsellor to dismantle the picture in the child's presence, because it is the child's story. To do so would be intrusive and might lead to undesirable symbolic interpretations by the child. However, it is important for the child to know that the picture will not be there when he returns for another counselling session.

If the counsellor takes a photograph of the arrangement of the symbols in the sand tray he can easily identify recurring themes and changes by comparing photographs from session to session.

Suitability of sand tray work

Children from about the age of five years and upwards enjoy sand tray work. Even adolescents and adults can find it useful. Younger children enjoy playing in the sand but are not developmentally able to engage in the symbolic use of the media.

As with working with miniature animals, sand tray work is ideally suited to individual counselling. It is an open-ended and expansive activity, because it allows the child to explore any possibilities within the limits of his own fantasies. The size and edges of the sand tray provide a sense of limitation and boundary without inhibiting the internal explorations of the child. Sand tray work encourages the child to focus on internal processes. It can also invite the child to be adventurous and interactive, with the counsellor's encouragement.

Further information about sand play can be found in Lowenfeld (1967) and Ryce-Menuhin (1992).

◆ ◆ ◆ ◆ ◆ ◆ ◆

19 Working with clay

Clay is an excellent material to use when working with children because its physical properties are both inviting and useful therapeutically. Most children find that the texture of clay makes it pleasant to touch and manipulate. It is easy to make shapes with clay and to change these shapes in size and appearance. Many children engage readily with clay and become absorbed in feeling, stroking, pressing, punching, squashing and shaping it. They find the tactile and kinaesthetic experience pleasant and satisfying. In some ways, the clay can almost become like an extension of these children, as though it were a part of them.

Clay enables a child to be creative. During this creative activity, emotions within the child are likely to emerge and to be expressed through the activity. Clay allows a child to express a very wide range of emotions: a child may serenely stroke the clay, or aggressively punch it, or pull it apart in frustration. Thus emotions which the child is holding in are likely to be expressed outwardly, and with cathartic effect.

Because shapes made in clay are easy to change into new shapes, this medium invites the child to continue working by developing existing themes and exploring new themes.

Clay is a three-dimensional medium. This allows the child to have more creative freedom than when working in two dimensions with paint or when drawing. Using clay, the child is free to create shapes which can be realistic, imaginary or symbolic. For example, a child could create a shape in clay to represent a monster. This shape, representing the monster, could be realistic and look like an animal, or it could look like a fantasy figure, or it might have a particular symbolic shape, or it might just be a roughly shaped piece of clay.

Working with clay can be particularly rewarding for children who feel inadequate about their creative skills, because it is a medium which can be used with very little skill – there is little chance of failure. Additionally, the counsellor does not need to impose any expectations or rules, so the child can feel free to express himself confidently by responding to his inner experiences without unnecessary restraint.

Because clay stimulates tactile and kinaesthetic senses, it allows children who have shut down or blocked their sensory and emotional experiences to get in touch with them again. As these children become fully engaged in working with clay, their increased sensitivity to kinaesthetic sensation is likely to result in the useful expression of emotion. The counsellor can expect to see behaviours which are likely to reflect the child's inner processes. The counsellor needs to observe the child's non-verbal and verbal responses, and to respond to these by using appropriate counselling skills.

Materials required when using clay

Soft, pliable clay is required. It is important that the clay is not too wet or sticky, because if it is, working with it will be unpleasant. The clay should not be too coarse and gritty, or it will be rough on the skin. Clay can be bought in blocks, of about 30cm by 20cm by 10cm in size, from a craft shop.

We prefer to work with clay on the floor, rather than on a bench, so that the child can more easily join with the clay, work right beside it, and move between clay sculptures. Children can work with clay on a vinyl floor, but the floor needs to be washed afterwards, and this is time consuming. Usually we work on a groundsheet, which can be folded up after use and washed at our convenience. The groundsheet should be large enough to provide an adequate work space, and to have room for both the child and the counsellor to sit on it comfortably.

A piece of thin wire or nylon fishing line, of about 40cm in length, with wooden handles on each end, is needed to cut the clay into pieces. If this is used like a cheese cutter, the clay can easily be separated into pieces. It can sometimes be useful to have tools for sculpting the clay, including wooden spatulas, stiff paintbrushes, and plastic knives and forks. A garlic press to extrude the clay can also be of value.

Clay dries out during use, especially in rooms where there is heating, air conditioning, or fans. To prevent this from happening, a bowl of water, with a sponge which can be squeezed to drip water over the clay, is required to keep the clay moist.

Some children become anxious because clay is messy. To deal with this, we provide plastic aprons, and easy access to a sink and running water.

In summary, the materials required when using clay are as follows:

- A large block of clay
- A groundsheet
- A plastic apron
- A wire for cutting the clay
- Sculpting tools
- A bowl of water and sponge
- Access to water for cleaning up

Goals when using clay

Asking the child to make clay shapes to symbolize or represent important people, objects, feelings or issues in her life, provides the child with an inviting opportunity to tell her story. As she does this the counsellor can use counselling techniques to assist the child in exploring relationships, in understanding her past, and in developing insight.

Because clay allows the child to give an outward expression to internal processes which occur as she tells her story, it provides a connection or bridge, linking the inner processes of the child and the counsellor, and allowing the counsellor to share the intimate detail of the child's story. Thus, the counsellor has an opportunity to encourage the child to express her emotions and to address issues.

Clay is particularly useful in helping a child to project feelings, rather than leaving them bottled up. This projection occurs as the child acts out her emotions physically. For example, she may pound or punch the clay, or she may smooth or roll the clay. As this happens, the counsellor can assist the child to recognize and own the inner feelings associated with her physical expression.

Clay can allow the child to experience satisfaction and success by making a finished product.

It is very useful when working with children in groups. In a group setting, children can be encouraged to interact with each other as they work with the clay and gain insight and understanding of other children in the group, through sharing. This sharing can enhance the children's individual sense of belonging to the group. Additionally, clay work can be used to help children to discover the consequences of their behaviour when in a group.

In summary, goals of importance when using clay include those listed below.

Goals when working with clay individually and in groups

- to help the child to tell and share her story by using the clay to illustrate elements of her story;
- to enable the child to project her inwardly contained feelings on to the clay so that they can be recognized and owned;
- to help the child to recognize and deal with underlying issues;
- to help the child to explore relationships and to develop insight into those relationships;
- to enable a child to experience success and satisfaction in completing a creative task.

Goals when working with clay in a group

- to help the children gain insight and understanding of others;
- to increase a child's sense of belonging to a group;
- to help children to discover the consequences of their behaviour when in a group.

How to work with clay

In discussing how to work with clay we will use the following headings:

1 Starting work with clay
2 Using clay to address specific issues
3 Creating a dialogue between two sculptures
4 Terminating work with clay
5 Using clay in a group

1 Starting work with clay

We have found that a good way to start work is to invite the child to make friends with the clay. This technique is one suggested by Violet Oaklander. Making friends allows the child to relate to the clay in a personal way. We say to the child: *Pick up a piece of clay*, and then, *Hold the clay in your hands, and close your eyes.*

Some children may resist closing their eyes, but that's OK. The child is next given the following instructions, with time being allowed between each instruction for the child to complete the task:

Roll the clay.
Flatten it.
Pinch it.
Pull it to pieces.
Gather it all up together, and roll it again.
Poke a hole in it with one finger.
Tear a piece off and make a snake.
Wrap the snake around one finger.

The child is then invited to get in touch with the immediate experience of using the clay. The counsellor might offer this invitation by asking: *What was it like to make friends with your clay?* and then, *What did you like doing most?*

The child may say that he enjoyed the experience of flattening the clay. The counsellor might then ask the child: *What was it like when you were flattening your clay?*

The counsellor can then invite the child to repeat the most pleasurable part of the 'making friends with your clay' exercise.

2 Using the clay to address specific issues

After the child has made friends with the clay, the counsellor can encourage the child to create a sculpture. This sculpture will be targeted toward particular goals, so the counsellor's instructions need to be specific with regard to these goals. Here are some examples of possible instructions:

Make a sculpture which will let me know how you feel right now.
Make a sculpture with your clay which is like you when you were a baby.

*Make a sculpture with your clay which is like you when you were living in
your foster placement.*
*Make a sculpture with your clay which is like you when you visited dad on
access.*

Sometimes a child might say 'I'm no good at doing this', or 'I can't make
anything.' The counsellor can encourage the child by saying: *Just make any
shape to be like you when you were* —— (see suggestions above).

Sometimes it is useful for the counsellor to model for the child, by
shaping another piece of clay herself and talking about what she is doing.
For example the counsellor might make a sculpture with a lot of spikes,
bumps and holes in it to represent busyness, and might say: *I'm feeling very
busy right now, because I have a lot of work to do, and this is how my clay
looks.*

Once the child has made a sculpture, the counsellor may be tempted to
invite the child to talk about it. However, before this happens, it is
important to check out the child's current experience by asking a question
such as the following: *What was it like to make a sculpture of you when you
were a baby?* (or whatever the sculpture was about). Exploring the child's
current experience in this way will enable the child to get in touch with her
'here and now' experience. She has an opportunity to tap into her current
feelings and thoughts and to talk about these. There may then be emotional
release and exploration of issues.

The counsellor might make a statement to feed back one, or more, of her
observations. For example she might say: *I noticed that you took a long
time to make your sculpture* or, *I noticed that you were very careful when
you were making your sculpture of the baby.* The counsellor might then
invite the child to be the sculpture by saying: *I want you to pretend that you
are that baby* or, *I want you to pretend that you are that shape.*

Then, while the child is imagining that she is the shape, the counsellor
might explore the feelings which are symbolically represented by the shape
and texture of the clay sculpture, by asking: *Tell me how it feels to have
these bumps around here?* or, *What is it like to have these spikes sticking out
of here?*

Next the counsellor might invite the child to move the sculpture or walk
around the sculpture and view it from a different perspective. She might
invite the child to express her experience. For example, the counsellor
might say: *When you look at your sculpture from over here, is it the same, or
is it different from when you were over there?* and, *Tell me more.*

3 Creating a dialogue between two sculptures

After creating a shape to represent herself, the counsellor might ask the
child to make a second shape to represent either a significant other person
in her life, or an emotion which is troubling her. The counsellor can then
invite the child to alternately imagine that she is each of the shapes, and to
engage in a dialogue between them. For example, a child called Jane makes

a shape to represent her foster mother. The counsellor might then say: *Imagine that you are your foster mother* (pointing to clay representation of the foster mother). *What would you like to say to Jane?* (pointing to the clay which represents the child).

This process is then continued, with the child swapping between imagining that she is Jane and imagining that she is her foster mother, and thus developing a dialogue between the two.

In all of the work described above, an important goal for the counsellor is to invite the child to continue sharing more information about the sculptures and about herself. This sharing enables the child to recognize, own, and deal with emotional feelings, and to recognize and work through issues. During this process, the counsellor needs to remember not to be interrogative or intrusive.

4 Terminating work with clay

When the child and counsellor recognize that there is no more to be said, the counsellor can invite the child to make a decision about what to do with the sculpture. The child may wish to leave the sculpture intact, where it is, but should understand that the counsellor will need to break it up and add it to the rest of the clay after he has left. Another option is for the child to move the sculpture to a safe place, so that, although dried out, it will be available in the future. Alternatively, the child may want to pound the sculpture into one lump, and to add it to the rest of the clay. This closing activity is important for the child, as the clay represents a part of himself. A child's choice and action during closure can give the counsellor additional information about the child and his perceptions of the sculpture.

5 Using clay in a group

When working with a group, the counsellor might start by saying: *Make a shape which will let the other children in the group know how you are feeling right now.*

When all the children have finished making their sculptures, the counsellor can invite members of the group to look at one child's sculpture and to guess how that child might be feeling. Interaction between the children in the group is encouraged as the children try to guess what each sculpture suggests.

Next, the counsellor might say to the group: *Make a shape to represent yourself.* When all the children in the group have finished making their new sculpture, the counsellor can ask each member of the group the following question: *What can you tell me about your shape?*

Once again interactive discussion is encouraged. It is important to refrain from pressuring a child to talk about his shape if he doesn't want to do this. Sometimes the counsellor might ask a child: *Would it be OK if Johnny said something about your sculpture?* Assuming that the child says 'Yes', the counsellor can invite Johnny to comment by saying: *What would you like to say about Jane's shape?* This also encourages interactive discussion.

We have found that at the end of a group session using clay, most children will participate with interest, in making a group sculpture by combining their individual sculptures. This can help the children to look at their relationships within the group. To do this, the counsellor might say: *Look around the group and find someone else's sculpture which might fit with yours.*

If a child called Joanne says, 'I think that my sculpture would look good beside Millie's', then the counsellor asks: *Millie, would it be OK for you if Joanne put her sculpture next to yours?*

If Millie says 'Yes', then Joanne can be invited to move her sculpture. After this the counsellor can check out how Millie feels about the change: *Millie, what is it like having Joanne's sculpture next to yours?* Millie might say that it is too close or not close enough, in which case she might be asked: *Would you like to move your sculpture further away (or closer)?* She can then be invited to move her own sculpture to a more comfortable position and Joanne can be encouraged to express her feelings, now that Millie has moved her sculpture.

This process is repeated with other group members until a group sculpture is created involving all of the individual sculptures. By using this approach, members of the group are able to come to an understanding of the relationships in the group, and an understanding of their own and others' needs with regard to these relationships. This can be achieved without the children needing to verbalize all of their thoughts and feelings.

It is interesting to note that usually in a group there will be some children who prefer to leave their sculptures standing independently at a distance from other sculptures. This preference should be respected and valued, and can be seen as a preferred level of inclusion rather than as exclusion.

During group work, choices should be offered and respected at all times with regard to moving sculptures, the closeness of sculptures, and the impact of closeness or distance on the owners of the individual sculptures.

When the group sculpture has been completed, the counsellor should ask the group: *How did you feel when you were putting the sculptures together?* and, *Is there anything that you would like to do with the sculpture now?* The group needs to be given choices about what to do with the completed group sculpture.

Suitability of the medium

To use clay as a therapeutic medium requires the child to have the ability to abstract and symbolize. For this reason, the medium is most suitable for children from the age of six and upwards. Younger children enjoy playing with the clay and constructing representational forms. However, because of their immaturity, they are not able to benefit from the processes described in this section.

Clay is a medium which can be used in individual, family, and group counselling. It is open ended and expansive, allowing the user to manipulate, change and control it at will.

Because clay stimulates the senses, it allows the child to come into contact with feelings and emotions, so is most useful when working with children who are blocked emotionally: it enables them to access and express their emotions in acceptable and appropriate ways (for example children who are angry can pound and bash the clay). Further, it allows introspective private processing of issues to occur.

◆   ◆   ◆   ◆   ◆   ◆   ◆

20   Drawing, painting, collage and construction

In this section we will be discussing four different types of media. These media fit into a group because they can be used in similar ways and, if desired, they can be used together. The media to be discussed are:

1   Drawing
2   Painting
3   Collage
4   Construction

When using any of these media the focus is on creativity. All of them invite the child to explore, experiment and play. The child can use the media to make pictures, or symbolic representations of issues, feeling and themes related to her story, or to a part of her story. Hence, the child can visually develop a picture of her environment, and recognize her position in that environment. She can also use the media to explore any changes that have occurred in the environment, or changes which she may have made over a period of time.

Children can use the media to create sequences to express the chronological development of their personal stories, as in a comic strip. They can create different and more satisfactory endings for experiences which have had unpleasant outcomes for them.

The media allow a child to make strong statements in acceptable forms. For example, aggressive or socially unacceptable behaviour can be expressed in a painting. In this way, the behaviour is contained instead of being acted out. This enables the child to experiment with, and experience, negative emotions.

The media also allow the child to be constructive – and destructive, but in a useful way. For example, a child may destroy a picture he has created by scribbling over part of it which symbolizes something that angers him. If he wishes, he can totally destroy the picture by tearing it up and throwing it away.

Children who are not able to talk about their wishes and needs in connection with past, present and future situations may be able to do so by using the symbolic language of drawing, painting or constructive artistic creation.

All of these media are powerful because they allow children to express and communicate internal thoughts, feelings and experiences by using their own individual imagery and symbolism. Using the symbolic language of art, children can experience and deal with emotional feelings, and change by dealing with related behaviours.

When selecting drawing or painting, we need to remember that children will perform with various levels of skill depending on their developmental age. A counsellor must have some understanding of developmentally appropriate skill levels, so that the child's performance is not incorrectly interpreted as abnormal, and maximum benefit is obtained therapeutically when using the media.

Firstly consider very young children below the age of four. It is normal and appropriate for these children to scribble and to experiment by trying out new ways of drawing. They do not relate the colours used in their paintings to the actual colours of objects, but mostly use colour in response to their emotional feelings. Although the counsellor may not be able to understand the meaning of the child's drawing or scribble, the child knows what it represents. Usually children in this age group won't tell a counsellor what they have drawn, unless asked. Also, the child may sometimes change the meaning of the drawing first calling it a man, then a dog, and then Mummy going shopping. This can be confusing for a counsellor.

As the child develops, from four to six years, he will see his drawing or painting as something of value, which he has created. He may want to keep the drawing or to give it to someone.

From the age of five to seven years, proportions in drawings of the human figure tend to be unrealistic. A child may draw a person with hands which are large and out of proportion to the figure. This could be wrongly interpreted, with the counsellor making inappropriate assumptions about the size of the hands in an individual drawing.

At the age of seven or eight, a child may begin to draw figures on the bottom edge of the page, and to draw other things around those figures, such as the sky, birds, the sun or clouds. Colour is used more realistically. However, the child may draw 'X-ray' pictures, for example a picture of a house showing both the outside of the house and a view of the rooms inside. Similarly, a child might draw a picture of her pregnant mother, and include in the picture the baby inside the mother's 'stomach'. The child may also draw several different events, occurring at various stages in time, in the one drawing.

From the age of eight onwards, symbols become more complex in their meaning and drawings begin to reflect individual differences according to the child's needs and issues. There tends to be a fascination with detail and patterns at this stage. For example, girls may decorate dresses elaborately, and boys may draw elaborate designs on aeroplanes or rockets.

As the child moves into early adolescence, motivation when drawing becomes less focused on what the child sees, and more on the child's emotional or subjective experience. A younger child will draw or paint as though she were a spectator at a scene, and will try to represent her drawing in a three dimensional way by using perspective. By contrast, the early adolescent is more likely to draw or paint as if she were directly involved in the action, and to use colour in response to her emotions.

While there are noticeable age-related developmental stages in drawing and painting, there are some common ways in which children generally reflect their feelings by their use of line, shape and colour. A line has a quality of movement or action: it might suggest direction, orientation, motion or energy. A vertical line is upright and obvious. A horizontal line is calm and might be associated with the absence of motion, or with sleep. A diagonal line has a dynamic quality, and could suggest instability or loss of balance. Circular or curved lines are fluid, and could suggest a calm easy motion.

Similarly, colours have symbolic meanings which are generally accepted. These meanings can be helpful in enabling children to express their feelings. For example, if we asked you to think of any symbolism associated with green and red colours, what would you say? Many people would say that green colours are more often used to symbolize 'a relaxed state' and red colours are more often used to symbolize 'anger' or 'danger'.

Notice any rhythm which occurs in a drawing or painting. A child may express rhythm in the form of repetition of the same shape, or line, or colour, or direction. Rhythms within a child's drawing or painting are often related to the emotions the child is expressing through the work.

Materials needed

Materials needed for drawing

- Sheets of white and coloured drawing paper of various sizes
- Pencils
- Coloured felt pens
- Pastels
- Crayons
- A selection of fluorescent highlighters

Primary school children can work comfortably on A4 paper. Younger children usually find this size restricting and prefer larger sheets. Although generally children prefer to work on white paper, sheets of coloured paper sometimes appeal to children, especially those who lack confidence in their drawing abilities. We rarely provide erasers, but instead encourage children to try again if they are unhappy with their drawings.

Materials and equipment needed for painting with brushes

- Large sheets of butcher's or art paper
- Acrylic or poster paints

- Large hair brushes
- A plastic apron to protect clothing
- A horizontal working surface
- Access to water

The paper used for painting needs to be more absorbent than that used for drawing. Painting is best done on a horizontal surface; running paint may cause frustration.

Materials needed for finger painting

- Large sheets of butcher's or art paper
- A polythene sheet
- Acrylic or poster paints
- Paint containers for holding and squirting paint
- Spray containers of shaving cream
- Vegetable dyes
- A plastic apron to protect clothing
- A horizontal working surface
- Access to water

For finger painting, squeezable containers, with lids suitable for squirting paint, are useful. Alternatively, bowls of paint can be used. Shaving cream, used in conjunction with vegetable dyes, can add texture to the work. Access to water is essential.

Materials needed for collage

Essential materials include the following:

- Large sheets of white or coloured paper or card
- Craft glue or another fast-setting adhesive
- Scissors
- A stapler
- Masking tape
- Sticky tape
- String

The collage is created by gluing, stapling, or tying materials to a backing sheet of white or coloured paper or card. Sometimes we use cardboard, as this provides a stronger backing for firmer materials.

A range of materials suitable for sticking to the backing sheet are required. These might include any of the following:

Magazine pictures	Glitter (various colours)
Newspapers	Coloured stars
Feathers	Sequins
Fabrics	Leaves
Yarns	Cotton wool

Wood shavings	Sand
Sandpaper	Sawdust
Small pieces of foam	Highly textured wallpaper
Coloured wool	

Good collage work can be done using pictures and words cut from magazines and newspapers. This approach appeals to many adolescents.

Materials required for construction work

In construction work we can make use of any objects or materials which lend themselves to creating three-dimensional sculptures. Expensive materials aren't needed: creative construction work can be done using junk which would normally be discarded as household rubbish. Here are some examples:

Plastic containers	Lids
Old tins	Wire
Styrofoam packing	Bubble wrap
Cake cases	Pipe cleaners
Ice-lolly sticks	Matchsticks
Coloured paper	Coloured card
Boxes such as Band-Aid and toothpaste boxes	Cardboard tubes from paper towel rolls

Clearly, sculptures made from such materials involve fixing things together. Although glue is sometimes useful, most children become frustrated when waiting for it to dry. Hence it can be advantageous to use alternative ways of holding pieces of a sculpture together. For example, Styrofoam shapes can be connected with toothpicks, Velcro tape, or double-sided tape. Many other materials can be tied together with picture hanging wire, fishing line or string. Paper clips, staplers, masking tape and packaging tape can also be used.

Goals when using drawing and painting

Goals when using drawing and painting include the following:

To enable the child to tell his story

By drawing and painting, a child who has difficulty in telling his story verbally can describe and disclose information about himself, his family and his environment. He can do this either by direct representation of people and events, or indirectly in a projective way, through symbolic representation.

To enable the child to express repressed or intense emotional feelings

These can be expressed through the creative activity itself, or concretized in the symbols used in the drawing and painting.

To help the child to gain a sense of mastery over events which he has experienced or is experiencing

By drawing or painting a child can serialize the events in his life through the use of comic book representation and storytelling. He can then, by combining the creative elements of art and fantasy, experiment with changes to his story, and thus gain a sense of mastery.

How to use drawing and painting

Some children find it difficult to get started when they are invited to draw or paint. This may be because of a number of reasons, such as the following:

1 The child may have a poor self-image.
2 The child may have been conditioned into copying rather than creating.
3 The child may have had negative messages about her ability to draw.
4 The child may be being oppositional.

To deal with a child's difficulty in getting started we can use warm-up exercises.

Warm-up exercises

We often start by using the warm up exercises as described below. The first two of these are known as 'Chasey' and 'Mr Squiggle'.

Chasey With a large sheet of paper, the counsellor uses a coloured felt pen to run around the paper, continually changing direction, while the child, using another pen of a different colour, tries to follow and catch up with the counsellor. After a while the counsellor stops holds the drawing up and says, *Oh, I wonder what we've made? Can you see anything in this picture?* and, *Does it look like anything to you?* If the child has no suggestions the counsellor might make a suggestion of her own.

Mr Squiggle The child is invited to draw lines, or scribble on the page, and the counsellor then uses these lines to make a picture. For example, a counsellor might add eyes and whiskers to a scribble to create a cat.

Warm-up exercises to help a child to get in touch with feelings When a child says, 'I can't draw' or 'I don't want to draw', the counsellor needs to focus on the child's feelings. The first step is to help the child to get in touch with her bodily experience. We might say to the child: *Close your eyes*, and then, *Notice what your body is feeling.*

Additionally, the counsellor might say something like: *Notice that your elbows are resting on the table*, and, *What does that feel like?* A question might then be asked about the child's feet resting on the ground. The child can be invited to draw her feet. The counsellor might say: *Can you feel your feet on the ground?* and *Draw me a picture of your feet on the ground.*

To provide some contrast, we can say to the child: *Stand up, close your eyes, and reach for the ceiling* and then, *Draw the feeling of standing up straight and reaching for the ceiling.* The child could also be invited to curl up in a tight ball on the floor, and then to draw what that felt like.

After doing these exercises, we might then ask the child about a recent experience. For example: *What did you do just before you came to this session?* The answer might be, 'I rode my bike down the street.' The counsellor can then ask questions such as the following:

What did it feel like to ride your bike down the street?
What did it feel like having your feet on the pedals?
What did it feel like having your hands on the handlebars?

Once the child is in touch with how his body felt, the counsellor can invite him to draw the feeling by saying: *Draw me a picture which will tell me how you are feeling right now.*

The purpose of the warm-up exercises is to get the child in touch with his feelings, and to help him to start using the media.

Making use of drawing and painting

For children from the age of eight or nine years and upwards, drawing or painting which involves fantasy is invaluable. It allows them to release socially unacceptable emotions, such as hate and anger, and to express secrets and desires.

The counsellor might start by asking the child to create her own world on paper, using shapes, lines and colours, and might say: *Think about your world as lines, shapes and colours. Use the whole page to show me where the people, places and things are in your world.*

When the drawing or painting has been completed, the counsellor might explore the relationships between shapes by noticing the closeness of some shapes to others, or the distance between some shapes and others. The counsellor might then use a feedback statement to encourage the child to talk about the significance of these relative positions. For example the counsellor might point to some shapes and say: *I notice that this shape here is a long way away from this shape here.*

The technique of using shapes, lines, and colours, can also be used effectively to help children to draw their families. For example, the counsellor might say: *Think of each member of your family and draw them as if they were a shape, a line, or a colour on the page.*

Sometimes the counsellor might want to help the child to find out more about himself as an individual. A good way of doing this can be to invite the child to imagine that he is a tree. The counsellor might say: *Imagine that you are a tree and draw a picture of yourself as the tree.*

Sometimes children need prompting and help to get started after being given the above instruction. In this case the counsellor can ask questions to help the child to get in touch with his creativity. For instance we might ask:

What kind of tree are you?
Do you have fruit?
Are you large?
Are you tall?
Do you have flowers?
Do you have many flowers, or just a few?
What do you look like in the winter?
Do you have thorns on your branches?
Do you have large leaves or small leaves?
Do you grow next to other trees, or are you on your own?

Following this, we might invite the child to describe his drawing by saying:
Pretend to be the tree and tell me what it is like to be in this drawing.

We often find that children identify strongly with the tree they have
drawn. This is very useful in helping a child to start working on personal
issues.

Useful topics for drawing or painting

Suitable topics can be addressed by using the following instructions:

Draw a picture of when you were a baby.
Draw a picture of your headache.
Draw a picture of your anger.
Draw a picture of your worry.
Draw a picture of where you would like to be if you were magic.
Draw a picture of your dream.
Draw a picture of your nightmare.

With any of the above drawings or paintings, it might be useful to explore
how the child feels, if he has included himself in the drawing. For example,
if the child has drawn himself as a baby, the counsellor might ask: *I wonder*
how that baby feels?

If there were other people or objects in drawing, then the counsellor
might point to one of them and say: *Pretend to be this person (or object)*
and *I wonder how you feel?*

Painting has additional value because of its texture and the flowing
quality of paint, so it is more powerful in allowing the child to connect with
his emotions. When using painting we might sometimes say to a child:
Paint a picture of how you feel right now or, *Paint a picture of how you are*
when you are sad (or happy).

Children seem to be able to represent feelings more easily with paint than
with drawing. When drawing, they tend to be more representational.

Finger painting

Some children are frightened of making mistakes. A good way to desen-
sitize them is to get them to experiment with shaving cream or finger paint.

Let the child squirt shaving cream on to a polythene sheet, then colour the shaving cream by dripping food colouring on to it and mixing it in.

Finger painting is best done on a large sheet of butcher's paper using plastic containers of acrylic paint which can be squirted or splashed on to the paper. The child can then be encouraged to move the paint around with her fingers. Plastic aprons are strongly recommended! Once the process has started, the counsellor can say to the child: *Let's see if you can show me how you're feeling by making a picture out of the paint.*

Finger painting involves tactile and kinaesthetic experiences. It can be soothing and flowing or it can encourage expansive and less controlled expression. Finger painting allows the child to make pictures and to change them quickly, or to cover them up or erase them with more paint. The size of the paper is the only restraint or boundary, so the child can feel free and be expressive. Finger painting is sometimes best used as a warm-up exercise for children before they begin creating more representational images with the use of brushes.

Collages

Collages add yet another dimension to the creative expression of children. Similar instructions can be given to the child to those used for drawing or painting. Additionally, collage allows the child to make connections between the texture of objects (such as cotton wool, sawdust, feathers, etc.) and emotional feelings. To help a child to make such a connection, the counsellor might say: *How does this sandpaper feel?* The child might reply, 'Scratchy.' The counsellor might then ask: *If you were that piece of scratchy sandpaper, how would you feel?*

Collage is a good medium to use when asking a child to make a self-portrait. A self-portrait in collage can help the child to become more fully aware of her perception of herself and can give her the opportunity to move from superficial descriptions to greater self-disclosure. We might begin by inviting a child to choose any of the materials provided to create a picture of herself, then make statements like: *I notice that you have chosen the crunchy sawdust for your hair. What is it like to have hair that is crunchy like sawdust* or, *I notice that you have chosen feathers for your arms and legs. What would it be like to walk around on feathers?*

Collage can be used with older children to explore their perceptions of issues and events in their lives. Older children will often use pictures and words of varying font sizes to make statements about current or past issues which are of concern to them. Depending on the materials available, collage can sometimes move into the activity of construction.

Construction or sculpture

Many of the suggestions given for drawing, painting and collage can be adapted for construction work or sculpture. For example, the counsellor might say: *Make a tree to represent you.*

Construction and sculpture are often useful for children who are clumsy or awkward, or who have experienced little success in their lives. As the child creates the sculpture, the counsellor can observe the child's responses to failure, success, decision making, problem solving, and completing tasks. In instances where the construction may take time to complete, the counsellor can observe the way in which the child deals with delayed gratification and can then make statements of observation about the child's behaviour like: *I notice that you are hard on yourself when you make mistakes,* or *When things don't work out right, you seem to give up easily.* The child's awareness of his behaviour is raised, so that relevant issues can be addressed.

Suitability of drawing, painting, collage and construction

All of these media are very suitable for use in individual counselling. Drawing can also be used effectively in groups and in family counselling. Similarly, finger painting can be used effectively in group work.

Construction, collage and painting are most effectively used with pre-school and primary school children. From early adolescence to late adolescence, drawing and sometimes painting are the most useful of these media.

Finger painting is the medium most likely to elicit open, expansive and expressive behaviours in the child. Drawing, and to some extent painting, lends itself to more representational and introspective behaviour. Construction, and to some extent collage, promotes the expression of more functional and less emotionally expressive experiences. Construction and collage also promote the exploration of insight and understanding of the child's own behaviour.

◆   ◆   ◆   ◆   ◆   ◆   ◆

21   The imaginary journey

We have included the imaginary journey in this book because we believe that it can be a useful tool in achieving the various goals listed in this chapter. However, the imaginary journey is a very powerful technique and as such needs to be used with care and only in situations where it will be helpful to the counselling process and to the child, and where there is confidence that it will not have any detrimental effects on the child. We strongly recommend that the imaginary journey should only be used by fully trained and experienced counsellors who are able to judge when its use is appropriate, or by new counsellors under the close direction of a competent supervisor who is able to judge that its use is appropriate. Having said this, we believe that this technique can help many children.

Most people, in their daily lives, go on imaginary journeys from time to time. They allow themselves to daydream or to fantasize about what has happened or might have happened in their lives, about what is currently happening or might be happening, and about the future. In a similar way, guiding a child on an imaginary journey allows the child to freely explore, in her imagination, real and imaginary scenarios from the past and present, and to fantasize about possible scenarios for the future.

Taking a child on an imaginary journey involves telling the child the outline of a story and allowing her to fill in the details from her own imagination and experiences. Thus, when the counsellor guides the child on the journey, she creates the scenes along the journey, but leaves the child to create in her imagination the people, the objects and the activities within the scene. Consequently the child is provided with an opportunity to create scenarios which are projections of her own inner world, in total privacy, and to explore the most personal themes and ideas which emerge spontaneously from within herself. As the child moves through the journey, memories, emotions and fantasies may be triggered, so that she becomes aware of them and can work through them with the help of the counsellor.

During the imaginary journey, the child becomes deeply involved in the processes occurring within herself as she finds, enters and explores the scenarios which are her own creation. It is as though she establishes an intimate personal relationship with herself through which she gains in self-knowledge.

In this chapter we will describe two different imaginary journeys which we have found to be useful. Imaginary journeys need to be carefully designed so that the child and not the counsellor is in control during the journey. It is important to word instructions so that the child has choice about what she does and does not do. The child must also be able to leave the journey whenever she wants.

Goals when using the imaginary journey

The imaginary journey can be used to help a child to get in touch with experiences which may have been very painful for him, and may have been repressed. Equally, it may be used as a way of helping a child to renew contact with happy or pleasant experiences from the past.

By sharing his experience of his journey with the counsellor, the child can deal constructively with memories which have been brought into focus by the journey. He can work through emotional feelings which those memories have triggered, and address troubling thoughts and beliefs. The imaginary journey enables the child to get in touch with his inner pain, and then to deal with that pain through the counselling process.

An imaginary journey can provide a child with an opportunity to gain mastery over past issues and events, so that he can feel as though he had an active role in those events, and was not just a passive and helpless observer. Consider the case of a child who had witnessed and been troubled by the bullying of one of his friends in the playground. He might feel guilty because he ran away and deserted his friend. In the imaginary journey he might reconstruct the scene, but instead of running away he might do something different, such as punching the bully on the nose, or telling a teacher about the bully. Although these alternatives are not necessarily appropriate or acceptable for the child, they allow him to experience some sense of power and control. The counsellor can then help the child to look at the alternative behaviours and their consequences, and as a result to feel better.

During the journey, the child can, in her imagination, change something she has done or said in the past. She can say or do things which might give her a sense of completion or satisfaction with regard to past events in her life. Consider the case of a child whose father has died. The child might, in some way, feel responsible for her father's death. In the imaginary journey she might visualize her father, and might say something to him which she needs to say in order to make her feel better.

Most importantly, the imaginary journey encourages the child to tell her story, and helps her to develop insight into her own behaviour, the behaviours of others, and the possible reasons for the occurrence of events in her past. The journey provides an opportunity for the resolution of issues and for the exploration of alternative behaviours or options.

In summary, goals when using the imaginary journey include the following:

- to enable the child to tell his story;
- to help a child to get in touch with, and work through, painful experiences that have been repressed;
- to help a child to re-experience happy or successful events;
- to help the child to experience imaginary completion of unfinished scenarios or events, with resolution of related issues;
- to help a child to gain mastery over past issues or events;
- to help a child to discover alternative behaviours or options which might have more satisfactory outcomes for him;
- to help the child to gain insight into his own behaviour and the behaviour of others;
- to help the child to understand the reasons why past events occurred.

Materials needed when using the imaginary journey

The child needs to be relaxed when going on an imaginary journey. A quiet room, with no intruding noises from outside is required. Preferably, the lighting should be pleasantly subdued rather than bright and glaring. In the room, the child needs a comfortable place to sit or to lie. We usually provide an adult-size bean bag for this purpose, because it gives children a choice of sitting or lying. Allowing for this choice is important because some children feel vulnerable when lying down. This is particularly true for children who have been sexually abused.

On completion of the imaginary journey the child will need paper and felt pens to draw a picture related to the journey.

In summary, materials needed are:

- A quiet room
- A large bean bag
- Drawing paper
- Coloured felt pens

How to guide a child on an imaginary journey

We begin the imaginary journey by encouraging the child to sit or lie comfortably on a large bean bag. We then say to the child something like: *In a minute, I'd like you to imagine that you are going on a journey. I will help you to go on the journey by telling you about some of the things that you might see on the journey. The things I will tell you about are only my suggestions, so you can ignore them if you like.*

Before proceeding further, it is important to tell the child that during the journey she may stop at any time she likes. We might say: *If you don't like the journey, stop going on it, and let me know. Do you think that you could do that?* and, *If you do want to stop going on the journey what will you do? Will you say something? What do you think you would say?* or, *Would you signal that you wanted to stop?* and, *How would you do that?*

It is important to give the child permission to ignore any directions which the counsellor might give, but which the child might not like. To give this permission, the counsellor might say: *During the journey, I may suggest that you imagine that you are doing some things. If you don't want to do these things, don't do them. Instead just imagine that you are doing something that you would like to do, or stop going on the journey altogether.* We then invite the child to sit comfortably on the bean bag by saying: *Firstly though, move around on the bean bag until you are comfortable.*

When guiding the child along the journey, we use a quiet tone of voice and talk slowly, so that we do not intrude on the child's relaxed mood and his attention to the journey. As we guide the child along, we leave pauses between each instruction, to allow the child to fill in details of the story by using his imagination, and to allow him to fully experience the journey in his imagination.

We will now describe two examples of imaginary journeys. We call the first of these examples, 'My secret place' and the second, 'The country house journey'.

My secret place

We start the journey by saying: *You are going to go on an imaginary journey – if you want, you can imagine that I am going on the journey with you, or you can imagine that you are on your own if that is what you would like to do. If you want to, you can close your eyes.* We then say the following sentences leaving pauses between them: *Imagine that you are walking down a hallway. Notice whether it is light and airy or dark and dismal. Notice the colours of the walls, the floor and the ceiling. Notice how it smells. Imagine that as you walk slowly down the hall-way you are looking around. There are doors all along the hall. Have a closer look at one of the doors. Notice what it looks like, how big it is, and what the door handle looks like. Imagine that you touch the door handle. When you are ready, you can open the door if you want to. If you open the door you will find yourself looking at a scene which you remember. Look at the scene from the doorway – look around. Notice anyone who is there. Maybe you can see yourself in the scene. If you wish you can imagine that you are yourself in the scene. If you want to you can look around – you can look at any people who are there – you can look at them one at a time.* (Time needed) *You may want to say something to someone and they may say something to you.* (Time needed) *Now imagine yourself standing in the doorway ready to leave. Is there anything that you want to do or say before you leave? If there is do it now.* (Time needed) *Imagine yourself going back through the door into the hallway – closing the door – and walking back down the hallway. Now leave your imaginary journey and notice that you are sitting on the bean bag. When you are ready, open your eyes and without talking look around this room.*

After this, we ask the child to draw a picture of the journey, because by doing this the child will re-connect with important parts of the journey, and will concretize these in the drawing. By giving some permanent expression to the experience of the journey, the child is more easily able to explore, and to share, the emotional and cognitive experiences related to the journey. We ask the child to draw the picture by saying: *Stay silent. Now take a piece of paper and some felt pens, and draw a picture of your journey.*

Next, the counsellor needs to help the child to process her experience of the journey. Before discussing this we will give our second example of an imaginary journey.

The country house journey

We begin by saying: *You are going to go on an imaginary journey – if you want you can imagine that I am going with you on the journey, or you can imagine that you are going on the journey by yourself, if you would prefer to do that. If you would like to close your eyes, close them.*

Then, talking slowly and softly with a pause between each sentence or phrase as appropriate, we say: *Picture yourself walking down a long dirt road. On either side there are tall trees. It is sunny and warm. In the distance you can see a house. Imagine that as you get closer to the house you can see the garden around the house. Imagine yourself walking through the garden to the front door which is partly open* [pause], *pushing the door open* [pause], *and walking inside. It's cool and dark after being out in the sun. It takes you time to get used to the light and when you do you may be surprised by what you see. There may be people there or it may be empty. Imagine that you look around the room and the house, touch things you want to touch, and talk to people you want to talk to* [pause]. *When you are ready to leave, imagine yourself going back out of the front door* [pause], *walking through the garden to the road* [pause], *and walking back down the road. Now leave your imaginary journey* [pause] *and notice that you are sitting on the bean bag. When you are ready, open your eyes and look around* [pause]. *Now I would like you to draw a picture of your journey. You can draw any part of it or all of it.*

Before processing the child's picture it is important to allow the child to take as much time as she needs to finish drawing whatever seems relevant to her.

Processing the child's picture and journey

When the child has finished her picture the counsellor can help the child to process her drawing by asking one or two questions about the drawing and the journey. For example:

What can you tell me about your picture?
What was it like to go on the journey?
What was it like to walk down the road?
What was it like being in the house (or hallway)?
What was it like opening the door?
Did you want to stay or did you want to leave?
Would you have liked to have done anything different on your journey?
Did this journey remind you of something which has happened to you before?

By asking these questions, information may emerge connecting the journey, or part of it, to an authentic experience from the child's life. This might give the child an opportunity to tell important parts of his personal story. Thus the counsellor needs to use the full range of counselling skills (see Part 3) in helping the child to deal with painful emotions, troubling thoughts, and issues of concern. During this process, the counsellor can help the child to redefine distorted memories in a more emotionally comfortable way and to challenge self-destructive beliefs.

Some children may not be able to draw a picture, or may not want to draw one. In this case the counsellor can directly process the imaginary journey by using some of the questions listed above which do not relate to a picture, but relate directly to the imaginary journey itself.

After the journey, a child may be able to share a great deal of useful information and this will enable him to make progress therapeutically. However, some children will be unable to share anything: they may not feel safe about sharing private information which emerged in the journey, and it is important to respect their right to say nothing. When a child is unable to share, it is still possible that therapeutic processing will occur privately within the child.

Suitability of the imaginary journey

Please note the caution at the start of this chapter with regard to the use of the imaginary journey. The imaginary journey should never be used with children who have known psychotic tendencies, or seem to be out of touch with reality, or who are disoriented with respect to time, place or person. The imaginary journey is also not recommended for children with low ego strength, because the activity might be too challenging for them. Nor is it recommended for children who are dissociative following trauma.

The imaginary journey is most suitable for children from early adolescence onwards. Some primary school children can also benefit from the use of this technique. It is suitable for individual counselling, but not for group work. The imaginary journey is open and expansive because it provides an opportunity for the child to make changes to the way that she remembers things. It encourages introspective and private thoughts in the child, which she can usually share with the counsellor.

◆　◆　◆　◆　◆　◆　◆

22　Books and stories

In this chapter we will consider the following:

- The use of story books in counselling children.
- Helping children to create therapeutically useful stories.
- The use of books for educational purposes within the counselling process.

The use of story books for counselling children

We invite you, the reader, to think for a moment about the nature of children's stories. Do stories have special qualities which make them suitable tools for use in counselling children? We think that they do. Children's stories involve people, animals, fantasy figures and all kinds of inanimate objects such as trains, rocks, clocks and flowerpots. The people, animals, fantasy figures and objects are given personalities, beliefs, thoughts, emotions and behaviours. Most importantly, as a story unfolds, themes develop, issues emerge, and the characters and objects in the story respond with particular thoughts, emotions and behaviours. When a child listens to a story, she may identify with a character, or a theme, or an event within the story. If she does this, then she is almost certain to reflect on her own life situation. Her interest in the thoughts, emotions, and behaviours of the characters in the story allows her to, at some level, share the experience of the story book characters and to project on to these characters beliefs, thoughts and emotional experiences of her own. Thus, she can projectively work through her own emotional turmoil. Additionally, a child will often recognize the relationship between events and themes within a story and events and themes in her own life. When this occurs she has an opportunity to work directly on her own issues.

Creating stories

An alternative to reading a story from a book is to encourage the child to create her own story: the child is certain to project ideas from her own life on to the characters and themes in the story. She may even include herself as a character in the story, or may describe events which have occurred in her own life, in the story. Once again, as when reading a story book, the child is provided with an opportunity to explore her own issues, thoughts, emotions, and behaviours, either projectively or directly.

Books for educational purposes

Sometimes, as counsellors, we need to teach children new behaviours which are more appropriate than the ones they have previously learnt. Consider, for example, children who have been sexually abused. Often such children have learnt to be trusting, and to have open boundaries. Additionally they may have been taught to be polite to adults and to be compliant. Such children need to learn about appropriate boundaries and to realize that it is appropriate and necessary to say 'No' when their boundaries are at risk. Books can be used in an educational way with regard to a number of other issues and/or areas of knowledge, including abuse, violence, social skills, anger management, sex education, separation, divorce and death.

Goals when using books and stories

General goals when using story books or when creating stories

- To help the child to recognize his own anxiety or distress by identifying with characters or situations in a story.
- To help a child to discover themes and related emotions which recur in his life from time to time. For example, the child may discover that he has a fear of being left alone, a fear of betrayal, or excessive feelings of responsibility for others. By becoming aware of such feelings, the child can deal with them and move towards a resolution of related issues.
- To help a child to think about and explore alternative solutions to problems. This goal can be achieved by changing stories so that they have different outcomes.

Goals specific to the use of story books

- To help a child to normalize events in his life by letting him know that others have had similar experiences. This goal can be achieved by reading stories which have themes similar to his own experiences.
- To help reduce stigma related to socially unacceptable experiences. Children who have experienced sexual abuse or domestic violence feel better about themselves when they know that other children have been through similar experiences and have had similar feelings. They can discover this by reading stories about other children having similar experiences.

- To help the child to recognize that some events are unavoidable. For example, a child who has become ill and has to go to hospital may be helped by reading a book about another child going to hospital, and may thus identify with some of that child's fears and hopes.

Goal specific to creating stories

- To help a child to express wishes, hopes and fantasies. This is particularly useful for children who are experiencing painful life situations, and are telling untrue stories to avoid the pain of facing reality. For example, a child who has no parents might be ashamed of being different from his friends, and might find it too painful to tell them the truth. Consequently, he might tell his friends that his parents are famous people who are working overseas. By using storytelling, the counsellor is able to help the child to recognize that his stories are not true, but may be expressions of wishes.

Goal when using books for educational purposes

- To help educate children in appropriate beliefs and behaviours. Books commonly used in this way are those related to protective behaviours, anger management, and social skills.

Materials needed when working with books and stories

We make use of a variety of story books which cover different themes and situations, including the following:

- making friends
- families
- rejection
- magic
- monsters
- fairy tales
- fables

The classic fairy tales and fables such as 'Little Red Riding Hood', 'The Three Little Pigs' and 'Hansel and Gretel', are extremely useful. They encourage the child to work projectively and also to talk directly about himself, his family and significant others.

We also have story books which are useful for helping children to identify and own their feelings. For example, we have books on cheating, bullying and temper tantrums.

Additionally, we have a collection of books which we use for educational purposes on topics such as:

- the development of skills which reflect self-esteem issues
- sexual abuse
- protective behaviours

- domestic violence
- sexual development

For creating stories, we use the following materials:

- large sheets of white paper
- felt pens of assorted colours
- an exercise book with widely spaced lines
- a cassette recorder with built-in microphone

How to use books and stories

Storytelling is an interactive process between the child and the counsellor. Usually children don't like writing in counselling sessions. Many of the children who come to see us have previously had unsuccessful experiences when attempting to be creative by writing stories. Because of this, we try to make story writing an easy, enjoyable and positive creative experience. Usually, as a child develops a story, we write the story down using a felt pen and a large sheet of paper. Sometimes we also use a tape recorder to record the story.

Children generally need some modelling by the counsellor before they fully understand the process of story making. We usually begin by saying to the child: *Today we are going to be telling stories to each other*, and, *I will begin, and sometimes I might stop, and when I stop, I would like you to fill in the gaps.* This allows the counsellor to choose a theme and to encourage the child to explore pertinent issues for himself.

The counsellor can then continue the story by saying: *The story will have a beginning, a middle, and an end*, and, *I will begin. Once upon a time there was a prince and this prince liked . . .*

The counsellor can then stop in mid-sentence and invite the child to say what it was that the prince liked. The child might respond by saying, 'To ride his horse in the country.' The counsellor could then continue: *As he rode around the countryside, he realized that . . .*

Once again the counsellor can stop in mid-sentence, so that the child fills in the next part of the story. The storytelling can continue in this way until there is an outcome, or an end.

When the story is complete (it has usually been taped) we like to play it back and to ask the child to identify with any character in the story by asking: *Who would you like to be the most in this story?*

The child can be further encouraged to explore his own behaviour if we ask: *If you were a prince would you have done the same as him or something different?* and, *What would you have done?*

Finally, the counsellor can then thank the child for the story he has told.

An alternative is to encourage a child to tell stories about a picture she sees. The counsellor might present the child with a picture from a magazine, or a photograph, and ask the child to tell a story about the people, animals or objects it. It is useful, once again, to remind the child that the story should have a beginning, a middle and an end. However, these stories can be short and brief.

For children who find it difficult to make up stories, it is better to use story books, fairy tales, or fables initially. This can help to familiarize the child with the way in which stories develop and can help him to recognize the way in which stories can relate to his own personal experiences.

When using stories from books, we sometimes use old and familiar tales such as 'Little Red Riding Hood'. This story is very useful, because it raises issues of disempowerment, fleeing, helplessness and rescue. We might read the story to the child, and then invite her to identify with one of the characters. After this, we might invite the child to think of alternative solutions to different situations in the story. For example, after reading 'Little Red Riding Hood', if the child identified with Grandma, we might ask: *How could grandma have been more powerful so she could have outwitted the wolf and not have been pushed into the cupboard?*

We might then encourage the child to think of several different alternatives by asking: *What else could Grandma have done when the wolf tried to push her into the cupboard?* and, *If you had been Grandma what would you have done?* We might then be able to affirm the child's bravery, courage and resourcefulness.

Story books written around topics such as domestic violence or sexual abuse can be used to help a child to understand that other children have similar experiences. This enables a child to feel the same as some other children and to feel less of a victim. Such stories allow the child to identify with, or to reject, similarities between themselves and characters in the story. They may also invite the child to disclose more information about her own experiences.

We often use books as a way of educating children with regard to important beliefs and behaviours. Books can be used to address a wide range of issues such as protective behaviours, stranger danger, secrets, and inappropriate touching. They can be used by the counsellor to help the child to explore choices and options about future behaviour. For example, a book might encourage a child to say 'No' to a stranger. The counsellor can then check out whether the child believes that he has the ability to say 'No', and can help the child to practise saying 'No' in a loud voice. The child and the counsellor can then engage in role plays that teach appropriate behaviours.

When using books for educational purposes, we like to give the child a copy of the book to take home and to share with his family or care-givers.

Suitability of books and stories

Books and stories can be used with children of pre-school age through to late adolescence. They are particularly suitable for young children, who are used to listening to stories and find them comforting.

Books and stories are most suitable for use in individual counselling or in parent–child counselling. They enable children to be expansive in their thinking. However, work can be focused by the selection of specific topics or subject matter.

Helping children to make up their own stories is very useful when working with children who are naturally creative and have good language skills. This approach will not appeal to children who are less gifted.

◆ ◆ ◆ ◆ ◆ ◆ ◆

23 Puppets and soft toys

When we use puppets and soft toys we invite the child to create and direct a drama, in which the puppets and soft toys *are* the characters. In the drama, the child projects her own ideas on to the puppets and soft toys, gives them their personalities, chooses their behaviours, and puts words into their mouths.

Children enjoy using puppets and soft toys because they are easy to manipulate. They require very little preparation, and are familiar toys for most children.

It is important for a new counsellor to understand the difference between the drama created when using puppets and soft toys and the drama involved in imaginative pretend play. In imaginative pretend play (see Chapter 24), the child role-plays, identifies with, and effectively becomes a character, or some characters, in the drama. By contrast, when using puppets and soft toys, the child uses stories and other dramatic events, and projects ideas from these on to the puppets and soft toys. He sees them as separate from, and external to himself, and can, without restraint, attribute to the puppets and soft toys, beliefs, behaviours and personalities which he believes are quite different from his own.

There are also differences between the use of puppets and soft toys, and the use of stories. Stories give the child an opportunity to express fantasies, and to explore conflict situations. They also enable the child to deal with important issues and feelings even when it is too difficult for the child to talk about these directly. Puppets and soft toys are similarly useful and also add an extra dimension to storytelling. Through puppets and soft toys, the child becomes directly involved in creating and speaking the dialogue of the story, and in manipulating the puppets and soft toys to act out the story. By doing this the child becomes involved in, and personally connected with the story. This enables her to more easily make the link between her own emotional feelings and those of characters in the story.

The dramatic sequences created when using puppets and soft toys provide children with a way of dealing indirectly with issues which might be difficult for them to own as personally theirs. The indirect approach of puppetry protects the child's inner pain from direct exposure; instead it is disguised as belonging to the puppets or soft toys. At the same time, the child can gain confidence in talking about relevant issues, and has the opportunity to develop the courage to directly own and confront those issues when she is ready.

The drama allows the child to project his beliefs, behaviours and personality characteristics, and those of significant others, on to the puppets and soft toys. For example, as the child creates the dialogue of the drama, he can replicate the personality and behaviours of a hated person, or of a loving friend from whom he may have been separated. Consequently, puppets and soft toys provide a safe outlet for the expression of fantasies with regard to the interactions of others, and his own interactions with them.

During the drama the counsellor can intervene to help the child to express, understand and work through his issues, thus bringing about change.

Some individual puppets and soft toys have inherent symbolic attributes. For example wolves can be dangerous, monkeys can be entertaining and mischievous, and policemen may be helpful or authoritarian. Teddy bears are soft, cuddly and nurturing, or may need to be nurtured.

Goals when using puppets and soft toys

Puppets and soft toys can be used to achieve the following goals:

- to gain mastery over issues and events;
- to be powerful through physical expression;
- to develop problem-solving and decision-making skills;
- to develop social skills;
- to improve communication skills;
- to develop insight.

To gain mastery over issues and events

When using puppets and soft toys the child has an opportunity to re-enact unpleasant experiences. Through doing this the child can gain mastery over the experience. For example in the actual life experience the child may have been passive and disempowered. In the re-enactment, the puppet or soft toy on to which she projects her experience, may behave in a more powerful and active way. The drama can be repeated several times with the puppet becoming progressively more successful in dealing with the situation, until the child becomes satisfied.

By using puppets and soft toys in combination with familiar fables, fairy tales and stories the child can restructure past events so that victims are empowered, consequences are just, and opportunities are given for issues and feelings to be expressed. This process is useful to the child psychologically: it moves her from a psychological space where she feels helpless and powerless into a new space where she has a sense of her own inner power and a sense of an improved ability to control her own actions and responses. Thus the child moves from being disempowered towards empowerment.

To be powerful through physical expression

An ideal way for the child to express feelings of power and strength is through the use of selected characters or puppets. Similarly, emotions which may be unacceptable can be expressed and exaggerated without fear of reprimand. Clearly, these processes are useful for children who have become submissive as a consequence of past experiences or who have low ego-strength.

To develop problem-solving and decision-making skills

Often children find it difficult to explore a range of solutions to their problems because they are inhibited by their expectations of the likely demands and restraints which they think will be imposed on them by others. However, by creating a drama with the puppets or soft toys they can safely explore a range of alternative solutions. The counsellor can then relate these to the child's own life situation.

To develop social skills

To help the child to develop social skills, the counsellor becomes involved in the child's puppet play. The counsellor then creates situations which require the child to respond by using her own puppets or soft toys. These responses can then be received negatively or positively by the counsellor's puppet. In this way the child can indirectly explore the appropriateness or inappropriateness of her own social behaviour.

To improve communication skills

Using puppets and soft toys in a drama demands both verbal and non-verbal activity by the child. Consequently, communication about imagined or real events or issues is encouraged. This enables the child to develop insight into the effect of various communication styles, and thus to develop improved communication skills. Also the child can identify with the characteristics and behaviours of the puppets and soft toys. By doing this she has a way of indirectly experimenting with alternative relationships, and can, if she wishes, explore issues such as separation and closeness and communicate these needs openly.

To develop insight

When a child creates the dialogue between puppets, she has to consider the various and sometimes conflicting points of view of the individual puppets in her drama. Consequently, she will develop insight which will hopefully enable her to recognize and understand other people's points of view, in her own life situation. This might be useful in helping her to develop a more meaningful understanding of past events in her life.

Materials needed when using puppets and soft toys

We like to use both puppets and soft toys. Our puppets are glove puppets; the type where a child puts his hand into the puppet and uses his fingers and thumb to move the mouth and ears, and to change the facial expression.

Unlike puppets, we can't change the facial expressions of soft toys. However, they do have the advantage that it is easy to use several of them at the same time.

It's useful to have a variety of puppets and soft toys, so that different types of characters and personalities can be represented. We suggest that a suitable range should include the following:

- family figures suitable for representing a mother, father, grandmother, sibling, baby, uncles, etc.;
- fantasy figures, including a devil, a ghost, witches, fairies and a magician;
- wild animals, farm animals and domestic animals; for example wolves, sharks, bears, elephants, horses and rabbits;
- some soft toys which have a degree of disguise. These might include a masked person, a clown and a faceless person.

How to use puppets and soft toys

Because we use puppets and soft toys similarly, we will only refer to puppets in the following discussion, although this discussion applies equally to soft toys.

There are four ways of using puppets:

1   Allowing the child to use the puppets spontaneously.
2   Inviting the child to create and direct a puppet show.
3   Combining the use of puppets with well-known fairy stories or fables.
4   Using puppets in dialogue with the counsellor.

Allowing the child to use the puppets spontaneously

We usually begin by letting the child know that we are going to play with the puppets. We invite the child to select whatever puppets appeal to her. This can give valuable information. For example, children tend to pick up most of the puppets and then to discard them after checking out their shape, size and other features. When the child has selected her puppets, she will usually spontaneously start up a dialogue between some of them. If she doesn't, we model this by selecting a puppet and talking through the puppet to the child. For example, when counselling a child called Samantha, we might select the puppet bear, speak as though the bear were talking and say: *Hello, Samantha. Have you come to play with me today?* We can then invite the child to begin her puppet show by introducing the characters. We might ask: *Why don't you show me all of the characters in your play and introduce them to me one by one?*

As the child introduces the characters, the counsellor can engage in conversation as each character is presented. For example, the counsellor might say: *Hello Teddy, I'm looking forward to this show. Are you?* or, *Hello Teddy, nice to meet you, I like your big red bow tie.*

This participation by the counsellor helps the child to feel more comfortable about the activity, sets the scene, and allows the child to project herself on to the characters.

Some children find it easy to make up a story and to act it out. Others find it more difficult. With these children we usually suggest themes for them to use, which are likely to address issues or events relevant for the child. For example, we might suggest themes concerned with being moved from the family home into care, or regarding access visits with an absent parent, or themes which reflect helplessness, fear or abandonment.

With some children we use a more formalized puppet show approach as discussed in the following paragraphs.

Inviting the child to create and direct a puppet show

We start to create a puppet drama by saying to the child: *Together, we are going to make up a play using these puppets and soft toys. You can choose the characters in the play. One of the characters is very lonely, frightened and uncertain about what is going to happen to him. Another character is strong and powerful and the boss. There are three other characters in this play. Would you like to choose the characters now?*

After the child has introduced the characters (as discussed previously), the counsellor needs to help the child to devise a theme and to start the puppet show. The content of the story that emerges will give clues about the child's preoccupations and his ways of dealing with these.

We usually invite the child to act out her puppet 'show', or puppet 'play', on a table with the child sitting on the floor behind the table, which serves as a miniature stage. Some children like to use props in their drama such as sticks, balls, pillows and blankets. However, too many props can lead the child into dramatic imaginative pretend play (see Chapter 24) instead of helping the child to focus on projecting ideas on to the puppets or soft toys.

Generally, we sit opposite the table like an audience watching the child's dramatic play. Naturally, we intervene to ask questions, make comments, and to assist with the creation of the drama, when appropriate.

At different times during the drama, the counsellor might intervene and talk directly to one of the characters, in an attempt to discover more about that character's behaviour within the play. For example, the counsellor might ask the bear: *What does it feel like to be left outside the house while the others are having a party?*

Children will inevitably project different aspects of themselves on to the various characters. For example, a child may project the mischievous part of himself on to the monkey who causes trouble between others, and at the same time project his wish to magically change the situation on to the wizard. During the process the counsellor might encourage the characters to persevere with particular behaviours, so that the child becomes aware of the way in which other characters respond. For example the counsellor might say: *Wizard, do that again because I think it might work this time.* This gives the child an opportunity to evaluate the consequences of particular behaviours, and to make decisions with regard to suitable responses for other characters in the play.

An alternative to the above idea is for the counsellor to suggest a change in the behaviour of one of the characters. For example, the counsellor might say to the wizard: *Wizard, I don't think that what you are doing is working. I wonder what else you could do?*

Some children resent intrusions from the counsellor and with these children the counsellor may need to watch a puppet show without interrupting. However, following completion of the show, the counsellor might discuss with the child various parts of the drama, or aspects of the drama. A discussion such as this could be started by the counsellor asking questions such as: *Who, of all the people or things in the story, would you most like to be?* or, *Who in the story would you not want to be?* It would not be helpful to ask a child, 'Who are you in this story?' Such a question could be confusing, because clearly a child will project parts of herself on to all of the characters.

Sometimes asking a child what happens to the characters in the story after the play has finished can be useful in helping a child to look at outcomes.

Combining the use of puppets with well-known fairy stories or fables

With some children, when using puppets, we make use of well-known fairy stories or fables to directly address specific issues. When doing this, the child is invited to use the puppets to act the story out. We then help the child to restructure the story so that more satisfactory outcomes are achieved. For example, a victim may become empowered, or alternative solutions to a problem situation may be discovered. A counsellor might get a child to act out the story of 'Little Red Riding Hood' using puppets or soft toys. After the drama has finished, the counsellor might ask: *What else could Grandma have done when the wolf decided he was going to eat her?* The child might suggest that Grandma could have run out of the house to seek help. The counsellor can then encourage the child to act the drama out once again using this alternative idea.

Using puppets in dialogue with the counsellor

Sometimes by using a technique of dialogue between a puppet and the counsellor, a child may be enabled to discover solutions to her own problems.

Soft toys and puppets can also be used in direct one-to-one interaction with a child. We sometimes use a particular teddy bear, which we describe as being wise, experienced, knowledgeable and magical. This soft toy can be helpful to a child who is having difficulty discussing certain issues. For example, a child may be frightened about going to school for fear of being bullied but not feel comfortable enough to talk about this. We can suggest to the child that Teddy is often pretty good at knowing what children are thinking. We might say: *Teddy sometimes knows what children are thinking. If he sits on your lap, he might be able to tell me about the things which are troubling you.*

We can then ask the child to hold the bear on her lap and direct the following comments to it: *Teddy, Jenny is having some problems, I wonder if you know what they are?* The child is then invited to respond on behalf of the bear: *Jenny, can you tell me what Teddy is saying?*

Some children may not feel comfortable doing this. In this case, the counsellor can hold the bear so that its mouth is close to her own ear and pretend to be listening to the bear. The counsellor can then repeat what the bear is supposed to have told her, and might say: *Teddy says that he thinks that your problem might be about going to school. I wonder if he's right or if he's wrong?*

The child can then be encouraged to engage in ongoing dialogue between the counsellor, the bear and herself. She can be asked to listen to the bear and to repeat what he 'tells' her. Thus she becomes the voice of the bear and is enabled to say what she would like through the bear.

Suitability of puppets and soft toys

Puppets and soft toys are useful when working with pre-school and primary school children. Interestingly, some early adolescents find them appealing, however they are generally more suitable for the younger age group.

Puppets and soft toys are ideal to use in individual counselling sessions, but can also be used in groups, where each child selects and characterizes a particular puppet or soft toy.

Using puppets and soft toys allows the child to explore and expand her thinking and encourages her to be interactive and sometimes adventurous. They can also be used to convey moral messages and to educate: for example, concepts of protective behaviours could be explored.

◆ ◆ ◆ ◆ ◆ ◆ ◆

24 Imaginative pretend play

Imaginative pretend play is the naturally occurring play of young children. They enjoy pretending to be someone else, such as a doctor examining a patient, or a mother feeding her children. In their play, they dress up and make use of props, for example empty food packets when they are pretending to be shopping. Thus, they combine the use of objects, actions, words and interactions with imagined people, to produce a drama.

Although very young children between the ages of two and three can mimic the roles of familiar adults in their lives, they need to use real objects, or toy replicas of them, in their representational play.

Older children from the age of four and upwards rely less on real objects in their imaginative pretend play. In this age range, they are generally able to use unrelated objects to symbolize, or take the place of, objects which are involved in their play. For example, a wooden block might be used as a telephone. These older children are also capable of substituting actions for objects, in their imaginative pretend play. For example, a child may raise his clenched fist to his mouth, as a substitute for a cup, when pretending to drink. Because older children are able to engage in abstract thinking, they can easily play the roles of fantasy characters like superheroes, monsters and fairies.

In imaginative pretend play the whole child becomes totally involved in acting out a character within an imagined situation. The child becomes an *actor* in the fullest sense.

Imaginative pretend play sometimes, but not always, includes the use of social skills. When social skills are involved, we refer to the play as socio-dramatic play. The use of social skills occurs when using imaginative pretend play in the form of verbal and non-verbal interaction between the counsellor and the child while the child is role-playing.

Imaginative pretend play involves the child's use of objects and replica objects. Some children can't use objects in this way, and are unable to engage in imaginative pretend play. Such children fondle, stack, pound or manipulate objects in much the same way as a baby would. This immature play might be due to any of the following:

- The child may have language difficulties, or cognitive delays.
- The child may have been deprived of a stimulating play environment, and consequently lack the experience needed to engage in imaginative pretend play.
- The child may be inhibited as a result of previous emotional traumas, abuse or neglect.
- The child may be shy or cautious about taking risks in play.

Because children between the ages of three and five normally engage in imaginative pretend play as a natural part of their development, the absence of such play is significant. A child with little ability to engage in imaginative pretend play may have limited personal resources for working through emotional issues.

By using imaginative pretend play a child can act out significant obser-vations with regard to her life and the people in her life and she can achieve a number of useful goals.

Goals of imaginative pretend play

Imaginative pretend play can be used for the following purposes:

1 to enable a child to externalize and articulate ideas, wishes, fears and fantasies both verbally and non-verbally;
2 to enable a child to express underlying thoughts or thought processes;
3 to achieve cathartic relief from emotional pain;
4 to enable a child to experience being powerful through the physical expression of emotion;

5   to allow a child to gain mastery over past issues and events;
6   to provide an opportunity for a child to develop insight into current and past events;
7   to help a child to take risks in developing new behaviours;
8   to help a child to practise new behaviours and to prepare for particular life situations;
9   to give a child the opportunity to build self-concept and self-esteem;
10 to help a child to improve communication skills.

Materials and equipment needed for imaginative pretend play

The materials used in imaginative pretend play can evoke strong responses in children. They often stimulate fantasies and sometimes trigger specific issues. For example, a magic wand, may have strong appeal to a child who would like to have more control over his environment and relationships.

We need to have a wide variety of props so that we can prompt children to enter into specific imaginative pretend play scenarios which are individually relevant, and which might achieve the goals listed above. Some props need to be directly representational and realistic so that younger children can use them easily; others can be less representational, for use by the older age group.

We have in our play room the following equipment and materials to encourage imaginative pretend play (some of these are also listed in Chapter 15):

Furniture and associated items

Toy stove
Toy kitchen cupboard
Toy washbasin
Child's table and chairs
Doll's bed
Doll's pram
Baby doll's bath
(the above items should be large enough for a small child to use when engaged in family role plays)
Plastic crockery, cutlery, pots and pans
Play-Doh (useful for making pretend food)

Dolls, soft toys and associated items

Rag dolls to represent adults and children of both genders
Baby doll
A variety of soft toys including a teddy bear and a monkey
Dolls' clothes
Feeding bottle
Dolls' nappies
Pillow and sheets for pram

Dress-up materials

Dress-up clothes
Hats
Ties
Belts
Adult shoes
Sunglasses
Wigs
Make-up (non-allergenic and which can be washed off easily)
Jewellery
Swords
Badges
Assorted masks
Doctor's or nurse's set
Old camera
Crowns
Magic wands
Old watches
Handbags
Wallets
Purses
Shopping baskets
Lengths of coloured material
Blanket
Sheets (to make a Wendy house)
Telescope
Hand mirrors
Wall mirror
Hairbrush and comb
Toothbrush
Toy telephone
Toy vehicles
Empty food packets
Play money
Cardboard boxes
Wooden blocks

How to use imaginative pretend play

Imaginative pretend play is play which starts to occur at the point along the child's developmental continuum where the child is ready to move from playing directly with objects to using objects in symbolic representation. From that point onwards the child can engage in make-believe. Whenever a child uses imaginative pretend play to experience a make-believe world, she can experiment by using an unlimited variety of roles and behaviours. Additionally she can transform her original perceptions about life issues and situations into new and different perceptions.

It is the counsellor's responsibility to provide an environment in which the child can create and enter an imaginal world, and then use the experience therapeutically. In providing the necessary environment the counsellor needs to do the following:

1 Provide a physical place, including materials and equipment, to help the child to enter her make-believe world.
2 Use the relationship between the child and herself to help the child to participate in, and benefit from, her imaginative pretend play.

With regard to item 1, we have already discussed the requirements for a play therapy room (see Chapter 15), and have listed equipment and materials required for imaginative pretend play earlier in this section.

With regard to item 2, it needs to be recognized that the counsellor has a choice of roles, and that appropriate choice will significantly influence the therapeutic effectiveness of the play. We need to remember that most young children don't need an adult to be present as a play partner. However, they do need someone to provide time, space, props, and sometimes themes and experiences. They need someone to act as a facilitator to help them to start playing, sustain their play, modify and extend it. Children who have limited play skills may need not only a resource person and facilitator, but also an adult who will join in their play to help them to improve their play skills.

So when working with most children a counsellor should adopt the role of facilitator. For the child with limited play skills there are three alternative roles which the counsellor can assume. These roles involve parallel play, co-playing and play tutoring.

Parallel play When parallel playing the counsellor sits next to the child and copies the child's play. For example, if the child is sitting near the dolls' house and rearranging furniture, the counsellor will sit beside the child and also rearrange furniture. The counsellor may then make comments about what he is doing. For example the he might say: *I am going to put this chair against this wall so that the mother and father can watch television more easily.*

By making this statement, the counsellor does not intrude on the child's play by commenting on that, but does provide a model of imaginative pretend play which includes verbal communication about what is happening. Because the counsellor has initially copied the child's play, the child is likely to see her own play as important and valued. Thus parallel play gives the counsellor the opportunity to model new ways of using available materials, and can encourage the child to play longer.

Co-playing In co-playing, the counsellor joins in with the child's play and can influence the child's play by responding to the child's actions and comments and asking the child for instructions. For example, if a child is already engaged in play as a mother looking after and feeding a young baby (doll), the counsellor might ask: *What should I do now? Dolly hasn't eaten her cereal and I'm her big sister.* This gives the child an opportunity to join with the counsellor in the imaginative pretend play. However, the child might reject the counsellor's involvement by saying something like, 'She doesn't have a big sister.' Alternatively, the child might respond by attempting to feed the doll with the pretend cereal, or by instructing the counsellor (big sister) to feed the doll.

The aim of co-playing is to influence the play and to enrich it by adding new elements. In the example given, the new element introduced was the non-compliance of the baby doll.

Play tutoring   Play tutoring, although similar to co-playing, does differ. In play tutoring, the counsellor can begin the play theme rather than join in on a theme which the child has already started. Secondly the counsellor assumes more control and direction over the play. In play tutoring the counsellor uses questions, statements and reflection of content to help the child in his play. For example, the counsellor might ask: *Are you the doctor, or the mum?* and, *Are you in the house or in your car?*

The counsellor might also make statements such as: *Here's a car, you can use this to go to the shops* (as he offers the child a toy car).

Alternatively the counsellor can reflect content and might say: *You've put out five plates. I think there must be five people in this family.*

Such statements, questions and reflection of content help the child to use more imaginative pretend play skills by drawing the child's attention to new uses of materials. The counsellor can also model new role-playing behaviours by becoming an active participant and taking on a role herself. For example, if the child were to assume the role of a doctor treating a sick child, the counsellor could assume the role of the mother of the child. Such role-playing and modelling can help the child to gain new play skills.

Although play tutoring can be helpful it can also be intrusive. It is desirable for counsellors to limit the amount of play tutoring and to move back into the role of an observer as soon as the child's play is developing and being maintained.

In summary, a counsellor needs to be able to act as a facilitator, and to use co-playing, parallel play and play tutoring at appropriate times when working with children who are involved in imaginative pretend play.

Starting the imaginative pretend play session

Before starting the session, we make sure that the play therapy room is set up with the equipment and materials which will be needed to stimulate imaginative pretend play. Sometimes we select particular props and equipment, because we wish to explore specific themes in a certain way. However, generally we provide the full range of equipment and materials so that the child can freely choose what she wants to use. When the child enters the room, we usually begin by saying something like: *Today, we are going to spend some time playing with the things in this room.*

Because the equipment and props are appealing to most children, the child will generally begin to explore what is available. The child will usually select some of the props, and begin to dress up and to imitate particular characters. Younger children usually move straight to the 'home' corner where we have the kitchen furniture (see Figure 15.1, p. 86), and begin to play roles that are familiar to them. For example, they may pretend to cook a meal as a mother, or start to look after a baby doll. When the child begins to engage in this kind of play, the counsellor can engage in play with the child, if appropriate, or simply observe the child, the themes and the sequences of the play. The counsellor can then choose opportunities as the play progresses to make statements, ask questions and provide feedback about what the child is doing.

Having started the session, the counsellor can take opportunities, as they arise, to help the child to achieve specific gaols.

How to use imaginative pretend play to achieve specific goals

We will now discuss ways to use imaginative pretend play to achieve each of the ten goals which we listed previously.

How to use imaginative pretend play to enable a child to externalize and articulate ideas, wishes, fears and fantasies both verbally and non-verbally

This goal will occur naturally as a consequence of imaginative pretend play. Such play allows the child to re-create his world in a symbolic and dramatic way. This is done spontaneously as the child creates a script and directs the 'players', both animate and inanimate. These players include himself, the dolls and soft toys, and perhaps even the counsellor. In the drama some children will spontaneously express their wishes, fantasies and fears, and the counsellor can retain the role of observer. However, for other children the counsellor can enrich the fantasies, wishes and ideas of the child through co-play. The counsellor might do this by exaggerating the role assigned to her, or by behaving in a paradoxical way and thus encouraging the child to become more forceful in expressing the ideas, fears, wishes, or fantasies being acted out. However, the counsellor needs to stay strictly with the role assigned to her by the child, otherwise she will intrude on and inhibit the child's personal expression.

How to use imaginative pretend play to enable a child to express underlying thoughts or thought processes

To do this the counsellor needs to spend time observing the child's play without interference. The child is then allowed, through free association, to use the imaginative pretend play time to explore unconscious wishes or desires. During this process, it is useful for the counsellor to reflect thoughts, feelings and content back to the child. For example the counsellor might say: *When Dolly is naughty she gets locked in her room. I wonder what it would be like for her to be locked in her room?* This enables the child to explore her own issues related to being trapped.

How to use imaginative pretend play to achieve cathartic relief from emotional pain

Imaginative pretend play is a way of giving a child an opportunity to 'act out' his feelings and problems, and thus to achieve emotional release or catharsis. When this happens, the imaginative pretend play is in itself the therapeutic intervention, because the process of play is healing in itself. When seeking to achieve this goal, the therapist needs to be totally non-directive and must provide a safe environment and an empathic relationship with the child.

How to use imaginative pretend play to enable a child to experience being powerful through the physical expression of emotion

By using play tutoring, the counsellor can model powerful fantasy roles for the child. The child can then be encouraged to act out powerful roles not previously experienced as applicable to himself, and can experiment with these roles with the aid of suitable props. The roles of rescuer, adventurer, nurturer or healer can be modelled by the counsellor, and can then be encouraged in the child. Once a child has assumed a powerful role the counsellor can move back into a position of co-playing, to support that role.

How to use imaginative pretend play to allow a child to gain mastery over past issues and events

The counsellor can invite the child to use imaginative pretend play to re-create an unpleasant or painful experience where the child felt helpless and disempowered. As this is acted out in the form of a mini-drama, the child can be encouraged to be more actively involved in events that may previously have been experienced passively. This can be achieved by inviting the child to repeat the mini-drama several times. With each repetition, the child is encouraged to experiment with new behaviours which are more powerful and involve taking more control. Thus, the child moves from a victim position and gains a sense of mastery over events that had been threatening. The counsellor can help by highlighting the process which the child uses. For example, the counsellor might say: *You didn't just tell that burglar to go away, you pushed him out of the door as well. I think you must be feeling very brave.* This helps the child to understand that he is becoming more in control of the situation.

How to use imaginative pretend play to provide an opportunity for a child to develop insight into current and past events

Imaginative pretend play gives an opportunity for the child to learn about himself, develop insight into current and past events, and provides him with an opportunity to change in a safe environment without judgement or pressure.

To help to achieve this goal, the counsellor can invite the child to create a drama which includes events similar to those experienced by the child. During the drama, the counsellor can invite the child to successively change roles, so that she is first one character, then another, and then the first character again. By repeating this process a number of times, the child becomes involved in playing the parts of two different characters, and a dialogue, of the child's making, emerges between these two characters. Consequently, the child experiences what it is like to be both characters and will gain insight into the behaviours, beliefs and perceptions of others, and into current and past events.

How to use imaginative pretend play to help a child to take risks in developing new behaviours

In imaginative pretend play the child can experiment with new behaviours which she might initially believe are too risky to use in her real life. During imaginative pretend play she can try out new behaviours which would otherwise never be tried, in order to check out their likely consequences. The counsellor can help the child to take risks by reminding her that what is happening in the imaginative pretend play is make-believe, and will not have real consequences. The counsellor might say: *Let's pretend that you are magic and you can change things whenever they go wrong.*

With this assurance of an 'escape' the child is encouraged to enter into simulated risk-taking scenarios with safety.

How to use imaginative pretend play to help a child to practise new behaviours and to prepare for particular life situations

Consider a child who needs to be more assertive. In imaginative pretend play, the child could be invited to assume the role of a figure of authority such as a teacher. The counsellor can then co-play, by pretending to be a child subjected to the behaviours of the authority figure (the teacher). In order to help strengthen the child's authoritarian role, the counsellor might become provocative by pretending to be non-compliant. For example, if the 'teacher' asks her to go to the 'time out room', the counsellor might say: *I don't really feel like doing that. I'm just going to sit here in my seat.*

This provocative response challenges the child's role. Whether the child becomes more authoritative or not can then be discussed. The counsellor might say: *I noticed that you didn't make me go to the time out room. I wonder how you could have persuaded me to do what you wanted?*

How to use imaginative pretend play to give a child the opportunity to build self-concept, and self-esteem

Experimenting with various roles can help the child to discover dormant and undiscovered parts of himself. The counsellor can encourage the child to expand on qualities which are emerging by co-playing with the child in roles which will support the emergence of behaviours such as leadership, friendship, helpfulness, problem solving, cooperation and collaboration. The counsellor might assume the role of helpless victim, chaotic friend or forgetful adult, to highlight the contrast in the behaviour of the child and of the co-playing counsellor. The counsellor can then affirm the qualities the child is exhibiting. For example, if the child had been helpful in the role play, then the counsellor could say: *You are really good at being helpful. I wouldn't have been able to do that if I hadn't had your help.* This affirms the child's ability to be helpful.

How to use imaginative pretend play to help a child to improve communication skills

Dramatic scenarios in imaginative pretend play depend on both verbal and non-verbal communication. Thus, through the dialogue of play, a child can experience success or lack of success in verbal and non-verbal communication.

Unfortunately, some children do not make a verbal commentary on their non-verbal activity during role play and do not spontaneously engage in dialogue. To encourage the child to do this, the counsellor might reflect back to the child what the child is doing and invite him to share his thoughts with the counsellor. For instance the counsellor might say: *I notice that you are putting Dolly back to bed. What would you like to say to Dolly while you are putting her to bed?* This encourages the child to communicate rather than just to engage in non-verbal behaviour.

Suitability of imaginative pretend play

Imaginative pretend play is the play of children between the ages of two and a half to five years. It is a time developmentally when skills are rehearsed in preparation for later life.

When children reach school age pretending becomes more covert, and rather than act things out, older children engage in fantasizing. Children from the age of six to twelve turn towards reality and their play becomes more realistic because they realize that overt pretend play is not socially acceptable. The use of imaginative pretend play is therefore more appropriate for younger children.

Imaginative pretend play can be open ended and expansive allowing the child to explore options and possibilities without boundaries and to express feelings, issues and concerns with safety. It encourages the child to be interactive and adventurous. However, it does allow her to stay within boundaries if she wishes by using simple repetitive themes.

◆   ◆   ◆   ◆   ◆   ◆   ◆

25   Games

Games, some formal and others informal, are played by young children across all cultures. They are enjoyable, and also help children to develop physically, cognitively, emotionally and socially. Games require specific skills and these vary in complexity. Some games, such as Snap and Memory, have rules which are simple and easy to understand and remember. These games are suitable for young children between the ages of four and seven. Many games require a more complicated set of rules and are therefore more suitable for older children, between the ages of seven and eleven.

From a counselling perspective, games can be a useful way of engaging children who are shy or, for other reasons, reluctant to enter the counselling relationship. Playing a game with a child can create a relationship that may be a precursor to meaningful counselling. Games can also be used as the central focus of a counselling intervention to achieve goals such as those listed later in this section. These goals generally relate to the later stages in the Spiral of Therapeutic Change (see p. 46), and are particularly relevant to the stage where the child rehearses and experiments with new behaviours.

Games contrast directly with free play. In free play there are no rules; whereas a child's behaviour is restricted by the rules of a game. From these rules a child learns what the goals of the game are, learns how to play the game, and learns what limits and consequences there are in the game.

The use of games can be a good way to challenge and develop a child's ego-strengths. In games a child has to face issues such as losing, cheating, taking turns, missing turns, sticking to rules, failure, fairness, unfairness and being left out. Additionally, the use of games allows the child to experience, experiment with and practise responses to tasks involving communication, social interaction, and the solving of problems.

While some games challenge the child's own abilities, most involve the interaction of two or more players and a comparison between their performances. In many games, the behaviours of participants are interdependent, with the outcome depending on each player's behaviour. Consequently, these games involve a high level of social activity.

Developmentally, it is normal for children between the ages of seven and eleven to assess their own levels of competence by comparing their performance with that of others. The element of competition in games therefore provides a useful opportunity for a child to make an assessment of his abilities. In doing this he will become aware that he is good at some things and not so good at others. However, it does need to be recognized that children with low ego-strength may feel threatened by the use of games if the competitive element is over-emphasized. When using games in counselling, there needs to be a high level of friendliness, cooperation and collaboration. The emphasis needs to be on the personal skills required within the game playing exercise, rather than on winning or losing.

The personal skills a child needs when playing a game include impulse control, dealing with frustration, and the ability to accept the limits on behaviour which the rules of the game demand. The child needs to attend, to concentrate, and to persevere so that a game is followed through to its conclusion. Playing a game also requires the child to have a certain level of cognitive ability, because most games involve the use of numbers, counting and a level of logical problem-solving ability.

Historically, many games have mirrored or paralleled events in our culture, and have almost acted as practice grounds in which children could rehearse skills and behaviours used by adults in our society. A good example of such a game is Monopoly, which allows the child to experience the successes and failures of free enterprise trading through the 'buying', 'selling' and 'renting' of property. In the 1990s, with the increasing range of video and computer games, there are many more games available which can be played by individuals on their own. Unless these games can be played with two handsets, the nature of the social interaction is limited.

As counsellors, we try to keep ourselves informed about games which appeal to children of various ages and abilities. Understanding what each game offers enables us to make sensible decisions about which game to use in a particular counselling situation.

Materials needed when using games

Games can be classified into three categories according to what determines who wins:

1 Games involving physical or motor skill
2 Games involving strategy
3 Games of chance

Games involving physical or motor skills include Fiddlesticks, tiddly-winks, Operation, some simple board games like Hungry Hippo and Mouse Trap, and games where small bags of beans are thrown at targets. Additionally there are games such as basketball and handball which require a higher level of physical activity, and help children to work off energy or dissipate anger.

In games involving strategy, cognitive skill determines the outcome. These include noughts and crosses, Connect Four, Chinese chequers, chess, Cluedo, and many card games.

In games of chance the outcome of the game is clearly accidental. Games of chance include bingo, snakes and ladders, card games, and many games which use a dice or a numbered wheel.

We have included games from each of the three categories in our own collection. We usually select games which are suitable for two people, or very small groups, and which are suitable for the space available. We choose games where the pieces or parts of the game are unlikely to cause injury to participants or damage to property. For example, soft sponge balls or Velcro covered balls are selected in preference to harder alternatives.

It is also important to consider the time it takes to play a game. It would obviously be inappropriate to expect a young child to continue to concentrate throughout a very long game. Moreover, a game used in a counselling session needs to be completed within the time allocated for the session. Generally, we prefer to use short games which can be repeated several times in a session. Such games give a child several opportunities to become aware of his current behaviours and then to experiment with new behaviours.

Goals when using games

Games can be used by counsellors to:

1 build a counselling relationship with a resistant or reluctant child;
2 help a child to explore her responses to restrictions, limitations and the expectations of others;
3 provide an opportunity for a child to discover her strengths and weaknesses with regard to fine and gross motor skills, and/or visual-perceptual skills;
4 provide a child with an opportunity to explore her ability to attend, to concentrate and persevere with tasks;
5 help a child to practise social skills such as cooperation and collaboration, and to practise appropriate responses to disappointment, discouragement, failure and success;
6 help a child to practise problem solving and decision making;
7 provide an opportunity for a child to learn about relevant issues or life events, for example domestic violence, sexual abuse, stranger danger.

How to use games

We will now look at how to use games to achieve each of the above mentioned goals.

1 The use of games to build a counselling relationship with a resistant or reluctant child

Some children do not engage in the counselling process easily because they are shy or resistant. Games such as chequers, Snap, or snakes and ladders, can be used to help in the joining process between the child and counsellor. Involvement in the game provides a safe context with easily recognized boundaries for both child and counsellor. Consequently, the child is unlikely to feel threatened and will relax.

Sometimes, using a game in the way described results in direct counselling gains, because significant internal processes of the child are revealed during play. For example, when playing a game it might emerge that a resistant child is resistant because he is fearful, or angry, or frightened of making mistakes. He may also be uncertain about the expectations of the counselling process.

If, during a game, a counsellor notices particular issues emerging for a child, then these can be addressed through the use of statements, reflection of feelings and content, and questions. For, example a counsellor might notice that a child is fearful of failure, and might make a statement such as: *Playing this game might be a bit tricky for you. It's tricky for me too sometimes.*

By making this statement, the counsellor acknowledges the child's anxiety about performance. The counsellor might also reflect feelings by saying: *You seem to be anxious, when you are not able to do as well as you would like.*

The counsellor might also ask: *What will it be like for you if you lose the game?* and, *What will it be like if you win the game?*

By using counselling skills, such as those given in the examples above, the counsellor can help the child to start entering the counselling process during the game, by raising the child's awareness of thoughts and feelings that may be relevant to the child's issues.

2 The use of games to help a child to explore her responses to restrictions, limitations and the expectations of others

Although games can sometimes be useful for helping a child to become aware of troubling unconscious material, they are probably more valuable for helping her to deal with her responses to restrictions, limitations and the expectations of others. Clearly, games depend on rules, and these rules provide restrictions and limitations on the child. Also, when playing a game, the child will be subjected to the expectations of others (e.g. the counsellor or members of a group) with regard to her behaviour. Thus, she has an opportunity to confront, explore and work through issues that arise because of the rules of the game and the expectations of others.

Consider the example of a passive dependent child. Such a child may respond to the restrictions of a game by continually asking for help. In order to address the underlying behaviours of passivity and dependence, the counsellor might mirror the child's behaviour by asking the child for help. The child can then be commended for his ability to give advice. The counsellor can thus highlight the child's own capacity to deal with the restrictions and limitations of the game.

Some children will try to cheat when playing games. A child who cheats is attempting to avoid facing the painfulness of failure in an immature and socially maladaptive way. Such behaviour interferes with the child's development of the ability to cope with painful experiences. Instead of coping with painful experiences adaptively, the child creates an unreal or untrue outcome. To address this problem, the counsellor could help the child to confront reality by encouraging her to explore her wish to win, and then to contrast this with reality. For example the counsellor might ask: *I wonder what it would have been like if you had won?* and, *What was it like for you to lose?*

The child can then express what it would have been like to have been successful and to recognize what it was like to have been unsuccessful. Thus, the child is encouraged to experience rather than to avoid the feelings of failure, and to learn how to cope with these feelings. This approach is useful for many, but not all, children. Some require an intermediate step to help them to cope with reality. This is because for young children, around the age of four to six years, creating an unreal or untrue outcome is normal behaviour. 'Cheating' can be seen as an immature behaviour which is developmentally appropriate for this age group. With younger children the counsellor might use the following different approach.

Consider a dice game. The counsellor might suggest that the child can throw the dice twice, instead of once, each turn and choose the best outcome from the two throws. This gives the child more control over the outcome, because he can choose which dice result to use. Consequently, the pressure to cheat is reduced, and the child learns to comply with rules. The counsellor might then encourage the child to take risks when deciding which dice score to use. By using this process the counsellor has maximized the child's chance of winning, while at the same time helping the child to confront the reality of the possibility of failure.

3 The use of games to provide an opportunity for a child to discover her strengths and weaknesses with regard to fine and gross motor skills, and visual-perceptual skills

Games which involve fine motor skills include Hungry Hippos, Jenga, Barrel of Monkeys, Fiddlesticks, and some computer video games. Games which require gross motor skills include quoits, Velcro-darts, basketball, handball, hide-and-seek, hopscotch and Twister. All of these can be played with the counsellor as the second participant.

Games which involve visual-perceptual skills include Connect 4, Guess Who?, some video computer games, memory games, card games, and some board games, such as Battleship.

The counsellor can assist a child to ascertain strengths and weaknesses by engaging the child in the games described and by giving appropriate feedback. A recognition of strengths and weaknesses is helpful when exploring the child's self-esteem (see Chapter 26), and in enabling a child to deal with self-destructive beliefs concerning himself.

4 The use of games to help a child to explore her ability to attend, to concentrate and to persevere with tasks

During a game, a counsellor can address a child's behaviours by making suggestions and providing encouragement, information and positive reinforcement. Children are more willing to experiment with new behaviours, and to practise new behaviours, in a game playing situation than in other situations.

The simple act of taking turns can be helpful for a child with impulse control problems. Thus, a suitable game can be used to teach the child self-control. A child who has difficulty in attending and/or persevering, may be encouraged to complete a game by the use of a statement such as: *When you have won three hands we will stop the game.* By saying this, the counsellor provides the child with an opportunity to visualize an end to the game, and the child is able to practise and experience completion of a task.

5 The use of games to help a child to practise social skills such as cooperation and collaboration, and to learn appropriate responses to disappointment, failure and success

Playing games allows children to evaluate existing social skills, and to learn and practise new social skills. Social skills include observing non-verbal communication, matching affect, asking appropriate questions, giving information, cooperating, sharing and collaborating. Games can also help children to change attitudes and values which are socially inappropriate.

Board games which require children to answer questions or to respond to item cards as they move around the board are particularly useful in achieving the above goal, because they take advantage of the social and interactive nature of children. These games are best played in a group, so that behaviours can be affirmed or challenged within the group.

A popular game called the Ungame is useful when working with early adolescent groups. In a different way, The Talking, Feeling and Doing Game also enables social skills practice and does not rely on a group to be successful. While playing games such as these a counsellor can explore the issues and thought processes of the child as she is confronted with difficulties or obstacles. For example the counsellor might say to the child: *It seems as though you may be having difficulty responding to this particular item card. What is the hardest part about the instruction on this card for you?*

The counsellor may suggest alternative responses and behaviours during the game. Later, the child may want to practise them so that they can be generalized for everyday use.

Some games, such as Minefield, can be used to develop trust. In Minefield, the counsellor blindfolds the child and distributes paper plates on the floor of the room to create an imaginary minefield. The counsellor then guides the child, using only verbal instructions, so that she can move slowly across the room without stepping on a mine. The counsellor and child can then swap roles, giving the child an opportunity to lead the counsellor through the minefield.

6 The use of games to help a child to practise skills in problem solving and decision making

Most board games, and some card games such as Memory, involve the skills of selecting alternatives and taking risks in response to particular situations. Card games which have a high element of chance are a useful way of helping a child to understand that even when care is taken life may not always go according to plan.

Instant Replay is a game which is useful for helping children to learn and use rational problem-solving methods. In this game, the child is invited to tell the counsellor about a difficult event in her life. She is then asked what happened next, as a result of the event. She is also invited to say what she was thinking to herself during the event, with particular reference to her own part in the event. The child is next invited to think of other things she could have thought or done when she was in the situation. After these have been explored, the child is invited to speculate about what the consequences might have been for each of the new possibilities, and is invited to choose the best alternatives and to practise them at home and at school.

7 The use of games as educational tools about specific issues or life events (domestic violence, sexual abuse, stranger danger, etc.)

Specifically designed games such as Breakthrough are now available to help children to become aware of, and deal with, specific issues such as physical abuse, sexual abuse, divorce, domestic violence, pornography and stranger danger. These are often board games and they invite the child to respond to questions and to give answers which are then evaluated in terms of the myths or realities.

Suitability of games

As mentioned earlier games can be used either individually or with groups. They are most useful for primary school children and early adolescents. It is important to remember that children up to the age of about eight years old may have difficulty in consistently staying within the rules of a game, and regressed behaviour may occur. Games suitable for early adolescents require a high level of challenge in cognitive, social and problem-solving areas.

PART 5
THE USE OF WORKSHEETS

Most children are familiar with worksheets, because they are commonly used in schools for teaching purposes. Similar activities are often found in weekend magazines and daily newspapers.

Activities involving worksheets have many different forms, including answering questionnaires, working on quizzes, finding words, joining dots, looking for differences between pictures, finding hidden items in pictures, and matching similar items. Some worksheets include measuring scales, such as pictures of thermometers, or continuum lines which stretch from one extreme to another, to measure attitude, performance or other criteria. Clearly, well designed worksheets are inviting for children, who enjoy using them. Most importantly, from the counsellor's point of view, worksheets act as a springboard for discussion, because they tend to draw out and focus the child's thoughts about particular issues or behaviours.

Worksheets can be useful at various stages in the counselling process. At the beginning of a counselling session a worksheet can be used to help a child to begin to look at, and then to explore particular issues. When a counselling session, or series of sessions, is ending, worksheets can be used to reinforce recently acquired ideas, beliefs and behaviours, and to help the child to consolidate problem-solving skills. By using worksheets, the counsellor actively facilitates change (see Chapter 13).

Worksheets can be used to help a child to:

- begin to look at particular issues, so that these issues can be explored;
- consider new ways of thinking and behaving;
- explore, understand and develop problem-solving and decision-making skills;
- make choices about how she might respond to a particular social situation or event, and to explore the possible consequences of these responses;
- recognize differences between old and new behaviours;
- affirm and/or reinforce concepts, ideas, beliefs and behaviours which have been explored or discussed during counselling;
- develop a plan so that learnt skills are generalized into the child's environment.

Additionally worksheets can be used in a group as a way of helping children to share different points of view.

We will focus on the use of worksheets for the following purposes:

1 Building self-esteem (Chapter 26)
2 Social skills training (Chapter 27)
3 Education in protective behaviours (Chapter 28)

In each section, we will provide a selection of worksheets which we have designed for specific purposes. You are welcome to photocopy these for your own personal use when working as a counsellor for children. Please remember, however, that they are copyright, and must not be used for other purposes. We find they are easiest to use if they are enlarged to A4 size.

◆   ◆   ◆   ◆   ◆   ◆   ◆

26   Self-esteem building exercises

From a very early age a child begins to form an image, or picture, of herself. This image or picture is generally referred to as the child's *self-concept*, and is largely based on the way in which the child is treated by the significant people in her life. These people, through their responses, give the child information about herself, and about her behaviours. As a consequence, she will develop both positive and negative attitudes towards herself.

We need to stress that self-concept is not the same as self-esteem. The image, or picture, which the child has of herself is her self-concept. That is how she sees herself. The value she puts on this image is the measure of her *self-esteem*. Self-esteem therefore is an indication of the extent to which a child values herself.

It is important, when counselling children to recognize the difference between self-concept and self-esteem. Although many children with a generally positive self-concept will have high self-esteem, this is not always the case. Some children see themselves as having many positive attributes: they may be clever academically, good at sport, and articulate, and as a result have a positive self-concept. However, they may not value these attributes, so may have low self-esteem and feel bad about themselves. Some very capable children, who have high expectations of themselves, see themselves as unsuccessful and unworthy when their performance doesn't match their personal aspirations. Their fear of failure raises their anxiety and their self-esteem is threatened. The opposite also happens: some children may see themselves as being unintelligent, poor at sport and inarticulate. However, they may like the way they are, and have high self-esteem.

The value and judgement which a child places on her self-concept, that is, the level of a child's self-esteem, will inevitably have a major influence on her adaptive functioning. Her beliefs, thoughts, attitudes, emotional feelings, behaviours, motivation, interest and participation in events and activities, and expectations for the future, will all be significantly influenced by her level of self-esteem. Additionally, the child's ability to enter into, and sustain meaningful relationships, will be dependent on her self-esteem.

Children with high self-esteem tend to have the following characteristics:

- They have a greater capacity to be creative.
- They are more likely to assume active roles in social groups.
- They are less likely to be burdened by self-doubt, fear and ambivalence.
- They are more likely to move more directly and realistically towards personal goals.
- They find it easier to accept differences between their own levels of competence and that of others in areas such as academic performance, peer relationships and physical pursuits. They also tend to worry less about differences in physical appearance. They are able to accept these differences and still to feel positive about themselves.

Many children who come for counselling help do not have the attributes listed above. Instead they feel helpless and inferior, incapable of improving their situation, and believe that they do not have the resources to reduce their anxiety. They have low self-esteem.

Some children with low self-esteem strive for social approval by behaving in ways which are over-compliant, or by pretending to be self-confident when they are not, while continuing to receive negative responses and feedback. They are struggling to feel good about themselves.

Generally, the self-esteem of a child remains fairly constant and stable over a period of several years. However, self-esteem can, with appropriate interventions, be influenced either directly or indirectly. A counsellor can help a child to raise his self-esteem.

Interventions to directly enhance self-esteem usually involve the use of praise and performance feedback to improve both the child's self-concept and self-esteem. However, although useful, this type of direct intervention is not always the most effective way to bring about improvement in self-esteem. Alternatively, or additionally, we can use an indirect method. An indirect approach targets specific areas, such as the child's performance as a student, his relationships with peers, or his motor performance. Clearly, a child's self-esteem is likely to improve if he can acquire competence and confidence in these areas.

We believe that for most children work in a group provides the best opportunity for self-esteem improvement. Children can realistically and positively evaluate themselves through the process of group interaction. Specific areas of skill development can easily be targeted through exercises and activities.

Although, in our view, group work is generally the most effective way of enhancing self-esteem, some children may not have the ego-strength or behavioural characteristics to enable them to satisfactorily participate in a group process. These children may have come from environments where they have had few experiences of love and success, and where domination, rejection and severe punishment have resulted in a high level of damage to the child's ego. They may have become submissive and withdrawn, or may have responded by becoming extremely aggressive and dominating. Because such children may be unable to fit comfortably into a group, their self-esteem needs are most appropriately met through one-to-one counselling. When working with children such as these, worksheets are useful. Such children are usually adept at avoiding and deflecting away from any discussion which focuses on their incompetencies, limitations and anxieties. Worksheets can be used to help them to focus and to target significant topics.

Some self-esteem programmes focus on helping the child to recognize and accept his own personal attributes, strengths and limitations. This is rather like saying, 'This is what you have got. Make the most of it.' Although this approach can be useful, we do not think that it is sufficient, because it limits the child's potential to change.

We like to emphasize not just the child's acceptance, but also the child's *ownership* of all of her qualities, both negative and positive. Imagine that you were given an old paintbox and worn paintbrushes and with them the instruction, 'These are yours to use. Paint a picture and do your best.' Now imagine that instead you were given the same paintbox and brushes and a different instruction, 'These are yours to *keep*. Paint a picture and do your best.' The second instruction implies ownership and subtly changes the user's attitude, responsibility and commitment to the proposed use of the paints. In both cases you might well choose to paint a picture. However, in the second case you might also be interested in *caring for and improving* the paintbox and brushes so that they can be maximally useful for you in the future. Similarly, by stressing the ownership of a child's attributes we believe that we help that child to more fully discover herself. By doing this she is more likely to develop strategies to deal with and manage those characteristics of herself which she perceives as negative.

If a child is prepared to accept and own her strengths and limitations, then she is likely to accept responsibility for developing and learning to improve on, and manage, her limitations, believing that she solely is responsible for the changes within herself.

Self-esteem is heavily influenced by the ability to interact in a socially adaptive way. Social skills are of such major importance that we have devoted a separate chapter (27) to social skills training.

If a child's self-esteem is to be enhanced, he will need to do the following:

- discover himself, so that he has a more realistic self-concept;
- recognize and understand his strengths and limitations;
- establish goals for the future, and devise and implement a plan to achieve these.

For each of these three areas we have prepared three worksheets. A summary of these worksheets and their uses is given in Table 26.1.

Table 26.1 *Self-esteem worksheets*

Topic addressed	Worksheet number	Title	Page number
Discover yourself	1	*I can do anything . . .*	169
	2	*Where am I? . . .*	170
	3	*My choice . . .*	171
Strengths and limitations	4	*Inside-out*	172
	5	*News headlines*	173
	6	*Jump the hurdle*	174
Goals for the future	7	*Balance your life*	175
	8	*These are my wishes . . .*	176
	9	*Picture yourself . . .*	177

In the following paragraphs we will discuss ways to use the worksheets. Please remember that the worksheets are not intended to be sufficient in themselves: they provide the stimulus for discussion of the relevant issues.

Discover yourself

The worksheets are designed to help children to discover themselves so that they can have a more realistic self-concept. These worksheets give children permission to do the following:

- express various polarities within themselves;
- examine which parts of themselves they expose freely to others and which parts of themselves they hide;
- discover how they can make choices about what they do;
- discover how they can make choices about when to do things by themselves and when to do them with others.

The three worksheets are entitled: *I can do anything . . .* (worksheet 1, p. 169), *Where am I? . . .* (worksheet 2, p. 170) and *My choice . . .* (worksheet 3, p. 171).

I can do anything . . . stimulates discussion about which parts of himself the child feels most comfortable in expressing at different times and in different situations. For example, a child may feel powerful and strong when with his peers, yet submissive with his parents. When using this worksheet we encourage discussion to focus around the belief that it is OK to behave differently in different circumstances, and we explore the need to be adaptive and considerate of others.

Where am I? . . . allows the child to develop a visual picture of those parts of himself which he can comfortably let others see and those parts of himself which he prefers to hide. Discussion can then explore the risks which might be involved if he were to expose the hidden parts of himself to others. By connecting the characters on the page to parts of the tree, the child is encouraged to explore the possibility that hidden parts might grow to become an exposed part of the tree for others to see and appreciate.

My choice . . . encourages the child to begin to view her life in terms of activities which fit into particular categories. It invites her to identify activities within categories and to create a picture about herself. This picture can help the child to discover how much time she spends in particular activities and to decide whether or not she would like to make changes. During a counselling session a child can be encouraged to make some choices or decisions about whether she would like to change parts of the picture she has of herself.

Strengths and limitations

In designing worksheets related to strengths and limitations, our goal is to help the child to:

- identify strengths and limitations;
- discover resources within himself which he can use to enhance his self-esteem;
- identify any thoughts and self-destructive beliefs he has about himself, which prevent him from changing to becoming stronger;
- discover how to care for himself;
- recognize mistakes as opportunities for learning and changing.

The three worksheets that deal with strengths and limitations are: *Inside-out* (worksheet 4, p. 172), *News headlines* (worksheet 5, p. 173) and *Jump the hurdle* (worksheet 6, p. 174).

Inside-out allows the child to identify three separate components of herself: her body, her emotional feelings and her thoughts. The worksheet then provides suggestions to help the child to discover new ways of caring for her body, her emotional feelings and her thoughts. The worksheet also helps the child to recognize and own behaviours which prevent her from developing her strengths.

News headlines highlights a specific incident in the child's life where he has made a mistake. It gives the child an opportunity to process a negative experience but to focus on the positive outcomes of that experience.

Jump the hurdle attempts to encourage the child to be flexible in his thinking, to consider taking risks and to discover the issues which prevent him from making new and different choices.

Goals for the future

Following through on plans and goals is an indicator of confidence and belief in oneself. In this section we attempt to encourage the child to combine his wishes and dreams with reality. We have designed three worksheets to address the topic of goals for the future: *Balance your life* (worksheet 7, p. 175), *These are my wishes* . . . (worksheet 8, p. 176) and *Picture yourself* . . . (worksheet 9, p. 177).

I can do anything . . .

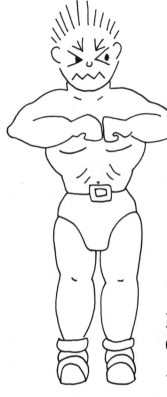

I AM THE GIANT GUNGA.
I CAN MOVE BRIDGES WITH ONE HAND.

I am the Empress
. . . . and I am
able to . . . .

I AM THE WISE ONE CALLED . . . . AND I CAN . . . . .

I am the quiet one called . . . . and
I can . . . .

I AM THE BRAVE SPIRIT THEY CALL . . . . . AND I'M ABLE TO . . . . . .

Worksheet 1

Where am I ?. . . .

Sometimes we hide parts of ourselves and only let others see what we want them to see. We do this for many reasons. Can you think of some?

Imagine that the tree is you, and the characters around the tree can represent parts of you. Draw lines from those characters which are like you to the tree. Draw a line from the character to the roots of the tree if you hide that part of you, and a line to the branches if you like others to see that part of you.

Can you draw another part of you here? Where does it fit?

Worksheet 2

My Choice . . .

Plot your interests by selecting those activities from the categories below which appeal to you most and placing them on the chart. Do this by using a coloured felt pen to identify a particular activity (put a coloured dot beside the activity). Then put a dot of the same colour on the grid to indicate how much time you spend doing the activity during an average day, and whether you do the activity alone or with others.

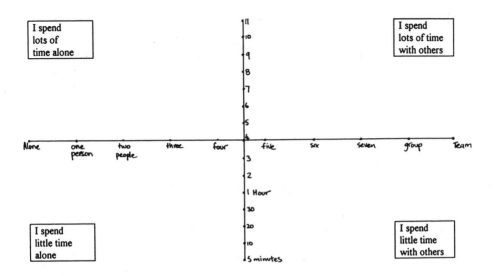

Working	**Travelling**	**Learning**	**Looking after your body**
Housework	Car	School	Eating, sleeping, washing
Chores	Train	Music lessons	Grooming
Shopping	Bus	Visiting counsellor	Exercising: dancing, skateboarding,
Job	Bike	Homework	gym, soccer, surfing, or other sport

Socializing	**Relaxing**	**Being occupied alone**
On the phone	Listening to music	Hobbies, e.g. models, craft,
Visiting a friend	Reading	drawing, cooking, collections,
Having a friend over	Daydreaming	jigsaws, Lego, gardening,
Talking with adults	Meditating	magic tricks, playing on the
Playing a game	Watching TV	computer
Helping someone		

You may want to add more . . . .
Look at the chart. What have you discovered about yourself?

Worksheet 3

Inside-Out

Here is a list of things which you may think about, feel emotionally, or experience in your body. Use a red pen to connect the items listed to the figure which would be most affected.

- Eat lots
- Hunch shoulders
- Bite nails
- Feel tense
- Headache
- Hold them in
- Clench teeth
- Pretend that I don't have them
- Let them out when I'm not ready
- Stress out
- Fiddle with things
- Think that people don't like me
- Should work harder
- Stomach ache
- Slouch
- Worry about tomorrow
- Look shabby
- Pretend I've got them (when I really
- Shouldn't take risks   haven't)
- Sleep a lot
- Should behave better
- Think the worst will happen

BODY

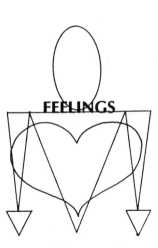

FEELINGS

THOUGHTS

Now here are a few suggestions to help you to take care of yourself. With a green pen connect them to the figure which would benefit the most.

- Ring a friend
- Relaxation
- Watch TV
- Ask for help
- Accept my mistakes
- Tell myself that I am lovable and capable
- Listen to music
- Count to ten
- Remember that I am made up of opposites
- Take a bath
- Read a book
- Bake a cake
- Blow gently 10 times (like blowing out candles)
- Talk to someone else
- Go for a walk

Worksheet 4

NEWS HEADLINES

DAILY COURIER

Today . . . .

committed the worst crime in history.

While the rest of the world slept the

small town of Pinchgut was

astounded at the news that . . . .

. . . .

. . . .

. . . .

. . . .

Many people said . . . .

. . . .

. . . .

. . . .

However, a few said . . . .

. . . .

. . . .

. . . .

In a statement by . . . .

it was clear that . . . .

. . . .

. . . .

The outcome will be that . . . .

. . . .

will . . . .

. . . .

. . . .

| Worksheet 5 |

Changing your mind
is OK.

Jump the Hurdle

Changing your mind means that you discover the hurdles which stop you from exploring new and different experiences, and from making new and different choices.

WOULD YOU RATHER crawl through
a long dark tunnel to get to the
best fun park in the world

OR play with a friendly tiger

Who, or what, would you need to help you so that you could change your mind?

WOULD YOU RATHER
fly an aeroplane

OR drive in the Grand Prix

WOULD YOU RATHER
sit in a tub of live snails

OR walk along a thin bridge over
a harmless snake pit

Worksheet   6

BALANCE YOUR LIFE

Each day we find ourselves doing things in one of the categories listed below.

- Occupying ourselves alone
- Relaxing
- Mixing with others socially
- Looking after our bodies
- Learning
- Working
- Travelling

Colour the box red for the category which best fits with what you are doing now . . . .
GREAT!! You've got the knack . . . . . NOW . . . . . . Begin the daily journey below - each time when you come to a blank square draw in it the symbol which best represents what you would be doing at that time.

SCHOOL DAY

START	Get out of bed				Go into class			Morning break

Arrive home			Time to go home				Lunch	Back to class

						Go to bed		

WEEKEND DAY

START	Get out of bed							Lunch

Dinner								

						Go to bed		

What would you like to change?

Worksheet	7

These are my wishes . . .

Wish 1, for today . . . .

Wish 2, for tomorrow . . . .
. . . .

And then wish 3, for the future. .
. . . .

Worksheet 8

Picture yourself... then, now, and in the future

At each stage on the time-line write down:
1. What you have achieved or what you hope to achieve.
2. Who, or what, you need or needed to help you achieve these things.
3. Mark an X to show where you are now.

Retirement

Adulthood

Secondary school

Primary school

3 months

Balance your life encourages the child to view her daily life in terms of various categories. This worksheet gives the child a picture of how her day is divided. It presents her with information about whether, for instance, she spends most of her time learning and not much time relaxing. The child is then encouraged to think of ways in which she might change her daily life to achieve a more satisfactory balance across each of the categories.

These are my wishes allows the child to fantasize about his life and to think about what he would like in the present, in the near future and in the long term. When using the worksheet, we encourage the child to be as imaginative and creative as he can be.

Picture yourself allows the child to plan the big picture of her future by examining the past, looking at the present and preparing for the future fulfilment of dreams and wishes. The child is encouraged to identify what she has achieved, and wants to achieve, and who or what she needs to help her to achieve her goal.

◆　◆　◆　◆　◆　◆　◆

27　Social skills training

As mentioned in the previous section, a child's self-image and self-esteem are dependent on the child's skills in relating to peers and adults. These skills contribute to self-esteem because a child with good social skills is likely to build satisfying relationships and to receive positive feedback from others. A child with poor social skills is likely to have unsatisfactory relationships and to receive negative feedback.

Many of the emotionally disturbed children who have come to see us for counselling help, have had poor social skills. Consequently, these children have had dysfunctional interpersonal relationships. Often, they have also engaged in socially unacceptable behaviours which have resulted in painful consequences for them.

Poor social skills can occur as a result of poor modelling by adults. Additionally, children who have experienced trauma often develop socially inappropriate behaviours: they may become aggressive or overly compliant. Other children develop irrational and self-destructive beliefs which set them up to mistrust others, and to misinterpret the behaviours of others.

It is clear that poor social skills lead to problems, not only in childhood, but also later in life, so it is very important for children with poor social skills to receive appropriate training to help them to improve their skills so that they can enjoy their social interactions and feel good about themselves.

What are the characteristics of children with poor social skills? How are they different from other children?

We believe that the following characteristics are typical of children with poor social skills:

- Often they don't adapt their behaviour to accommodate the needs of others.
- They tend to choose less socially acceptable behaviours.
- They have difficulty in predicting the consequences of their behaviours.
- They misunderstand social cues.
- They are unable to perform the social skills required for particular situations.
- They often have an inability to control impulsive or aggressive behaviour.

There are three components to social skills training, which are essential if the training is to be effective and useful:

1 We need to help the child to gain clear ideas about what constitutes socially adaptive behaviour.
2 We need to help the child to discover how to use appropriate social skills.
3 We need to help the child to generalize the skills learnt, so that they can be put into practice in the various social situations of the child's own environment.

In order to meet the requirements of these components it is preferable to use a combination of group work and individual counselling.

Group work provides an opportunity for children to identify and discuss acceptable and unacceptable social behaviours as these behaviours occur in the group. It also enables the practice of new behaviours.

In individual counselling, we use worksheets to help the child to think about her current behaviours and their consequences, to recognize alternative behaviours, and to make choices about how she intends to respond to particular social situations in the future. Working individually gives the child the opportunity to examine her own responses and choices without pressure from others. Clearly, this is an individual task, as each child is different, and has her own unique social environment. Once the child has chosen appropriate skills for use in particular situations, we can help her to devise a plan of action. In this plan the child needs to decide on the best time to use the selected skills within the various situations of her environment. Thus she is able to think about ways in which to generalize learnt social skills into the various settings of her own unique and individual environment.

After the child has attempted to carry out her plan of action, she can be invited to evaluate the success of the plan, and to modify it if necessary for future use. We can also help the child to think about possible responses to any new problems that may arise as a consequence of her use of new social skills.

There are three major areas which need to be addressed when training children in social skills:

1 Identifying and expressing feelings
2 Communicating with others
3 Self-management

Table 27.1   *Social skills worksheets*

Worksheets for IDENTIFYING AND EXPRESSING FEELINGS			
Issue addressed	Worksheet number	Title	Page number
Identifying own feelings	10	*Find a feeling*	187
	11	*Artemus is anxious!*	188
Identifying others' feelings	12	*Guess what?*	189
	13	*Your body*	190
Expressing feelings	14	*The volcano*	191
	15	*Fighting fear with Felix*	192

Worksheets about COMMUNICATING WITH OTHERS			
Issue addressed	Worksheet number	Title	Page number
Making friends	16	*Conversation starters*	193
	17	*??Questions??*	194
Being left out	18	*Advice for Jim*	195
	19	*Gumbo gossips*	196
Solving conflicts	20	*Fighting!*	197
	21	*Terry, Tyrone and Me*	198

Worksheets on SELF-MANAGEMENT			
Issue addressed	Worksheet number	Title	Page number
Chilling out	22	*Look before you leap*	199
	23	*Choices and options*	200
Consequences	24	*If – then – but*	201
	25	*Crime and punishment!*	202
Sticking up for yourself	26	*Saying 'no' made easy*	203
	27	*Reward yourself*	204

A child needs to be able to identify his own and other people's feelings if he is to relate adaptively. He needs to be able to communicate effectively in ways which validate his own needs and are respectful of others' needs. He also needs to manage his own behaviour effectively so that it is socially acceptable.

In each of the three areas listed above, we have identified three specific issues which can be explored and have prepared two worksheets for each issue. A summary of these worksheets and their uses is given in Table 27.1, and copies of the worksheets are included in this chapter.

Identifying and expressing feelings

To function adaptively, so that they can relate easily with others, children need to be able to: identify their own feelings, identify other people's feelings and express their own feelings.

In the following paragraphs we will discuss ways to use worksheets which we have designed to address the three issues listed above. The worksheets are not intended to be sufficient in themselves; they provide the stimulus for discussion of the relevant issues.

Helping children to identify their own feelings

The following worksheets help children to identify their own feelings: *Find a feeling* (worksheet 10, p. 187) and *Artemus is anxious!* (worksheet 11, p. 188).

Quite often, we find that children are unable to label the feelings which they are experiencing. For some children, this may be because they have had confusing information about feelings. For example, a child might have been told by his mother that he was 'just tired', when he was actually behaving in an angry way. Other children may have difficulty in recognizing the differences between feelings which are fairly similar: for example feeling disappointed might be confused with feeling sad, and feeling embarrassed might be confused with feeling shy.

Find a feeling helps the child to identify particular feelings by relating them to events and situations. *Artemus is anxious!* presents the child with a list of situations she might find anxiety provoking. The worksheet also invites the child to consider situations and events, specifically relevant to herself, which might make her anxious.

Helping children to identify other people's feelings

The following worksheets help children to identify other people's feelings: *Guess what?* (worksheet 12, p. 189) and *Your body* (worksheet 13, p. 190).

Once a child has learnt to identify his own feelings and to match them with situations and events, he is more likely to be able to predict or guess how other people might feel in particular situations.

Guess what? invites the child to guess how other people, shown in the picture on the worksheet, might be feeling. By using this worksheet, the child might also, in his imagination, project himself into situations similar to those depicted, and discussion about specific events and issues might ensue.

Your body encourages the child to use observational skills. The child is asked to consider how people use their bodies, and the expressions on their faces, to indicate how they are feeling. Following on from this exercise, the child might be invited to think about his own body language, and how he uses this to express his emotions.

Helping children to express their own feelings

The following worksheets help children to express their feelings: *The Volcano* (worksheet 14, p. 191) and *Fighting fear with Felix* (worksheet 15, p. 192).

Once a child can identify her own feelings and recognize the feelings which other people are expressing, she needs to learn how to express her own feelings clearly and appropriately. This means expressing feelings in ways which are comfortable for both the child and the other party involved.

The Volcano is specifically targeted at the expression of anger. When using this sheet each point on the volcano is discussed. For example, once the child has identified what kinds of things make her angry, she may look at the bottom of the volcano, where sitting on angry feelings can be imagined. The child might be encouraged to talk about what it would be like to sit on angry feelings, what might happen if she did, and what that might be like for other people. She could then be asked whether she could identify other children or people who sit on their anger. Moving up the volcano to the level where anger is allowed to ooze out provides an opportunity for the child to explore a different way of expressing anger. Once again, the kinds of behaviours which she might see in others, when they let their anger ooze out, can be identified. At the top of the volcano is the explosive angry reaction. Here the child is encouraged to examine the appropriateness and inappropriateness of this kind of expression of anger. Remember that worksheets are a springboard for further discussion.

Fighting fear with Felix encourages the child to explore possible reactions to fear, and to look at his own reactions to fear.

The situations listed might not be relevant for a particular child, so when using this worksheet we usually invite the child to tell us of his own experiences of fear. He can then explore his reactions during such experiences. *Fighting fear with Felix* also allows the counsellor to normalize the feeling of fear. This is very important because some children believe that feeling frightened is abnormal and is not OK.

Communicating with others

Once children can identify feelings in themselves and in others, and can begin to express their feelings appropriately, they are more likely to be successful in communicating with others. Social communication involves an exchange between two (or more) people. Necessarily, one individual initiates the communication and the other responds. In early childhood, this peer interaction is based on shared play activities. However, as children grow older, the interaction becomes more focused on peer acceptance and intimacy. Friendships tend to move from being physical with a focus on actions, towards relationships with an increased awareness of the feelings and emotions of others. In middle childhood, between the ages of about seven and eleven, children have more social contacts and are able to identify 'best friends'. With the establishment of best friends they begin to demonstrate commitment to each other. Aggressive interactions tend to decrease and friendships tend to involve more verbal interaction. At this stage it is important for children to be able to communicate adaptively, or they will not be able to establish satisfying social relationships. Additionally, they need to learn to deal with the emotional consequences of situations that inevitably occur in childhood, such as being left out, being ignored, being in demand as a popular child, or being ridiculed.

In order to help children to learn appropriate communication techniques, we have devised worksheets to address the following issues:

- Making friends
- Being left out
- Solving conflicts

Making friends

The following worksheets help children learn how to make friends: *Conversation starters* (worksheet 16, p. 193) and *??Questions??* (worksheet 17, p. 194).

Conversation starters suggests several different ways in which a child could start a conversation during her first day at a new school. The child is asked to identify those conversation starters which would be OK to use. She is also invited to think about the responses she might get if she were to use one of the other starters which she hadn't chosen. This worksheet helps the child to think about suitable conversation starters when in new situations and helps her to explore the anxiety related to going into new social situations.

??Questions?? teaches children how to use questions and answers to start up and maintain a conversation. The worksheet invites the child to ask questions beginning with 'what', 'where', 'how', 'when', 'why', and 'who', in order to discover information about a picture. Each time the child asks a question about the picture, the counsellor responds creatively, so that a story develops. For example, the child might ask, 'What caused that puddle on the floor?' In response the counsellor might reply, *There is a hole in the roof and the house was built right under a giant waterfall*. As the child asks more questions, the counsellor can develop the story, using humour if she wishes. Similarly, the counsellor can use questions to encourage the child to tell a different story about the picture. Later, the child and counsellor might take turns in asking questions and developing a story together.

By doing this exercise the child learns to use questions and answers to initiate conversations. She also learns to listen, and to take turns. The child can then practise these skills in her social situation when sharing interesting or exciting information with peers.

Being left out

The following worksheets are for this purpose: *Advice for Jim* (worksheet 18, p. 195) and *Gertrude & Grommet Gumbo – the Gossips* (worksheet 19, p. 196).

Being left out is something which children experience from time to time both at school and at home. *Advice for Jim* helps the child to explore his reactions to being left out. It also allows the counsellor to invite the child to talk about times in the past when he felt left out, and to discuss the ways in which he reacted. The counsellor can then validate the child's feelings and encourage the child to explore alternative ways of responding.

Gertrude & Grommet Gumbo – the Gossips looks at the way in which gossiping damages social relationships, with the consequence that children get left out. This worksheet helps the child to learn suitable responses to use when another child is inviting him to join in gossiping. Additionally, it allows the child to explore the reactions which he experiences when he is left out as a result of gossiping.

Solving conflicts

The following worksheets help children to learn how to solve conflicts: *Fighting!* (worksheet 20, p. 197) and *Terry, Tyrone and me* (worksheet 21, p. 198).

Resolving conflicts in interpersonal relationships requires understanding, skill and practice. It is important for a child to identify the reasons why conflict occurs and to understand her own responses to conflict. *Fighting!* invites the child to think about possible reasons why fights occur. The child is also encouraged to talk about conflict situations which have occurred at home and school, and to think about how these happened.

Terry, Tyrone and me explores a number of different ways of responding to conflict. When the dots have been joined, Terry can be seen to be a tortoise, whose responses might be timid, fearful and unassertive, coming from a position of helplessness and victimization. In contrast, Tyrone is a troll, whose responses might be aggressive, bullying, controlling and powerful. The counsellor can encourage the child to explore assertive ways of dealing with conflict when she thinks about her own responses in the 'Me' section of the worksheet. The counsellor can also validate the child's emotional feelings, whether they be fear or anger, in a conflict situation.

Self-management

To be socially competent a child must be able to identify and express feelings, develop skills to communicate successfully with others, and at the same time be aware of, and manage, his own behaviour. Being aware of his own behaviour helps him to be sensitive to feedback cues from others, and to be aware of the timing and pace of his own behaviour during interactions. In managing his own behaviour he needs to be able to understand and recognize consequences, to recover after social errors, to present himself in a way which is socially acceptable, and to reinforce his own social behaviours in a positive way.

In order to help children to learn self-management skills we have devised worksheets to deal with the following topics:

- Chilling out
- Consequences
- Sticking up for yourself

Chilling out

The following worksheets help children to learn how to chill out: *Look before you leap* (worksheet 22, p. 199) and *Choices & options* (worksheet 23, p. 200).

Chilling out is the opposite to being impulsively reactive. After a provocative or annoying event has occurred, chilling out involves the following:

1 STOP: Don't respond reactively, instead withhold action.
2 THINK: Take time to think about and to assess the event. Work out what seems to be the best way of behaving.
3 DO: Practise the way you wish to behave and then do it.

Look before you leap uses the STOP, THINK, DO, plan (Petersen and Gannoni, 1994), which is widely used by students in schools when experiencing difficulties with self-management. The worksheet encourages the child to identify behaviours which she might sometimes use, but which could lead to unsatisfactory consequences. When using this worksheet, the counsellor might work with the child to identify a particular situation which recurs in the child's life. A plan, using new behaviours, can then be developed by the child. After the child has carried out the plan, its effectiveness, in terms of outcome, can be evaluated. If the child believes that the plan was unsuccessful, then alternative solutions can be explored, a new plan devised, and the child can practise once again.

Choices & options allows a child to explore the consequences of alternative actions which can be taken at different points in time. It can be useful for the counsellor to invite the child to think about how she feels emotionally while she is making a choice at one of the decision boxes on the sheet. Thus, though the task is cognitive, the importance of recognizing emotional feelings when making decisions is highlighted. This is important, because choices can be heavily influenced by emotional responses.

Consequences

The following worksheets address the issue of consequences: *If – then – but* (worksheet 24, p. 201) and *Crime & punishment!* (worksheet 25, p. 202).

If a child is to be able to self manage her behaviour, then she will need to have a clear understanding of the nature and appropriateness of the consequences of behaviour. *If – then – but* is unique in that it invites children to explore both the positive and negative consequences of particular behaviours. The worksheet also helps the child to realize that by making some adaptive behavioural decisions, there may be some loss of immediate gratification. This worksheet can be used as a starting point to help the child to consider new choices and options, and to plan to use new and different behaviours. If the child then experiments with these new behaviours in her own environment between counselling sessions, the positive and negative outcomes can be subsequently evaluated. If necessary, a new plan can then be developed.

Crime & punishment! allows the child to examine his concept of the seriousness of particular unacceptable behaviours. It also allows the child to explore the appropriateness of consequences of, and punishments for certain behaviours.

Sticking up for yourself

The following worksheets help children to learn to stick up for themselves: *Saying, 'No' made easy* (worksheet 26, p. 203) and *Reward yourself* (worksheet 27, p. 204).

While the main thrust of exploring self-management is about restraining or restricting outbursts of aggressive or other inappropriate behaviour, it should be emphasized that self-management also means the child rewarding herself for her own positive achievements and valuing herself as a unique individual.

There are many situations where children feel pressured into behaving in ways which may compromise their own beliefs, values and ambitions. Good self-management must include the ability to say 'No', when it is appropriate to do so. However, saying 'No' to peers is not generally easy for children to do. It can result in the child being ostracized, being unpopular, being criticized, or being ridiculed by peers. *Saying 'No' made easy* gives the child some practical ways of responding to pressuring situations by peers. The worksheet allows the counsellor to explore with the child the ease with which he might be able to use some of the suggested statements. This worksheet can also be used to help the child to invent his own ways of saying 'No'.

Reward yourself allows the child to reinforce her own positive social accomplishments. In the shields the child can write or draw something she has done that she feels proud of. The worksheet also provides an opportunity for the child to practise telling somebody about her accomplishments in a way which is appropriate, acceptable, and likely to encourage further affirmation or reinforcement of positive behaviour.

Summary

In designing the worksheets in this chapter we chose the areas which we believe are the most significant in helping children to develop social skills. It is clear to us that there are many more behaviours, feelings and situations which could be usefully explored by using worksheets. Perhaps you, the reader, would like to design some worksheets of your own. Doing this could be both useful and satisfying.

◆ ◆ ◆ ◆ ◆ ◆ ◆

Find A Feeling

Draw a line from the sentence to the face to show how you would feel if . . .

My pet
was run over

I had a bad
secret which I
couldn't tell

My mother
talked to
the neighbour

I heard a
thumping
noise in the
middle of
the night

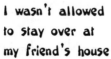

I wasn't allowed
to stay over at
my friend's house

I fell off my
bike in front
of my friends

I didn't study
for my spelling test

I was caught cheating
on my test

Worksheet 10

Artemus is Anxious !

Can you help Artemus find out what makes him feel anxious?

Artemus is a bit like you . . .

Draw a line from Artemus to the things which make him feel anxious.

- Going to the doctor or dentist

- Being called to the Principal's office

- Wondering whether Mum or Dad will be in a good mood tonight

- Not understanding the rules of a game

- Having to ask questions in class

- Remembering what time you have to be home

- The spelling test tomorrow

- . . . .

Worksheet 11

Guess what ?

Your Body

We can guess how people feel from the way they use their bodies and the expressions on their faces.

How do these people feel?

Circle the body part used to express the feeling.

THE VOLCANO

What makes you angry?

I get angry when . . . .

Find the spot on the volcano which is most like you when you get angry.

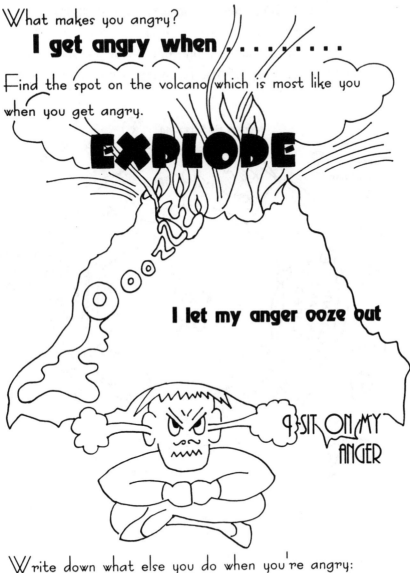

EXPLODE

I let my anger ooze out

SIT ON MY ANGER

Write down what else you do when you're angry:

. . . .

Worksheet 14

Fighting FEAR with Felix

Everyone feels frightened sometimes. Some things are more scary than others. Draw a red line from Felix's head to a spot on the life saver to show what you would do in each of the following scenes if you were scared.

Conversation starters

Put a tick in the box next to the conversation starters which would be OK to use on your first day at a new school.

. . . . what's wrong with the conversation starters you haven't ticked?

Worksheet 16

?? QUESTIONS ??

Look at this picture. Ask three questions beginning with:

a) What . . . . . .   d) When . . . . . .

b) Where . . . . .   e) Why . . . .

c) How . . . .   f) Who . . . .

to find out more about it.

Worksheet 17

Advice for JIM

Jim needs help. He has a brother who always gets to go with Uncle Ben. Jim's brother is often invited to spend the night with Uncle Ben, so that he can get up early and help his uncle on the farm.

Every time Jim asks to go, Uncle Ben says, 'Next time. You're a bit young yet.'

- What do you do when you feel left out?
- Put a circle around your answers.

GET ANGRY

Cry

Make a FUSS, so that people pay attention

TELL SOMEONE
HOW I FEEL

Don't say anything

Worksheet 18

GERTRUDE & GROMMET GUMBO
THE GOSSIPS

The Gumbos say untrue things about people to other people
= THEY GOSSIP =
Gossiping can hurt and make you feel left out.

If people ask you questions about others you might get caught gossiping.
Here's a good rule:

> IF YOU CAN'T SAY SOMETHING NICE - DON'T SAY ANYTHING AT ALL

Tick the things you could do or say if people try to gossip.

☐ 'Let's talk about something else.'

☐ 'I don't know them very well, so I can't know if that's true.'

☐ 'I think you're gossiping.'

Tick the things you could do if people gossip about you.

☐ Gossip about them (it would serve them right!).

☐ Talk to the 'Gumbo' gossipers, and ask them not to gossip.

☐ Ask someone to help you to solve your problem.

Worksheet 19

FIGHTING !! ! ! !

Fights happen when people:

TEASE	GOSSIP	TELL TALES
CHEAT	STEAL	SHOVE
BULLY	LIE	HIT
BREAK PROMISES	SHOW OFF	DON'T BELIEVE

See if you can find these words in the square below and circle them:

A	N	C	F	H	M	P	Q	U	W	A	B
B	R	E	A	K	P	R	O	M	I	S	E
Z	L	B	U	L	L	Y	A	T	S	P	Q
F	G	K	T	E	L	L	T	A	L	E	S
O	E	S	T	E	A	L	O	Q	F	R	S
G	L	C	Z	X	D	S	P	A	W	K	I
M	R	H	F	S	C	H	I	T	L	O	A
P	N	E	B	K	G	O	S	S	I	P	W
W	I	A	D	P	H	V	X	Z	E	D	J
Z	D	T	E	A	S	E	J	B	A	J	Z
K	S	H	O	W	O	F	F	H	W	B	I
X	D	O	N	T	B	E	L	I	E	V	E

When you were in a fight, what caused it? . . . .

. . . .

. . . .

Can you think of any more reasons why fights happen? . . . .

. . . .

Worksheet 20

TERRY, TYRONE AND ME

We can choose to respond to people who want to fight by asserting ourselves in a firm but non-threatening way.

Join the dots to find Terry.

What do you think would happen if Terry got into a fight?

Join the dots to find Tyrone.

What do you think would happen if Tyrone got into a fight?

Write on the dotted lines what you would do if you got into a fight.

Worksheet 21

LOOK BEFORE YOU LEAP

	True	False
* Sometimes I say things & later regret it --------------	☐	☐
* Sometimes I make a decision without thinking ---	☐	☐
* Sometimes I do things without listening to the rules -------------------------	☐	☐
* Sometimes I go ahead without reading the instructions -----------------	☐	☐
* Sometimes I don't listen to both sides of the argument -------------------------------	☐	☐
* Sometimes I make arrangements without listening to the details -----	☐	☐
* Sometimes I take messages and leave out most of the information ---	☐	☐

If you answered 'True' for 5 or more of the above then you need to 'chill out'

Chilling out means going slow, not hurrying and using the
STOP - THINK - DO plan.

STOP - and discover what the problem or task is.

THINK - of three things you can do to solve the problem or task.

DO - Choose the one which is best for you.

Worksheet 22

Choices & Options

There are many ways to respond when we have trouble with our friends.

* Take a coloured pen & trace the path you would like to take if you were Sue. At each decision box, think about how you might feel when making a choice.

* In a different colour trace a path you would like to try.

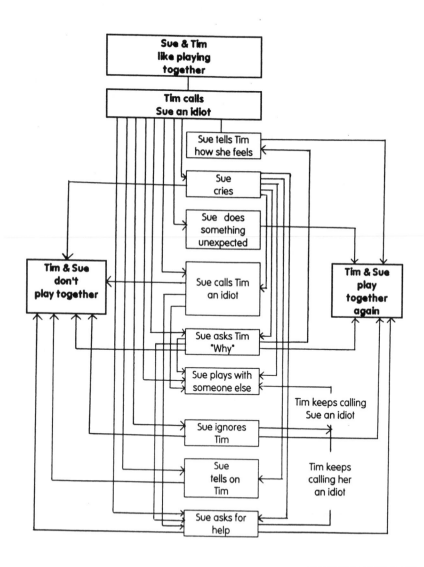

Worksheet 23

If = Then = But

Fill in the blanks! Here is an example:

If I borrowed my mum's bike without permission,
Then . . . I would get to the video shop faster,
But . . . I'd probably be grounded for the weekend.

Now fill in the missing parts of the following 'if - then - buts'.

If I cheated in my spelling test,
Then . . .
But . . .

If I skipped school tomorrow,
Then . . .
But . . .

If I tell my best friend that she hurt my feelings,
Then . . .
But . . .

If I spend all the money I earned doing jobs, on one item,
Then . . .
But . . .

If I tell this secret I have,
Then . . .
But . . .

If I stay home and study for my test,
Then . . .
But . . .

Worksheet 24

CRIME & PUNISHMENT !

Here is a list of behaviours. Some are worse than others. The really bad behaviours would probably result in severe consequences.

- Rearrange the list in order of the worst to the mildest.
- On your list, write the punishment or consequence, which you believe fits the 'crime'.

CRIME	My list	Consequence
Murder		
Back-chatting		
Hitting		
Lying		
Stealing		
Interrupting		
Disobeying		
Bullying		
Name calling		
Gossiping		
Cheating		
Keeping secrets		
Telling tales		
Changing your mind		

Worksheet 25

Saying 'No' ... *made easy*

Match the responses you would use to the requests!
Draw a line to join them together.

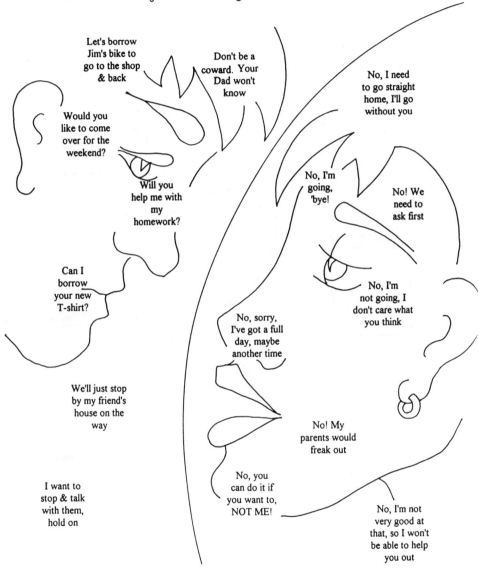

Let's borrow Jim's bike to go to the shop & back

Don't be a coward. Your Dad won't know

No, I need to go straight home, I'll go without you

Would you like to come over for the weekend?

Will you help me with my homework?

No, I'm going, 'bye!

No! We need to ask first

Can I borrow your new T-shirt?

No, sorry, I've got a full day, maybe another time

No, I'm not going, I don't care what you think

We'll just stop by my friend's house on the way

No! My parents would freak out

I want to stop & talk with them, hold on

No, you can do it if you want to, NOT ME!

No, I'm not very good at that, so I won't be able to help you out

Worksheet 26

REWARD YOURSELF

We often don't realize that we can be proud of many of the things we do or say. In each of the shields below, write or draw something you feel proud of, and could tell somebody about.

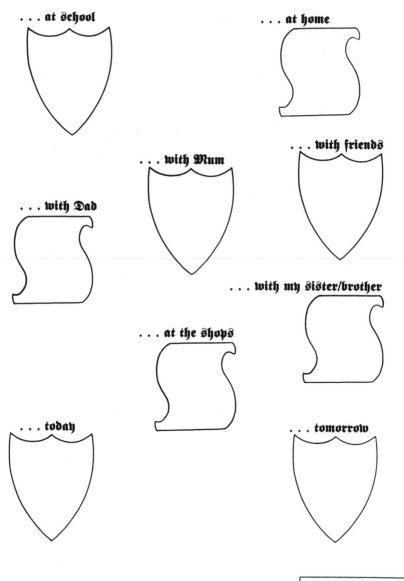

... at school

... at home

... with Mum

... with friends

... with Dad

... with my sister/brother

... at the shops

... today

... tomorrow

Worksheet 27

28 Education in protective behaviours

Protective behaviours education involves giving children the message, 'Look after yourself and keep yourself safe from harm and potential danger.' If children are to respond appropriately to this message, then they need to be able to:

1 Understand appropriate boundaries.
2 Be able to protect themselves from physical harm.
3 Be able to protect themselves from emotional harm.

1 Helping children to understand appropriate boundaries

If children are to be safe, and to feel safe, then they need to have a clear understanding of what boundaries are normal, desirable and acceptable in our society. They also need to understand the limits, expectations and behaviours relevant to those boundaries. Once children have this understanding they are more likely to be able to make decisions and to take action to live within and to protect those boundaries.

When helping children we need to consider developmental, family, social and cultural boundaries.

Developmental boundaries

As a child grows older and moves through the normal developmental stages, her social, emotional and physical boundaries change. When a child is an infant many people may be actively involved in physically caring for her: they may feed her, bath her and change her nappy. People from outside the family circle may, at times, play with her. Sometimes admiring strangers may touch her or hold her. As the child grows older she will become more discriminating and will start to set boundaries of her own. She will start to express her wishes about who should meet her physical, emotional and social needs. As the child begins to set her own boundaries, others are likely to become more respectful and less intrusive, particularly with regard to intimate needs. Certainly, children aged four or five are generally less accepting of strangers, and do not like them intruding on their physical or emotional space. Children in this age group are unlikely to be comfortable if a stranger gives them a cuddle or takes them to the toilet.

Developmentally appropriate changes to boundaries occur right through to adulthood, when intimate physical experiences are limited to partners, spouses, girlfriends and boyfriends.

When teaching protective behaviours, we must take account of those boundaries which are developmentally appropriate. It can also be important for a child to understand that behaviours which are not acceptable now may be acceptable later, when the child grows up and enters teenage or adult relationships. Similarly, she needs to understand that boundaries and behaviours which were acceptable when she was younger may not be acceptable now.

Family boundaries

Ideas about family boundaries are usually transmitted from generation to generation. What was acceptable in a mother's family of origin, or in a father's, is likely to be acceptable in the child's family. However, problems sometimes arise where a mother and father come from families with different attitudes and standards. It might be interesting for you, the reader, to think about your own family and identify which boundaries and behaviours have been passed down from a previous generation, and which ones are new.

Families vary, from those which are disengaged with very tight boundaries, at one extreme, to those at the opposite extreme, which are very enmeshed and have open and flexible boundaries.

In a disengaged family, the family is generally seen to be an independent nuclear family, which as a group does not socialize much with outsiders. Individuals within the family may function fairly independently, and there may be little communication.

By contrast, many enmeshed families live more of a community lifestyle. They extend their family to include relationships with aunts, uncles, cousins and friends, and may frequently engage in large family gatherings. Children in such families may freely and easily spend time with any of the members of their extended family. Possessions may be shared, holiday times may be spent together, and in times of need distant family members may be approached for help. Some people clearly enjoy this extended family atmosphere. However, for other people the lack of clear boundaries can be confusing and overwhelming.

When working with children on protective behaviours, it is essential to recognize the nature of the family system within which the child lives. We believe that often it is necessary to involve parents with their children in protective behaviours education. By doing this, the parents can be involved in the development of strategies for setting and maintaining sensible boundaries that provide safety and will also be acceptable in their particular family environment. Without parental cooperation, the child may be set up for failure.

Social boundaries

Social boundaries are those boundaries which are generally accepted as being socially appropriate in contemporary society. Some of the most important of these boundaries are enshrined in legislation. For example, there are laws which prohibit the expression of a variety of behaviours in public. Physical assault on one person by another is illegal. A sexual relationship between an adult and a child is illegal.

Social boundaries are most likely to be violated when family and cultural boundaries are strong, pervasive, and different from socially accepted norms. Consequently, counsellors may need to help a child, and/or the child's parents, to recognize differences between social and family expectations, so that sensible decisions can be made with regard to appropriate boundaries.

Cultural boundaries

Cultural boundaries are based on beliefs and values specific to a particular cultural or religious setting. People in different parts of the world have very different values and attitudes with regard to appropriate child behaviours and with regard to appropriate parenting strategies. What is permissible sexually and physically varies from culture to culture. Similarly, differences in what are considered to be appropriate boundaries are evident between people from different religions, and between people who are religious and those who are not.

Violation of cultural boundaries often has social consequences and therefore can result in significant emotional trauma. When counselling children, we need to remember that we will not be effective if we ignore cultural norms. Clearly, we all have our own personal values, and should use whatever opportunities we have to create a fairer and happier world. However, as counsellors we must recognize and validate cultural boundaries and thus be in a position to challenge them by suggesting changes, when it is appropriate and when the opportunity arises.

2 Helping children to protect themselves from physical harm

Part of protective behaviours education involves helping children to develop skills to protect themselves from physical harm. Situations where physical harm could occur might involve any of the following:

- Domestic violence
- Sexual abuse
- Peer pressure
- Peer relationships

Domestic violence

Often in families where there is violence between parents, children are not only witnesses of this violence, but are also subjected to physical abuse themselves. Sometimes children find themselves in situations where they try to prevent violence from occurring between their parents. In such situations they are at risk of being harmed physically, either intentionally or accidentally. Children are also at risk of physical abuse in families where parents or siblings have poor anger management strategies.

Children in situations such as those described need counselling help to assist them to develop protective behaviour plans which can be used in times of danger. Clearly, it is desirable for parents to be involved in the construction of such plans so that their children are assured of their support.

Sexual abuse

Sexual abuse involves misuse of power and control, making it hard for children to protect themselves because they do not have adult physical strength. Perpetrators may threaten to harm children physically if they attempt to resist, or if they disclose abuse. When sexual abuse occurs there is a high risk of physical harm. Perpetrators often penetrate the bodies of both female and male children, causing physical injury. Some perpetrators of sexual abuse use seductive techniques which can be confusing for a child. This confusion is exacerbated if the child is unsure about appropriate boundaries.

Counsellors need to educate children with regard to appropriate sexual boundaries, and to help them to develop strategies for protecting these boundaries. They also need to empower children so that they are able to report instances of inappropriate behaviour.

Peer pressure

Most children want to be accepted by their peers and are therefore highly susceptible to peer pressure. This is particularly true for pre-adolescent children. Consequently, children will often respond to dares and bets in ways which require them to perform physically in situations where they have limited skills or experience. For example, if a child swings on a rope over a waterfall, to prove that he is brave or courageous, he may incur serious injury. It follows that protective behaviours education must include information about how to resist inappropriate peer pressure.

Peer relationships

Social relationships among children focus heavily on being accepted, being popular, being brave, being tough, having skills, and having other attributes perceived by children as 'desirable'. Children often find themselves in situations where they are challenged and need to protect themselves physically from others. They are especially vulnerable in school playgrounds, where peer relationships can involve undesirable behaviours, such as bullying by individuals or groups.

As part of protective behaviours education, children need to learn skills and strategies to deal with the possibility of being harmed physically by peers.

3 Helping children to protect themselves from emotional harm

When children are young their emotional needs are usually met by adults. However, as children grow older they become more responsible for meeting their own emotional needs and need to develop skills to enable them to do this. They also need to learn skills to avoid emotional trauma whenever possible and to deal with it when it does occur.

For children emotional harm frequently occurs as a result of:

- Keeping secrets
- Being victimized
- Poor communication skills and lack of assertiveness

Keeping secrets

Sharing secrets is a strategy often used by younger children when developing 'best friend' relationships. This strategy allows children to signal to their peers that a relationship is exclusive. It is developmentally appropriate for young children to behave in this way, and such secrets generally don't cause problems for them. However, secrets between adults and children often cause marked emotional distress, especially when the secret involves the violation of social, family or cultural boundaries.

In families where violence is occurring, children often feel unable to talk about it to people outside the family. They feel compelled to keep the violent behaviour a secret, either because they are ashamed of it, or because they are afraid that there may be unpleasant consequences if they tell others. A child may also feel obliged to be supportive of one parent's behaviours even if these violate appropriate boundaries.

An important component of protective behaviours education is to help children to realize that having secrets can cause problems, and to help them to feel OK about divulging secret information, when that is appropriate.

Being victimized

For a variety of reasons children often find themselves as victims. In families, they may be victimized because they are the youngest, because they are the only female or male in the family, because they are the oldest, or because certain characteristics or behaviours have been attributed to them. At school, children may be victimized because they are the fattest, the thinnest, the slowest, the clumsiest, because they wear glasses, or because they have a disability. Behaviours and characteristics which are perceived negatively are often attributed to such children. Consequently they may be stereotyped as victims and may be unable to challenge the stereotype and the recurring victimization. As a result they commonly develop maladaptive behaviours such as becoming aggressive or over-compliant. This inevitably has emotional implications for future relationships and behaviours.

Communication skills

Children frequently suffer emotional trauma because they have poor communication skills and are unable to express their feelings or talk about their needs and worries. Children who are unable to discuss important issues with others may develop self-destructive beliefs which are emotionally damaging for them. They may also develop maladaptive behaviours in order to cope.

Children who have poor communication skills are unlikely to have the ability to stand up for themselves and to assert their rights. In situations involving peers or adults, this lack of assertiveness can result in feelings of helplessness and powerlessness, and in a perception of not being in control. Protective behaviours education should include some training in communication skills, in particular with regard to assertiveness.

The use of worksheets for education in protective behaviours

Following from the previous discussion, it is clear that children need to be able to make decisions so that outcomes for them will be positive in terms

Table 28.1   *Protective behaviours education worksheets*

Issue addressed	Worksheet number	Title	Page number
Boundaries	28	*Ages & stages*	213
	29	*My place, my space*	214
	30	*Rainbow road*	215
Behaviours for physical protection	31	*My safety plan*	216
	32	*Biffin the bully*	217
	33	*The 3 A's*	218
Behaviours for emotional protection	34	*Surpises & secrets*	219
	35	*From blame to fame!*	220
	36	*Crystal ball*	221

of their physical and emotional safety. They also need to have skills to solve problems if their physical or emotional safety is threatened, and to understand what behaviours are acceptable in society and what behaviours are not. They need to develop an understanding of limits, expectations and boundaries. Thus, if children are to develop protective behaviours, they must learn problem-solving skills, decision-making skills, and how to set appropriate boundaries.

We believe that these skills can be achieved through the use of work-sheets, and have designed worksheets to cover the following three specific areas (see Table 28.1):

1   Setting appropriate boundaries
2   Behaviours for physical protection
3   Behaviours for emotional protection

As before, the worksheets are intended to provide the stimulus for discussion of the relevant issues.

Setting appropriate boundaries

When helping a child to set appropriate boundaries we need to take account of the developmental needs of the child, and to consider the child's family system and wider social system. Additionally, we need to help the child to gain decision-making and problem-solving skills. We have taken all of these factors into account in the design of the following worksheets: *Ages & stages* (worksheet 28, p. 213), *My place, my space* (worksheet 29, p. 214) and *Rainbow road* (worksheet 30, p. 215).

Ages & stages presents three vignettes of situations which children might experience and invites a child to consider and to discuss the decisions that children of various ages would need to make. Consequently, the child is encouraged to recognize that appropriate decisions, relevant to a particular situation, might be different for children of different ages. For example, in vignette number one it would be developmentally appropriate for a young child to keep the door locked and seek an adult's help, whereas a teenage child might ask the stranger what he wants, while still protecting himself from danger.

My place, my space explores the issue of privacy within the home. It invites a child to consider what are appropriate personal boundaries, for children of different ages, within a family setting.

Rainbow road is designed to help children to explore social boundaries, and to consider the appropriate responses to the variety of people with whom they may come into contact. Children who have a poor under-standing of appropriate social boundaries are indiscriminate about the ways in which they greet and relate to strangers, or distant associates of their family. By colouring in the blocks at the top of this worksheet, using the rainbow sequence suggested, the child can visually recognize the continuum from intimate closeness to distant relationship. As the child colours in the 'road' from the START box, travelling in a spiral, the colours generally follow a rainbow sequence. However, this sequence is sometimes inter-rupted, highlighting the need to be alert in recognizing situations in which clear boundaries are needed, or when more open boundaries are acceptable. For example, when a child visits the doctor, personal touching for specific medical purposes is acceptable, even though the doctor may not be a close family member.

Behaviours for physical protection

The three worksheets here focus on domestic violence, peer pressure and sexual abuse. The worksheets are: *My safety plan* (worksheet 31, p. 216), *Biffin the bully* (worksheet 32, p. 217), and *The three A's – Alert! Avoid! & Action!* (worksheet 33, p. 218).

My safety plan is designed to help children to explore possible outcomes if they become involved in violent or physically threatening situations. It is specifically designed for use with children from violent homes, where it is often difficult for children to know whether to protect themselves or to defend the victim of the violence. The worksheet provides an opportunity for counsellors to help children to realize that the perpetrators of violence are solely responsible for the violence. The worksheet also encourages children to develop individual protection plans for their personal safety.

Biffin the bully aims to help children to label abusive behaviour. Clearly, even though abuse at any level is not OK, some abusive behaviour is not as severe as other abusive behaviour. Using this worksheet, the child is invited to plot abusive behaviours on a continuum from least serious to most serious. The child's attention can then be drawn to the fact that all of the abusive behaviours have been plotted within the international symbol which signifies, 'Not Permitted'. A strong message is therefore given that *all abusive behaviour is unacceptable*, no matter how minor it may be. Although the abusive behaviours are attributed to Biffin the bully, the child is invited to consider the possibility that Biffin may change. Hence the child can be encouraged to see that it is the behaviour and not the person who is to be criticized. While using the worksheet the child can be invited to think about and discuss bullying behaviour she might encounter at school.

The Three A's – Alert! Avoid! & Action! targets the protective behaviours which a child might need to use when encountering strangers, or in situations that might be antecedents for sexual abuse. The emphasis is on encouraging the child to be alert to the possibility of danger. The worksheet provides a list of questions the child can ask herself, in order to make the best decisions, when encountering possible threatening situations. After considering the questions, the child is invited to find a way through a maze in which she can either avoid danger by choosing her route carefully, or take action to deal with risky situations. Use of the worksheet gives the child strong permission to avoid situations that may be risky. It also invites her to think about what action she could take if she were to find herself in a potentially dangerous situation.

Behaviours for emotional protection

When exploring behaviours to prevent emotional trauma we will focus on secrets, victimization and communication skills using the worksheets: *Surprises & secrets* (worksheet 34, p. 219), *From blame to fame!* (worksheet 35, p. 220) and *Crystal ball* (worksheet 36, p. 221).

Surprises & secrets can be used to help a child to understand that surprises can be pleasurable, whereas keeping secrets can be uncomfortable. The child can then explore the idea that some secrets are not OK, and can consider the consequences of keeping, or disclosing, such secrets.

From blame to fame! explores the issue of victimization. Often, children who see themselves as victims believe that they are trapped in this role, and that there is no possibility of change. The worksheet promotes a more positive outlook by encouraging the child to construct assertive statements which could result in moving the characters in the illustrations from a 'victim' position to a 'hero' position. When using the worksheet, the child is first asked to imagine what each character in the illustrations might be thinking, feeling, and might like. We suggest that the counsellor should next invite the child to nominate a powerful hero (e.g. Catwoman or Superman). The child can then be asked what that hero might say, using assertive statements beginning with the words, 'I think . . .', 'I feel . . .', and 'I would like . . .', with reference to each illustration.

Crystal ball encourages children to verbalize their needs and to ask for things they have a right to have, rather than hoping that other people will guess or mind-read. The worksheet helps children to explore the pitfalls of guessing how others might feel, or might want. It helps children to recognize that other people too are unlikely to be able to guess what it is that they themselves need or want. Consequently they can learn that in order to get their needs met, they must state them clearly and firmly.

Ages & Stages

4 YEARS OLD: Miffy is 4 years old. Help Miffy to make the right decision about what to do when someone knocks on the door.

Smile & invite the stranger inside

Open the door & go & get a grown-up

Slam the door shut & run away

What would Taffy do?
What would Vanda do?

8 YEARS OLD: Taffy is 8 years old. Help Taffy to make the right decision about how to respond to Mr Nice at Church on Sunday.

Let him put his arm around me & ruffle my hair like he always does

Avoid him all morning. I could hide behind the wall!!

What would Miffy do?
What would Vanda do?

14 YEARS OLD: Help Vanda make the right decision about how to respond to Burford, a new friend, next door.

I'll let him kiss me today

We can stay out late & talk

I'm going to ignore him completely

What would Miffy do?
What would Taffy do?

Worksheet 28

My Place, My Space

Test your respect for privacy by circling true or false in response to the following questions:

- Toby is two years old. He should be allowed to bath on his own so that he has privacy.

    True   False

- Tina is sixteen years old. She needs to be able to spend time alone in her room if she wants to.

    True   False

- Simon is nine years old. If his bedroom door is closed, members of his family should knock before going in.

    True   False

- Mum & Dad should always be supervised by someone when they are together.

    True   False

- Samantha is thirteen years old. Everyone in the family should be allowed to read her diary without asking.

    True   False

- Matthew is four years old. When he is playing alone in the front yard his family should leave him by himself if he tells them to go away.

    True   False

- Roberta is seven years old. She should always let her uncle shower with her when he is visiting.

    True   False

Worksheet 29

RAINBOW ROAD

The boxes below represent the different ways in which we greet, or make contact with other people. Colour the boxes in as indicated.

Touch private places (Red)	Cuddle (Orange)	Hug (Yellow)	Shake hands (Green)	Wave (Blue)	Watch (Dark blue)	Ignore (Purple)

Sophie is your age & she is getting ready to go out. Along the way, she will meet many people. Sophie will need to decide how to greet these people. Can you help her? Follow Sophie's journey from the START box below. As you go, colour each box to match with the colours above, to show how you think Sophie should greet the people on her journey.

DR DRAKE	TAXI DRIVER	LADY AT THE BUS STOP	TICKET SELLER	MAN WALKING HIS DOG
BUS DRIVER	DAD	AUNTY JO	UNCLE BOB	MAN IN A CAR
SHOP KEEPER	MUM	START ME	NEIGHBOUR	
DAY CARE PERSON	TEACHER	BEST FRIEND	BOY NEXT DOOR	

My SAFETY Plan

Sometimes in families where adults fight, younger children may also get hurt. Mason lives in a family like this. Below are plans that Mason could use to look after himself. Follow the path that you think will lead to the best SAFETY PLAN for Mason, so that he can protect himself from being hurt.

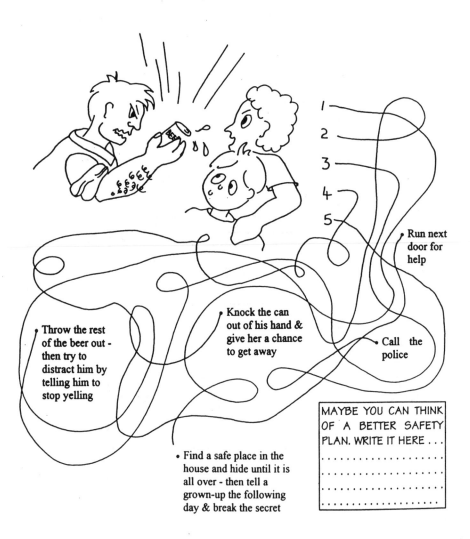

1
2
3
4
5

• Run next door for help

• Throw the rest of the beer out - then try to distract him by telling him to stop yelling

• Knock the can out of his hand & give her a chance to get away

• Call the police

MAYBE YOU CAN THINK OF A BETTER SAFETY PLAN. WRITE IT HERE . . .
. . . .
. . . .
. . . .
. . . .

• Find a safe place in the house and hide until it is all over - then tell a grown-up the following day & break the secret

Worksheet 31

BIFFIN THE BULLY

The words outside the circle describe abusive acts, things that BIFFIN THE BULLY might do.

Write each word along the line inside the circle. Place the words on the line from left to right according to how serious you think the abuse is.

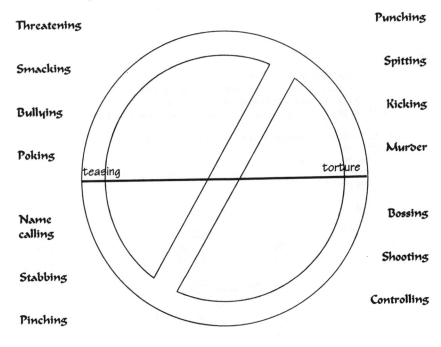

Threatening   Punching

Smacking   Spitting

Bullying   Kicking

Poking   Murder

teasing   torture

Name   Bossing
calling

Stabbing   Shooting

Pinching   Controlling

Making rude faces   Hair pulling

- Did you notice that all the words are now inside a symbol which means 'not permitted'?
- How many of these behaviours happen at your school?
- Can you add any other bullying behaviours?

- DO YOU THINK THAT 'BIFFIN THE BULLY' CAN CHANGE ?

Worksheet 32

The three A's – ALERT! AVOID! & ACTION!

Keeping physically safe sometimes means knowing how to protect your body from being hurt even when everything 'seems' OK. Have you ever felt as though you know that something isn't right but you can't put your finger on it? Taking notice of that feeling is called being *ALERT*.

Find your way through the maze below. You can *AVOID* risky situations by taking a path without obstacles. Alternatively, you can deal with obstacles by making decisions and then taking *ACTION* in order to stay safe.

As you travel through the maze, ask yourself these questions:

QUESTIONS:
- Is this person someone I know?
- When I am with this person do I feel safe and not worried?
- Will I be able to get help if things get out of control?
- Does Mum or Dad or someone else I can trust know where I am and will be?

If the answer to any of these questions is 'No', then use one of the following options:

OPTIONS:
- Say, 'No, stop that!'
- Make a fuss.
- Tell an adult

- Walk away
- Run to the nearest safety house
- . . . .

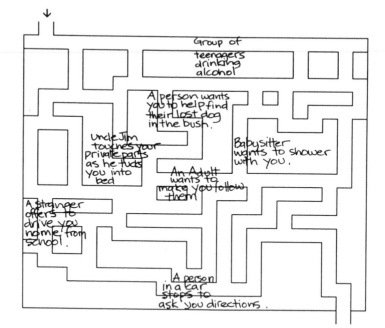

SURPRISES & SECRETS

Does Arthur have a secret or a surprise?
. . . .

Is it a good one?
. . . .

How does Arthur feel?
. . . .

Should Arthur tell?
. . . .

If Arthur tells what might happen?. . . . .
How will Arthur feel then? . . . .

Does Jenny have a secret or a surprise?
. . . .

Is it a good one?
. . . .

How does Jenny feel?
. . . .

Should Jenny tell? .
. . . .

If Jenny tells what might happen?. . . . .
How will Jenny feel then? . . . .

Does Dorothy have a secret or a surprise?
. . . .

Is it a good one?. . . . . .
. . . .

How does Dorothy feel?
. . . .

Should Dorothy tell? . . . .
. . . .

If Dorothy tells what might happen?. . . . .
How will Dorothy feel then? . . . .

QUESTIONS TO ANSWER:
* Is there a difference between secrets and surprises?
* What is the difference?
* Are there good secrets and bad secrets?
* Are there good surprises and bad surprises?

Worksheet 34

From BLAME to **FAME !**

Sometimes when we feel picked on, we blame others for how we feel and behave.
If we tackle the problem ourselves, we generally feel better.

Making statements that begin with:

* I think . . . . . .
* I feel . . . .
* I would like it if . . . . .

is a good way to start.

What do you think that you would say in the examples below?

	♦ Tony thinks that Bosco expects him to fetch things for him all the time.	I think . . . . . .
	♦ It makes him feel used & worthless.	I feel . . . .
	♦ He'd like to help Bosco sometimes but would like to say, "No" at other times.	I would like it if . . . .
	♦ He'd also like Bosco to say, "Please", & "Thankyou".	
	♣ Jack is the youngest in the family and **always** has to clean the family's shoes.	I think . . . . . .
	♣ His brothers did do this when they were his age.	I feel . . . .
	♣ He feels like he's missing out on doing other things, and also that this job isn't very important.	I would like it if . . . .
	♣ He'd like to do a different job sometimes, instead of the same one over and over.	
	♥ Tina is the only girl in the family.	I think . . . . . .
	♥ She is always having to look after her younger brother when her parents are busy.	
	♥ Tina loves her brother, but she doesn't get much time for herself & her friends.	I feel . . . .
	♥ Tina has 2 older brothers. They all get along with their baby brother really well.	I would like it if . . . .

Worksheet 35

CRYSTAL BALL

- By looking into the crystal ball you might GUESS how Kristel is feeling & also guess what it is that she wants.

- What could Kristel say so that you would KNOW what she felt and wanted?

Worksheet 36

PART 6
IN CONCLUSION

Although we have written this book as an introductory text we hope it will be a useful resource for both new workers and experienced counsellors by providing ideas for engaging children in the counselling process and helping them to work through issues. We hope that readers will be able to join their ideas together with ours for a useful purpose.

We have a strong belief in individual difference and in the need to respect the ideas of others. We realize that our readers may have strong commitments to particular theoretical frameworks and therapeutic models. However, we are hopeful that many of the ideas we have described in Parts 3, 4 and 5 can be adapted to suit different ways of working. We also realize that counselling approaches need to be varied to suit specific cultures, lifestyles, beliefs and values. We have not addressed particular cultural issues in this book but in this regard refer you to Ivey et al. (1993).

We respect the contributions made by different professions to the work of counselling children and have a strong preference for work with children to occur in multi-disciplinary teams wherever possible. Perhaps this is because we are convinced that our own personal differences as occupational therapist and psychologist have been significant in helping us to enhance the quality of the work we do with children.

We would like to reiterate that we do not believe that counselling children should be restricted to one profession or one environment. Often the counselling needs of a child can be met in the child's own environment by those workers, of whatever profession, who have direct access to that environment. For example, we have found that workers in women's refuges are often able to address a child's immediate needs. Similarly, teachers and counsellors in schools, and nurses and medical officers in hospitals, are generally able to provide a level of immediate counselling help which is especially useful because it addresses the child's needs within her own context. Nevertheless, it is important for workers to recognize their own limitations and to refer children to professionals with more specialized experience and skills when necessary.

We recognize that counsellors in many settings do not have the high standard of facilities which we enjoy in our private practice and in the Health Department where we work as child psychotherapists. However, these facilities are not essential. A counsellor armed with drawing paper and pens (see Chapter 20), a box of miniature animals (see Chapter 17), a box of symbols (see Chapter 18), and a few books has all the basic tools needed for useful counselling interventions to occur in any available space. This may not be ideal but we do not live in an ideal world and a counsellor with some portable aids can be of considerable help in enabling children to tell their story and thus to feel better.

Individual work with children may not always be the best approach. Sometimes family therapy can be more appropriate. We have found that an openness to working in different ways has been most useful. For example, although we generally work individually with children, we also make use of family therapy, couple counselling, parenting education, and individual psychotherapeutic work with parents, in seeking to address children's emotional and behavioural problems. Generally, we like to involve the parents, the child and the family in deciding which approach or combination of approaches to use. Sometimes we find ourselves acting simply in the role of case manager, coordinating resources available in the community with occasional follow-up.

Finally, we would like to stress the importance of training and supervision. This book is not intended to be sufficient in itself, rather it is a source of ideas. We believe that counsellors of children need to be properly trained by experienced and qualified professionals. Additionally we believe that all counsellors of children need ongoing professional supervision to ensure the quality of their work and to address the needs of specific children. Even though we, the authors, are both experienced counsellors, we still regularly discuss individual cases with another competent professional in order to get a different perspective and to keep a check on the influence of our own personal issues. Whether we like to admit it or not, our own issues will from time to time interfere with our counselling work. A good professional supervisor can identify these issues and help us address them so that they will be resolved and will not continue to interfere with our counselling work.

Bibliography

Adler, A. (1964) *Social Interest: a Challenge to Mankind*. New York: Capricorn.

Axline, V. (1947) *Play Therapy*. Boston: Houghton Mifflin.

Ayers, J. and James, C. (1986) *It's OK to Say NO*. New York: Creative Child Press.

Bandler, R. (1985) *Using Your Brain for a CHANGE – Neuro-linguistic Programming*. Moab: Real People Press.

Bandler, R. and Grinder, J. (1982) *Reframing*. Moab: Real People Press.

Bauer, G. and Kobos, J. (1995) *Brief Therapy: Short Term Psychodynamic Intervention*. New Jersey: Aronson.

Bowlby, J. (1969) *Attachment*. New York: Basic Books.

Bowlby, J. (1988) *A Secure Base*. New York: Basic Books.

Cade, B. (1993) *A Brief Guide to Brief Therapy*. New York: Norton.

Cattanach, A. (1992) *Play Therapy with Abused Children*. London: Jessica Kingsley.

Christ, G.H., Siegel, K., Mesagno, F. and Langosch, D. (1991) 'A preventative program for bereaved children: problems of implementation', *Journal of Orthopsychiatry*, 61: 168–78.

Clarkson, P. (1989) *Gestalt Counselling in Action*. London: Sage.

Corsini, R.J. and Wedding, D. (1989) *Current Psychotherapies*, 4th edition. Illinois: Peacock.

Dale, F.M. (1990) 'The psychoanalytic psychotherapy of children with emotional and behavioural difficulties', in V.P. Varma (ed.), *The Management of Children with Emotional and Behavioural Difficulties*. London: Routledge.

De Shazer, S. (1985) *Keys to Solution in Brief Therapy*. New York: Norton.

Dryden, W. (1990) *Rational Emotive Counselling in Action*. London: Sage.

Erikson, E. (1967) *Childhood and Society*, 2nd edition. London: Penguin.

Freud, A. (1928) *Introduction to the Technique of Child Analysis*, trans. L.P. Clark. New York: Nervous and Mental Disease Publishing.

Gardner, R.A. (1974) *Dr Gardner's Fairy Tales for Today's Children*. Englewood Cliffs, NJ: Prentice-Hall.

Geldard, D. (1993) *Basic Personal Counselling*, 2nd edition. Sydney: Prentice-Hall.

Gil, E. (1991) *The Healing Power of Play*. New York: Guilford Press.

Glasser, W. (1965) *Reality Therapy*. New York: Harper and Row.

Havighurst, R.J. (1972) *Developmental Tasks and Education*, 3rd edition. New York: McKay.

Heidemann, S. and Hewitt, D. (1992) *Pathways to Play*. Minnesota: Redleaf Press.

Ivey, M., Ivey, A. and Simek-Morgan, L. (1993) *Counselling and Psychotherapy – a Multicultural Perspective*. Needham Heights, MA: Simon and Schuster.

James, B. (1989) *Treating Traumatised Children*. Lexington, MA: Lexington Books.

Jung, C. (1933) *Modern Man in Search of a Soul*. New York: Harcourt Brace.

Klein, M. (1932) *Psychoanalysis of Children*. London: Hogarth Press.

Kohlberg, L. (1969) 'Stage and sequence: the cognitive developmental approach to socialization', in D. Groslin (ed.), *Handbook of Socialization Theory and Research*. Chicago: Rand McNally.

Lazarus, A. and Fay, A. (1990) 'Brief psychotherapy: tautology or oxymoron?', in J. Zeig and S. Gilligan (eds), *Brief Therapy: Myths, Methods and Metaphors*. New York: Brunner/Mazel.

Lowenfeld, M. (1967) *Play in Childhood*. New York: Wiley.

McMahon, L. (1992) *The Handbook of Play Therapy*. London: Routledge.

Maslow, A.H. (1954) *Motivation and Personality*. New York: Harper.

Millman, H. and Schaefer, C.E. (1977) *Therapies for Children*. San Francisco: Jossey-Bass.

Moustakas, C.E. (1973) *Children in Play Therapy*. New York: Aronson.

Oaklander, V. (1988) *Windows to our Children*. New York: Center for Gestalt Development.

Petersen, L. and Gannoni, A.F. (1994) *Stop, Think, Do: Manual for Social Skills Training in Young People*. Melbourne: ACER.

Piaget, J. (1962) *Play, Dreams & Imitations*. New York: Norton.

Piaget, J. (1971) *Psychology and Epistomology: Towards a Theory of Knowledge*, trans. A. Rosin. New York: Viking.

Ramzy, I. (1978) *The Piggle: an Account of the Psychoanalytic Treatment of a Little Girl by D.W. Winnicott*. London: Hogarth Press.

Reisman, J.M. and Ribordy, S. (1993) *Principles of Psychotherapy with Children*, 2nd edition. Lexington, MA: Lexington Books.

Rogers, C.R. (1942) *Counseling and Psychotherapy*. Boston: Houghton-Mifflin.

Rogers, C.R. (1955) *Client Centered Therapy*. Boston: Houghton-Mifflin.

Rogers, C.R. (1965) *Client Centered Therapy: its Current Practice, Implications and Theory*. Boston: Houghton-Mifflin.

Ryce-Menuhin, J. (1992) *Jungian Sand Play: the Wonderful Therapy*. New York: Routledge, Chapman and Hall.

Schaefer, C.E. (1990) *The Therapeutic Use of Child's Play*. New York: Aronson.

Schaefer, C.E. and O'Connor, K.J. (eds) (1983) *Handbook of Play Therapy*. New York: Wiley.

Schaefer, C.E. and O'Connor, K.J. (eds) (1994) *Handbook of Play Therapy – Advances and Innovations*. New York: Wiley.

Schaefer, C.E. and Reid, S.E. (1986) *Therapeutic Use of Childhood Games*. New York: Wiley.

Singer, J. (1973) *A Child's World of Make-Believe*. New York: Academic Press.

Sloves, R. and Belinger-Peterlin, K. (1986) 'The process of time limited psychotherapy with latency aged children', *Journal of the American Academy of Child Psychiatry*, 25: 847–51.

Sloves, R. and Belinger-Peterlin, K. (1994) 'Time limited play therapy', in C.E. Schaefer and K.J. O'Connor (eds), *Handbook of Play Therapy – Advances and Innovations*. New York: Wiley.

Smilansky, S. (1968) *Effects of Socio-Dramatic Play on Disadvantaged Pre-School Children*. New York: Wiley.

Spiegel, S. (1989) *An Interpersonal Approach to Child Therapy*. New York: Columbia University Press.

Thompson, C.L. and Rudolph, L.B. (1983) *Counselling Children*. Monterey, CA: Brooks/Cole.

Varma, V.P. (1990) *The Management of Children with Emotional and Behavioural Difficulties*. London: Routledge.

Walter, J. and Peller, J. (1992) *Becoming Solution Focussed in Brief Therapy*. New York: Brunner/Mazel.

West, J. (1992) *Child Centred Play Therapy*. London: Arnold.

Yorke, C. (1982) *Psychoanalytic Psychology of Normal Development*. London: Hogarth Press.

Zeig, J. and Gilligan, S. (eds) (1990) *Brief Therapy: Myths, Methods and Metaphors*. New York: Brunner/Mazel.

Index